As You Were

To War and Back
with the Black Hawk Battalion
of the Virginia National Guard

CHRISTIAN DAVENPORT

WILEY

John Wiley & Sons, Inc.

Published by John Wiley & Sons, Inc., Hoboken, New Jersey
Published simultaneously in Canada

For general information about our other products and services, please contact our Customer Care Department within the United States at (800) 762-2974, outside the United States at (317) 572-3993 or fax (317) 572-4002.

Wiley also publishes its books in a variety of electronic formats. Some content that appears in print may not be available in electronic books. For more information about Wiley products, visit our web site at www.wiley.com.

Library of Congress Cataloging-in-Publication Data:
Davenport, Christian, date.
    As you were : to war and back with the Black Hawk battalion of the Virginia
National Guard / Christian Davenport.
        p.   cm.
    Includes index.
    ISBN 978-0-470-37361-3 (cloth)
        1. United States—National Guard—Biography.   2. Iraq War, 2003—
        Biography.   3. Soldiers—United States—Biography.   I. Title.
UA42.D23 2009
956.7044'33092273—dc22
    [B]   2008045528
Printed in the United States of America

10 9 8 7 6 5 4 3 2 1

To my mother,
to my wife,
and to the citizen-soldiers, who go when called

Nostalgia, it comes from the Greek.
I researched it: straight from the Greek. *Algos*
means pain. *Nostos* means to return home.
Nostalgia: the pain of returning home.

— Tim O'Brien, *Going after Cacciato*

Contents

Acknowledgments

When I started this project I wanted to be the first journalist to extend the Pentagon's embedding program from Iraq to the home front. The best way to do that, I figured, was with a unit from the National Guard, which is, I believe, one of the most important, and most overlooked, American institutions; the Guard's citizen-soldiers face a sacrifice all together different from the active duty. They come home not to large military bases but to their old civilian lives and try to pick up where they left off, to be as they were.

I'm thankful, first and foremost, to the soldiers who allowed me to document their lives in this book. They signed on with gusto, and their faith in the project and their patience with me only reaffirmed my commitment to get it right. This is their story, and this book belongs to them: Mark Baush, Kate Dahlstrand (née Broome), Ray and Diane Johnson, Craig Lewis, and Miranda Summers.

By spending nearly two years writing about them, I entered not only their lives but those of their family and friends as well, who were to a person gracious and kind.

Colonel Robert E. McMillin II generously allowed me to embed with the 2-224th for three weeks near the end of its tour, and encouraged me to get to know as many of his soldiers as possible.

I'm also thankful to Lieutenant Colonel James W. Ring and Command Sergeant Major Susan G. Bentley (Retired), who kept the door open long after the battalion came home. Lieutenant Colonel Chester Carter (Retired) of the Virginia National Guard's Public Affairs office helped a great deal in arranging for me to meet up with the battalion. With the 2-224, I'd also like to thank Captain Aaron Loy, Major Walter "Keith" Nunnally, Chief Warrant Officer-4 R. J. Smith and Sergeant David Testa.

The seeds of this book began with stories I wrote for the *Washington Post*, my professional home since 2000. My editors, Leonard Downie, Philip Bennett, Robert J. McCartney, R. B. Brenner, Lynn Medford, and Phyllis W. Jordan, generously allowed me the time to pursue this project and encouraged me throughout.

Lynda Robinson of the *Post*'s Sunday magazine first suggested I spend a year following reservists coming home from war, and her faith and enthusiasm kept me going. Others at the *Post*, including David Fahrenthold, Marc Fisher, Mary Hadar, Peter Perl, David Rowell, and Suzanne Wooton, lent clear eyes, kind words, and inspiration.

By selecting me as one of its 2007 fellows, the Alicia Patterson Foundation, under Peggy Engel's excellent stewardship, allowed me the time to immerse myself fully in the book, without distraction.

I'm also indebted to Lieutenant Colonel Les' Melnyk, who opened up his files, not only at the National Guard Bureau but at his home as well. Our discussions about the military in general and the Guard in particular helped shape the tone and structure of the book. Chief Warrant Officer-2 John W. Listman Jr. (Retired), a historian with the Virginia Army National Guard Historical Collection, helped illuminate the long, grand history of the Virginia National Guard. Renee Hylton and Manny Pacheco of the National Guard Bureau were also immensely helpful.

In researching the Guard, I relied on many sources, none more so than Michael Doubler's definitive history, *Civilian in Peace, Soldier in War: The Army National Guard, 1636–2000.* I also relied on Lewis Sorley's biographies of Generals Creighton Abrams and Harold Johnson, and Laura Fairchild Brodie's fine work on the Virginia Military Institute.

My agent, Rafe Sagalyn, saw well before I did that my idea could indeed become a book, and helped greatly in shaping it. Eric Nelson, my editor at Wiley, immediately saw the full arc of the story and became not only a masterful editor, but a counselor and partner as well. Production editor Rachel Meyers and freelance copy editor Eric Newman cleaned up my unruly prose with their careful copyediting.

Through his close readings, my father, Gary, kept me, and the text, honest. My mother, Marolyn, was there, as always, with her sound judgment and encouragement.

Finally, I'm thankful to my wife, Heather, an unerring critic, who patiently read through several drafts and improved every one. She is my best friend and my love, always.

Introduction

In the spring, along the grand boulevards designed by a Frenchman to mimic Paris, all the nation's capital blooms with what seems an overnight Technicolor force—flowering pear trees, tulips, daffodils, and, of course, the famed cherry blossoms, which line the Tidal Basin like so many low-hanging pink and white clouds. It's a time of transition, spring heralded by the bloom.

Like thousands of other tourists descending on the city that day in April 2007, Miranda Summers and two friends had come to Washington, D.C., for the annual Cherry Blossom Festival. There was only a hint of cool in the air. The sun was bright. It was a wonderful day for sightseeing. But unlike her friends, Miranda had come for something besides the flowering trees. In her pocket was a patch that she had worn on the left shoulder of her flight suit while in Iraq, and she planned to lay it at the foot of the World War II Memorial.

Had Miranda shown the patch to her friends—both civilians who had never served in the military—they could have easily mistaken it for a frivolous ornament, the sort of thing you would stitch to a denim jacket next to a peace symbol or a Grateful Dead logo. The patch was round and bore what looked like the Chinese symbol of duality, yin and yang, with two tadpolelike swirls, one dark, one light.

In fact, the patch was the insignia of the Twenty-ninth Infantry Division, one of the oldest and most vaunted Army National Guard units in the country. During World War I, it suffered 5,500 casualties in France's Argonne Forest. In World War II, the Twenty-ninth stormed the beaches of Normandy on D-Day. Designed in 1917 by an army major, the patch represented how the division was composed of units that had fought on both sides of the Civil War: one half was blue, the other gray. But for the soldiers in Miranda's unit—the Virginia Army National Guard's Second Battalion, 224th Aviation Regiment—the patch was brown and tan, the better to blend with the Mesopotamian desert.

The soldiers of the 2-224th were as young as nineteen, fresh out of boot camp, and as old as sixty-two, having served in Vietnam. In civilian life, they were plumbers, police officers, college students, computer technicians, and insurance salesmen. In war, they were soldiers: cocky helicopter pilots, door gunners, and mechanics. The unit, an aviation battalion that flew Black Hawk helicopters and went by the call sign "Punisher," was based in Sandston, Virginia, just outside of Richmond. But the soldiers came from all over, from the southern part of the state, where the Civil War was still seen by some as the War of Northern Aggression, up through the Shenandoah Valley to the tony suburbs of Washington, D.C. One soldier's military retirement was put on hold so he could deploy. A few left pregnant wives at home. Others left lucrative civilian jobs, and some, like Miranda, who was called up a few credits shy of graduating from an elite liberal arts college, took leave from school.

The battalion's 350 soldiers were diverse—black, white, Hispanic, full-blooded American mutts—from varied walks of life. About one in ten was a woman. Some had seen combat before; many hadn't. Three were Vietnam vets, including fifty-eight-year-old Chief Warrant Officer-5 Ray Johnson, who shipped off to Iraq at a time in life when his wife thought he should have been thinking about retirement and tending to his grandchildren. Others were as green as Lieutenant Craig Lewis, who could give his civilian employer only a few days' notice and landed in a war zone fresh out of flight school having never flown a single official mission.

Those who had enlisted after 9/11 knew that at some point they'd be sent overseas; that was just life in the new National Guard. Some, like Captain Mark Baush, had served with the unit the last time it deployed overseas, to Bosnia in 2001 just as the Twin Towers fell. But there were many others, like Sergeant Kate Broome, who joined for the college benefits during peacetime and never thought they'd be called for anything more than the occasional flood or riot.

In short, they were typical National Guard citizen-soldiers.

For a year, they were stationed at Al Asad Airbase in deadly Anbar province, where they flew missions to some of the country's most dangerous hotspots—Baghdad, Fallujah, Ramadi. But now Miranda and her fellow soldiers were home, transformed into civilians almost as soon as they stepped off the plane. Two months had passed, and Miranda still didn't feel like a civilian. The war still hung with her and would, she knew, for some time.

This little self-created ceremony at the World War II Memorial would be a private act of celebration, a proclamation that she had returned home safe and alive. By performing this ritual at the altar of those who had come before, she would be officially joining the long continuum of soldiers returning from war. And that, she hoped, would allow her to put the war behind her and simply resume where she had left off, still believing such a thing was indeed possible.

She hadn't told the friends who had accompanied her to Washington all of this, of course. They wouldn't understand. Few did. Most of her friends, and even her family, didn't get why she had wanted to join the military in the first place and certainly would not have understood what she went through in Iraq. So while her two friends were taking in the beauty of the blossoms and basking in the springtime sun, she quietly excused herself and made her way over to the memorial.

As she drew closer, she noticed a dense throng of older men, with VFW hats, pins, and ribbons on their chests, around the spot where she had intended to lay her patch. They were clearly World War II veterans. Miranda hesitated, suddenly intimidated. Who was she to walk among the men who fought the Good War against Hitler, Mussolini, and Tojo? Who was she to place her patch at their monument, to tread on their pantheon, to assume that just because she had seen war they were both part of the same soldierly fraternity?

They were members of the Greatest Generation, lauded and lionized even still. At this very moment, there was combat raging in Iraq, and yet their war still seemed to dominate the national consciousness four decades hence. It was as if the country preferred nostalgia over the present reality. This grand memorial, with its fountains and soaring eagles carved into some of the most prime real estate in country—on the National Mall halfway between the Lincoln Memorial and the Washington Monument—was evidence of that.

As she entered the monument, Miranda passed a quote etched into the granite that read, "This was a people's war, and everyone was in it." In World War II, 16 million had served, from small towns and big cities across the United States. Everyone else at home was affected, everyone sacrificed, everyone knew someone who was fighting. Miranda's war could not have been more different. With armed forces of merely 2.2 million, only a tiny fraction of the American population saw action in Iraq. To the rest of the country, numbed to the point of indifference by the images on television, inured to the body count, the Iraq War was little more than an annoyance, something that didn't affect them.

In the three decades between Vietnam and Iraq, the line between those who served and those who did not had become one of the great fault lines in American society, along with race, class, and religion. In 1991, 68 percent of the U.S. Senate and 48 percent of the House had served in the military. By the time Miranda came home, only 29 percent of the Senate and 23 percent of the House knew what it meant to wear the uniform. Out of 535 members of Congress, only about a dozen had sons or daughters who had risked their lives in Iraq. Most of the country was more than happy to let other people's children go to war, and so Miranda and her fellow soldiers left for Iraq as anonymously as they returned. To come home was to realize that despite the myriad "Support the Troops" bumper stickers, most Americans had no idea what the war was like. They had not seen "the elephant," a term Civil War soldiers used to describe their experiences in combat. Instead of being a second coming of the Greatest Generation, Miranda was part of an invisible generation returning to a nation that had never been so divorced from its military and so unaffected by the war others were fighting.

The conflicts in Iraq and Afghanistan were the country's first extended military campaign since the Spanish-American War fought without some form of conscription, and it was being waged by a tiny sliver of the population: the 1 percent who volunteered to serve, while the rest stayed home, unburdened by so much as a tax increase to help cover the costs of war. There was no collective sacrifice, no rationing, no Rosie the Riveter urging, "We Can Do It!" There was only the 1 percent. In this war, as one historian said, the military went to combat while the rest of the country went to the mall. And without a draft, nearly half of that 1 percent belonged to the citizen-soldiers of the National Guard and Reserve, who were being called for two and three tours and at one point constituted more than half of the army's combat force in Iraq.

As Miranda and her fellow Guardsmen knew all too well, those who join today have little in common with those who enlisted during Vietnam, when the Guard was regarded as a haven for those looking to avoid the war. For hundreds of thousands of Guard members, the motto "Get Your Degree Tuition Free" had enormous appeal. In exchange for four years of one-weekend-a-month, two-weeks-a-year service, young Americans fulfilled their military obligation and learned invaluable skills for future civilian jobs, all while covering some of the skyrocketing costs of a college education.

During peacetime, few believed that the part of their contracts that said they may be called up in the event of a national emergency would ever mean they'd be shipped overseas for combat. They thought they would respond to the occasional hurricane or tornado when called up by their state's governor, who shares command of the Guard with the president. But ever since 9/11 when President George W. Bush invoked Title 10 of the U.S. Code, allowing a mass federal mobilization, Guard life has been transformed and its new motto represents the profound shift. No longer does the Guard advertise free education. Instead it offers: "The most important weapon in the war on Terrorism. You."

The Iraq War completely redefined what it means to be a citizen-soldier. Never before had Guard members been plucked from civilian life, sent overseas to combat, and then cast back into society, only to have to repeat the jarring process—disrupting families, stressing civilian careers—again and again. The war and the repeated deployments have transformed the Guard from a bunch of loosely trained backups derisively known as "weekend warriors" to a front-line force that is expected to perform every bit as well—and nearly as frequently—as their active-duty counterparts. The repeated deployments in Iraq have rendered citizen-soldiers more soldier than citizen. They are more likely to complete a tour of combat than four years of college. They know, as Major General Thomas J. Plewes, the head of the Army Reserve, said in March 2000, "We are no longer a force in reserve."

Miranda watched the old World War II vets from a distance and summoned her courage. She had earned that patch, had sacrificed so much, and now she was going to do what she had come here to do. She wended her way through the men, her head down, determined if a tad sheepish, and laid her patch on the ground. She stood still for a moment and stared at it, waiting for the sense of closure she had hoped for. But it did not come. There was none of the charged emotion, none of the pride of accomplishment. Instead, she felt the eyes of another generation of warriors at her back. Standing there, she felt foolish, as if, she would later recall, she were "praying in public."

"Is that a Twenty-ninth ID badge?" one of the old veterans called out.

It took a moment for Miranda to realize he was talking to her. "Yes, it is," she replied.

"From Iraq?"

"Yes."

Whose was it? The men, gathering around her, wanted to know. "Your brother's? Your boyfriend's?"

"No," she said firmly. "It's mine."

Yours? They were incredulous. This slight little blonde—who was no more than 5-foot-2 and couldn't have weighed more than 110 pounds—had been in Iraq? What could she have done?

"I was a supply sergeant," Miranda explained.

Of course, they nodded to one another. That seemed to satisfy their curiosity. She was in supply. Admin work, not combat. Which made sense to men in their seventies and eighties: Women don't fight in war.

"In the rear with the gear," they teased her.

Miranda, growing slightly agitated, was quick to correct them.

"Actually, I also served as a helicopter door gunner," she said.

At that, everything changed. The teasing stopped. Their smirks were wiped away. They looked at Miranda with pride. She had viewed the world through the crosshairs of a rifle sight and seen war. She had seen the elephant.

The largest of them, a monster of a man, a foot taller than Miranda at least, with a Butterball-sized gut and forearms like Popeye's, came over and buried Miranda in his arms. A hug from one veteran to another that transcended wars and gender and time, and said: You are one of us.

The old vet released her and the others came over to pat her on the shoulder. You done good, they said. You went to war and survived. That's the important thing. You're lucky to be alive, to be so young.

Now you have the rest of your life ahead of you.

PART ONE

MOBILIZATION

1

Miranda

No One Likes a Sulky Soldier

A few minutes past sunrise on the second Saturday of September 2005, the verdant campus of the College of William and Mary was a preternaturally quiet place, so still and lifeless it seemed Miranda had it all to herself. It would be several more hours before her classmates awoke to their frat party–fueled hangovers and headed to the cafeteria for restorative servings of greasy eggs and coffee and later to the cocoon of the library stacks.

Exhausted as she was on these early Saturday mornings, Miranda loved them and always found herself admiring the beauty of the campus. With its Georgian architecture, vast open spaces, and picturesque bridge on which, the legend went, a kiss could lead to marriage, William and Mary, in the heart of Virginia's Colonial Williamsburg, lived up to its impressive pedigree. Founded in 1693 by a charter from England's King William III and Queen

Mary II, the college was the second oldest in the country (behind Harvard) and the alma mater of Thomas Jefferson, whose life-sized statue stood sentry by a brick wall in the center of campus. William and Mary was known as the Ivy of the South, one of the most elite and exclusive colleges in the country. It was home to the best and the brightest students, who joked that the reason the library closed at 6 P.M. on weekends was that the administration thought they studied too much.

Miranda, a twenty-two-year-old senior history major, excelled here; she found great friends and was active in her sorority. But it was only during these Saturday mornings, when she was alone with the rising sun on her way to her one-weekend-a-month National Guard drill, that she felt comfortable enough to wear her uniform on campus, something she rarely did when the rest of the school was around to see her.

It wasn't that she was ashamed of serving in the army. On the contrary: Wearing the uniform was the fulfillment of a dream she'd had since she was a young girl growing up in Indiana. It's just that while William and Mary had a small but dedicated ROTC program, a student in camouflage was still a highly unusual sight, one that attracted the kind of bewildered, blinky-eyed stares that reminded Miranda of the cartoon bunnies in *Bambi*. It was almost more common to see a student streaking—another of the college's traditions—than a soldier decked out in a battle dress uniform like the one Miranda was now wearing: Her black boots polished and laced tight, creases crisp, a specialist's rank insignia on her collar, her beret perched delicately over her carefully primped blond hair so as not to ruin it for later that evening.

She had taken special care with her hair that morning, twirling it loosely into a bun so that it wouldn't come out a tangled mess. It was going to be a big night, and not just because the football team was going to demolish its intrastate rival the Virginia Military Institute later that afternoon. It was the culmination of rush week for the college's fraternities and sororities. Over the years, some chapters had been banned from campus for various alcohol-related infractions, but Greek life was still a big part of the college's social scene. William and Mary was, after all, where the fraternity system in America began with the founding chapter of Phi Beta Kappa in 1776.

Tonight was to be "Pref night," the crescendo of the mating ritual between pledges and the sororities who were courting them. Miranda and her sorority sisters had stayed up to near dawn discussing which girls they wanted to invite to join. The girls had winnowed their list of sororities to their top three preferences. Now after weeks of casual courtship, it was time for the sororities to sell themselves with a full press. After some negotiating with her army supervisor, Miranda had received special dispensation to leave drill early on Saturday afternoon so she could attend the festivities at Kappa Delta. Over the years, these drill weekends had caused her to miss so much—every single homecoming parade, big frat parties, and even a semiformal dance—but she was not going to miss tonight. Tonight she was not going to be a soldier. She was going to be a sorority girl. She was going to shed her uniform for a black satin dress like all the other Kappa Delta girls, lace her neck with pearls, and demonstrate that she was among the best group of coeds a young girl could ever hope to be associated with. What's more, Miranda had been chosen to address, tonight, on behalf of the sorority, the girls rushing Kappa Delta.

As much as she loved school, she couldn't help but feel somewhat detached this year. She had tried to get into her studies, and to indulge into the wonderful frivolity of rush week when the Kappa Delta sisters pulled all-nighters gossiping about the pledges—who was smart, who was cute, who would fit in. But she just couldn't help but feel apart from it all. "I feel like a ghost when I walk around campus," she had written in her journal just two weeks earlier. "It's like I'm not even here."

Now, with the campus vacant, the cleansing smell of the morning dew, everyone else tucked comfortably away in their dorm rooms, she felt her isolation.

All summer long, there had been rumors that the 2-224th was headed to Iraq. Suddenly, drill weekends had taken on a heightened sense of urgency. There were briefings on how to detect roadside bombs. The pilots and mechanics were feverishly trying to get all the Black Hawks in tip-top shape. The medics were performing their emergency drills with even more care and exigency. Now it appeared the only question was when they would all ship out. Miranda hoped it would be after Christmas, so she could at least finish the semester and graduate on time. She'd already interrupted her college career once to go to basic training, and with the possibility of a deployment looming, she had enrolled in summer school to make sure she'd have the credits to graduate early, if need be.

During the first week of school she had warned her professors that she might not be around to finish the semester. This news had come as a shock because few knew she was even in the Guard to begin with, a personal detail Miranda purposely did not advertise. The war did not exist at William and Mary, and Miranda did not want to be the sole manifestation of its ugly existence. As far as she knew, just one other student had left campus to join the fight. There had been a couple of peace rallies on campus, but nothing that rivaled the protests during the Vietnam War, when in 1968 students held silent one-hour peace vigils for seven straight days. By contrast, the Iraq War seemed an abstraction—something to lament and deride in coffeehouse chats, not something for students to fear or protest. It didn't involve them.

When Miranda broke the news to her professors that she might be called to serve, at least one said he had sensed the day would eventually come. He put his hands over his mouth and gasped, "I wondered how long this would take." Young men and women had been shipping off to war ever since 9/11, and it wasn't until now—four years later—that war had finally touched one of his students. Most of her professors were supportive and promised to work with her on independent projects from Iraq if necessary to make sure she would graduate on time. But one told her that to pass his class, she had to be there for it. "You have to make a decision," he said. "Are you a student or a soldier?"

I'm trying to be both, she thought. But she was starting to think that while she had a foot in both worlds, she belonged fully to neither.

As she made the hour-long drive to Guard drill that Saturday morning, Miranda wondered if this would be the weekend that the unit would finally get official word that it was going to Iraq. At the beginning of every drill, while standing in formation, she expected the battalion commander to break the news. She waited for an inspirational speech, a war cry. She imagined something like George C. Scott in the movie *Patton*, standing before that huge American flag, rallying the troops.

But formation on this Saturday came and went without news. No speeches. No talk of war. No bombast. Only more of good old "hurry up and wait," as only the U.S. Army could dish it out. At least the soldiers were all in this together. That camaraderie, the instant friendship that comes with enduring what soldiers some-times call "the Suck" of military life, was perhaps what she liked best about the Guard. In a way it mimicked the bonds she had with her sorority sisters. But at a time when neighborhoods and schools all across the United States had segregated themselves into neat little enclaves, the army was still one of the last places to get a genuine cross-section of society: whites and blacks, lawyers and firefighters, all working together. Where else did you find that? Not in small-town Indiana, where Miranda had grown up, and certainly not at William and Mary, where the scions of the powerful took their diplomas.

Only a few of her college friends knew that she might be going to Iraq, and Miranda had sworn them to secrecy. News like that would have spread quickly through the Kappa Delta house and across the campus, and she didn't want to be seen as anything other than just another student. Many of her sorority sisters had no idea she was even in the Guard. Miranda—with her penchant for *Vogue* magazine, stylish mid-back-length blond hair, and expressive hazel eyes she liked to accent with mascara—didn't fit the soldier stereotype. "It was like she was on the soccer team, or something," remembered Portia Ross, one of Miranda's best friends. The Guard "was this odd little hobby she had."

Her classmates just knew that she often was gone on weekends and could sometimes be seen on the treadmill running with a heavy rucksack on her back. She was a bit more serious, a bit more mature. It wasn't just that she had grown up in a Mormon household. Miranda had always been focused. While she would wear her uniform under the rare anonymity provided by her 7 A.M. Saturdays, Miranda changed back into civilian clothes before returning to campus. Even her roommate had seen her in uniform only once or twice. Miranda just didn't want to have to explain why she'd joined the army to people who didn't know the difference between a corporal and a captain.

In the rare instances when people asked her why she was in the army, she told them the truth: She desperately needed the GI Bill to pay William and Mary's $20,000-a-year tuition. But it was also an easily digestible answer that seemed to make sense to civilians. She knew that any other explanation—like patriotism or service or love of country—would have been met with consternation, if not outright disbelief. The rest of the story, though unspoken, was that Miranda would have enlisted even if the National Guard wasn't going to give her one cent. She loved the army. She even loved basic training. She loved that the military had lived up to all the corny recruiting ads, that she pushed herself and realized how much she could really accomplish. She loved the teamwork and the discipline, and getting up early and doing more by 9 A.M. than everyone else did all day. The army had taken a slight, insecure young woman and turned her into a damn good soldier: strong and strong-willed, able to run a six-minute mile, pump out sixty push-ups, and even order around a squad of soldiers without taking any of their guff.

If she had to pinpoint the genesis of her fascination with the army, it would be, oddly enough, seeing the film *Forrest Gump* in the fifth grade. Tom Hanks's character was the oddball outcast who with the army finally found a place where he fit in. During the awkwardness of adolescence, a place to fit in was exactly what Miranda was looking for. As a sixth grader she'd given a class presentation on Shannon Faulkner, the first female cadet who enrolled at the Citadel after the courts forced the once all-male military institution to admit women. When Miranda was thirteen, she begged her parents to let her join the Civil Air Patrol, an air force cadet program for teenagers. She often was the youngest of the group, and the only girl, but she toughed out the four-day camping trips. She forded rivers and rappelled down rocks just like everyone else. She even was able to catch her own food just as she was taught. And if the boys expected her to be squeamish at skinning a rabbit, they were disappointed. Soon the boys couldn't help but be impressed, and Miranda's confidence grew.

Her parents thought this would turn out to be a passing fad, something she'd outgrow. "We could think of much worse things she could be doing," her father, Carl Summers, recalled. "So we supported her."

He was a college professor with a doctorate in psychology, and a devout Mormon who taught his three children early on that they should decide not to drink or have premarital sex, so when the opportunities presented themselves they could say they had already made up their minds. Before she died of cancer when Miranda was fifteen, Miranda's mother was the chair of the Educational Psychology department at Ball State University in Muncie, Indiana, where Miranda spent most of her childhood. Carl Summers's second wife, Vanessa, was also an academic with a "Dr." before her name. Miranda was destined for a life of higher learning, her father felt—college and then graduate school. The army wasn't part of that picture. But during her senior year of high school, Miranda decided she was sick of school. She wanted a soldier's life, and so she'd forgo college and enlist. She was so determined that the best her father could do was strike a deal. Miranda would apply to the service academies: West Point or Annapolis. If she didn't get in, she'd go to a regular college.

She made the first cut of the Naval Academy's rigorous application program, but a knee injury kept her from passing the physical. So the following fall she enrolled in George Washington University.

She hated it from almost the moment she stepped on campus. She was a country girl from Indiana. George Washington was in the heart of Washington, D.C., and she didn't take to the big-city vibe. The whole place was just overwhelming. The only reason she had agreed to go in the first place was that her father had landed a job there teaching statistics, which meant she could attend at a reduced rate.

She complained to him that she didn't like her classes or her professors, and she wasn't making friends. All of this was true. But Miranda probably would have felt the same way about any college in the country. Then a couple of weeks into her freshman year, American Airlines Flight 77 hit the Pentagon two miles from GW's campus, and as the country was swept up in a patriotic fervor in the weeks that followed the 9/11 attacks, her desire to be a soldier intensified.

She waited until the end of the semester before dropping out and moving back to Indiana. She felt she owed her father that much. But shortly after arriving she looked up the Muncie recruiting offices of the Army National Guard in the Yellow Pages and called. "I want to join," she said. The recruiter promised to come and pick her up because she didn't have a car, but then never showed. When Miranda called back, he apologized and said he didn't think she was serious: The only people who call out of the blue to say they want to enlist are the prank callers who like to torture recruiters, he said.

Well, I'm serious, Miranda told him. A few days later she was on her way to the army's processing center. It wasn't until after she had signed the paperwork that she told her father what she had done because she knew he would disapprove—and he did, angrily, as if it were a personal betrayal: "How could you?"

The army, he thought, was "not exactly the ideal situation for a young woman," especially if she was his daughter. "I tried to talk her out of it," he recalled. "But there's a point where you push, and she pushes back. So I made a decision that if this is what you want, I'll support you."

He had been similarly disappointed when Miranda decided she did not want to be a practicing Mormon, like the rest of her family.

Just twelve years old, she informed her father, "I'm not going to lie about what I believe in." The decision came as a blow, but it was clear she'd made up her mind and wouldn't budge. There was no talking her out of it. And so Carl Summers decided to support her then, too. Before landing the job at GW, he had been out of work for a while and as a result was "going through a financial crisis at the time," he said later. "I couldn't support her, and the military must have looked like the best option."

Actually, it looked like the only option, which is what she told him: "This is how I'm going to get through college—on the GI Bill." The demands of the military—the weekends, the physical pain, the mind-numbing routine—would be worth it if it meant she could strike out on her own. But Carl Summers wanted to make sure she understood how serious this was. "Once you sign the dotted line, they own you," he said. And even though the Guard boasted that the only commitment for help with one's tuition was one weekend a month, just two weeks a year of service, he warned her that she could get called up for combat. She didn't dispute that, but quietly she thought, there's no way I'm going to war. So the following year, after graduation from basic training, she transferred to William and Mary and became one of a handful of citizen-soldiers on the campus.

After yet another formation without any news about Iraq, Miranda thought of sneaking out to her car to take a nap. She was exhausted after having stayed up so late the night before, talking about the different prospects rushing the sorority. She wanted to be in top form for Pref night. But she had a pile of socks in the supply room to distribute. The more quickly she handed them out, the sooner she could go back to the campus. As she got started, she noticed a sergeant passing out pieces of paper. Probably yet another bureaucratic form from Uncle Sam, she thought.

"Here's yours," the sergeant said, arm outstretched as if distributing Halloween candy.

"You are ordered to active duty as a member of your reserve component unit for the period indicated unless sooner released or unless extended," it read. "Report to home station 18, October, 2005. . . . Period of active duty: Not to exceed 545 days. Purpose: OPERATION IRAQI FREEDOM."

At last, here it was. But more than what the capitalized words portended, it was the two figures—18 October and 545 days— that stood out. Miranda shuddered when she realized that her report date was a little more than a month away, which meant she wouldn't be able to finish the semester on campus after all. If she couldn't get her professors to agree to let her finish her studies from Iraq, her graduation would be postponed until after the deployment, which at 545 days, or eighteen months, was going to be even longer than she had expected. Her heart sank when she thought she could be in her mid-twenties when she graduated.

Her father had been right after all. The army owned her, and now the steep debt of her many semesters' worth of college benefits had suddenly come due. But even though she had the legal orders in hand, with dates now set, she hoped that somehow they'd be pushed back just enough so she could finish the semester and graduate on time.

"I keep hoping and praying that I can push it off until December," she wrote in her journal. "I just want to graduate before I go. Somehow things seem to be going too perfectly for this to happen now. I can finally pay for school, I have the credits I need, the classes I need, great friends, great sorority. . . . Somehow, deployment just seems like an idle threat not intended for me, like chlamydia or West Nile [virus]. I just have so much faith that it will all work out. I suppose that I should be a little more upset about this, but something just keeps telling me that school, Iraq, and everything else is all part of the master plan for me."

But she wasn't going to Iraq today. Nothing was going to keep her from enjoying Pref night. Not the army. Not the deployment. Not war. She'd have time to worry about all that later. Pref night was the most important thing. She had a speech to give. Only now she'd have to do some last-minute editing. She had a secret she was finally going to share.

There was no point now in changing out of her uniform before returning to campus. She was going to Iraq. If people stared as she crossed campus back to the Kappa Delta house, she didn't notice—or care. Let them see me in uniform, she thought. She had other things to worry about. Plus, she was running late. She had only about a half hour to spare before the Pref night festivities were to begin, and despite the care she had given her hair that morning, her army beret still left it a tangled mess that only a good brushing and a curling iron could remedy. For a split second she paused to think about how surreal this all was: How can I be more worried about my hair than going to Iraq? But she was. Maybe it was denial. Maybe it was a deeply ingrained determination to lead a normal college life. Maybe it was the fact that Iraq was still an unimaginable abstraction, while a head of nearly unsalvageable hair was now staring at her in the mirror while the rest of the sorority was beginning to filter into the common room downstairs.

By the time the pledges, known by the more politically correct term "potential new members," or PNMs, arrived, Miranda and her Kappa Delta sisters were in their black dresses, and any of the exhaustion Miranda had felt earlier after a night of virtually no sleep was superseded by the nervousness she felt at the prospect of delivering her speech.

The PNMs who gathered in the living room of the sorority house seemed so young, so innocent. Even though she had been in the same position just a few years before, Miranda couldn't fathom how wonderful it must be to have what sorority would invite you to join as your chief concern. When it was time for her to speak, the sisters gathered all the PNMs into the dining room. The sisters stood behind Miranda, who began by saying how much the sorority had meant to her. "Kappa Delta is a chapter of women who accomplish. I have never seen a group of women with so many goals and aspirations, but moreover, I have never seen so many women achieve these things so often," she said, reading from a sheet of paper.

She talked about how the sorority had accepted her as a transfer student. How loving they were, how nurturing. "Kappa Deltas not only support each other, we support each other to an extreme that I can only call enabling," she continued.

Her sisters supported her, she went on, when, after 9/11, "I found myself feeling strangely disconnected from campus life. School was okay and I loved my sisters. But I started feeling like I belonged somewhere else, and that place was the army. I was scared to tell my sisters that I wanted to enlist. I thought manicured sorority girls would be the last people on earth to understand that I wanted to sleep in the mud and crawl under barbed wire. But when I finally brought it up, they were incredibly supportive.

"One of the first letters I got at basic training was from my big sister. The packages and letters kept coming, and seeing the brightly decorated letters in the mailbag would always make things seem a little better. My drill sergeants thought that it was hilarious that I was in a sorority, and they would make me do extra push-ups to get my letters that were on Kappa Delta stationery. I think that I have the dubious honor of doing more push-ups for Kappa Delta than anyone else here."

At that, everyone laughed. It seemed so incongruous to think of Miranda, the high heels–wearing sorority girl, as Miranda the mud-spattered recruit doing push-ups while being yelled at by drill instructors. But Miranda kept her head down, trying to focus on her speech.

"I found out this summer that instead of preparing for my senior year, I should be preparing to go to Iraq," she continued, hearing gasps from the sisters standing behind her. "Although I'd known it might happen for years, when I found out, I was scared and angry that things weren't going to go my way. I had to decide if I was going to come back to school this fall, knowing that I would never make it through the school year. I knew that I didn't have much time left before I leave everything I know for almost two years, and I had to make some choices about how I wanted to spend it."

Aside from the sounds of muted sobs, there was an almost funereal silence, and Miranda could feel her own tears rising. Even some of the PNMs standing in front of her, girls she barely knew, were crying. She pressed on.

"As I get more details and see that there is more of a chance that I'll be leaving before the end of the month than before the end of the year, I'm so thankful that I came back here. My officers, my parents, even the college ask me why I'm back at school this fall when I know I'm not graduating. The answer is simple: I know that I only have a few weeks left, and there is nowhere else on earth that I would rather spend it."

She rushed immediately into an adjoining room because she couldn't hold her tears back any longer, and she didn't want to break down in front of the PNMs. Portia Ross followed her in, and she and a couple of other sorority sisters huddled around her.

"Are you sure you have to go?" they asked. "Are you positive? Isn't there anything you can do to get out of it?"

"I'm going," Miranda said. "There isn't anything I can do."

Giving her Pref night speech about going to Iraq would be the hardest part, or so Miranda thought. But now the word was out on campus, and she became the Girl Who's Going to Iraq, the subject of stares and whispers. She loved her friends and classmates, but they sure could come up with some odd questions and observations about the war.

"Will you have to cut your hair?"

"Yeah, probably," Miranda said.

"Are you ready?"

"Yes," she said trying to sound confident, though she actually had no idea if she was prepared for this.

"Will you have to shoot anyone?"

"Only if I really have to," she said. But again, she had no idea.

And then there was the one girl who said, incredibly, "I thought only poor people went to war."

As Miranda soon realized, once you mention you're going to Iraq, everyone feels compelled to give an opinion of the war, and the opinion generally wasn't good. Not that Miranda was a die-hard supporter—she wasn't, and like the rest of the country she grew more disenchanted with the occupation the longer it lasted. But she was a soldier. And soldiers do what they're told, even if that means dropping everything and leaving a plush college life of cello lessons and Civil War history classes and Saturday afternoon football games. They pack their bags and go, knowing they may not come back. Miranda wasn't exactly thrilled to hear about what a waste of a war she was about to enter from people who did not have to worry about making out a will, or making sure they left specific instructions about how they wanted to be buried.

In her journal, she developed several "tips for breaking the news." Among them: "Do not slide the fact that you're going to Iraq into otherwise pleasant conversation. While it is completely okay to use it to get out of uncomfortable conversations, such as when sleazy guys ask for your number at bars (I'd give it to you . . . but I'm going to Iraq), this is not something good to say, when, say, people ask what your postgraduate plans are."

For the most part, she deflected talk of the war with humor. When people asked what Iraq would be like, she'd say it would be a heck of a lot better for her because she was bringing her ultrasoft, 800-thread-count bed sheets. When people asked her what they could send her in care packages, she joked that she was starting a deployment registry at Target, as if she were getting married. "I mean, getting deployed is a big moment in a girl's life," she'd joke. The more concerned her friends were, the lighter she kept the conversation, even boasting that she was going to bring a much-needed dose of style to the desert by wearing pink toenail polish every day of the deployment. This, she soon learned, was the sort of everything's-going-to-be-all-right insouciance that people wanted to hear from their resident soldier. Outside of a few close friends, no one wanted to hear about her worry, or about her frustration at having her life so drastically interrupted, and certainly not about her fear, which was focused on nothing as specific as death or injury or failure but rather on the ominous unknown that lay ahead.

"Keep a chipper attitude," she wrote in her journal. "No one likes a sulky soldier."

If she was a curiosity to her classmates, she was to her professors a physical manifestation of the war itself, a reminder of their own draft-fearing past and in a couple of cases a lesson to be quickly highlighted in class as part of the curriculum.

"Both of my teachers today announced to the class that it would be my last day and to wish me well," she wrote in her journal shortly before leaving campus in October. "I managed to not cry both times, although there was some definite lump in the throat action. I imagine that I had about the same look on my face that people get when a friend announces to the entire room that it is their birthday. I wasn't sure if I should smile, look sad, or pretend like the professor was talking about someone else. In both classes, I could hear gasps of true shock. It's uncomfortable to be a living, moving occurrence that proves that a largely unpopular war is not ignorable. I wished that life was like a movie, and there would suddenly be an American flag for me to stand behind while I placed my hands on my hips and boldly exclaimed that I would make the world free for democracy if it was the last thing that I do."

Her last Saturday night on campus, her sisters surprised her by throwing a good-bye party at which they presented her with a pile of cards she couldn't bring herself to read just yet because she knew they'd be too painful. The girls hung on her, sobbing into her shoulder, while she remained, for the most part, stoic, ever the good soldier. She was touched and moved, but all the teary hugs and farewells made her start to feel as if she were attending her own funeral. What she really wanted to do was party. She was going to

Iraq, damn it, and not even the most heartfelt sobs were going to change that fact. Enough, she finally declared to her sorority sisters. Let's get out of here. Let's get drunk and stupid and act like freshmen.

"I refuse to be a downer," she dictated. "And I refuse to let you guys be a downer around me. We're going to have a blast."

As she changed into her toga, Miranda shed her usually abstemious personality. Soon she was dancing with such childlike abandon that she was able, as if in a dream, to forget completely who she was and where she was going.

At about one in the morning, some of the frat boys announced they were going to streak the campus green, and Miranda convinced some of her friends to go along. As the boys ran wild, Miranda struggled to undo all the pins holding her toga together. But soon it slipped off, and she took off running across the grass in the moonlight, her sheet fluttering behind her like a cape in the wind.

2

Ray and Diane

Hurry Up and Wait

Ray Johnson told his wife, Diane, that he wouldn't be called up for Iraq, and she believed him. Why wouldn't she? He hadn't been called up for the first Persian Gulf war, or for Bosnia or Haiti or Kosovo or any of the other missions the National Guard had participated in since Vietnam. He hadn't even been called up after 9/11, though she had been sure he would be.

Now it was late 2005, nearly three years after the United States invaded Iraq. Ray was fifty-eight years old, a grandfather of seven, his hair almost all gray, and with a slight paunch starting to show. He was one of the Guard's oldest helicopter pilots—and the most experienced. In Vietnam, he'd flown hundreds of combat missions, and now he used that experience as an instructor pilot, training soldiers of another generation how to fly Black Hawks. And that, because of his age and rank, he assured Diane again and again, was how he'd stay.

"I'm not going to Iraq," he'd promise.

Even though Ray had been in the military for almost forty years, Diane had never viewed her husband as a soldier. Sure, he went off one weekend a month, two weeks a year for training. But she considered that his hobby. Some husbands played golf. Hers played army.

Ray never boasted about his soldierly credentials, and he hardly ever talked about Vietnam. Over the years he'd become expert in deflecting all questions about that war. Diane knew only a few details: that many members of his flight school class had been killed, and that he'd had some harrowing moments himself. And when he took her to the occasional reunion of Vietnam helicopter pilots, she realized he knew them only from other reunions, not from Vietnam. So many of the people he had served with in the war had been killed. It was a miracle, Ray had told her, that he had survived.

There was this, too: Vietnam had cost him his first marriage. He had married early, at twenty, and impulsively in the weeks before he shipped out. The union was a mistake that could not survive the separation. She waited until he came home from Vietnam to start the divorce proceedings.

Ray and Diane hadn't started dating until almost twenty years after his return from Vietnam, and by then he already considered the war ancient history, best left alone. They were both divorced, living in North Carolina. She was thirty-two, working as a librarian. He was a forty-one-year-old police officer and hospital medevac pilot. They met through a mutual friend who thought they'd make a good match. Why the friend thought that was a mystery to Diane, especially when she asked what Ray did for a living.

"He's a cop," the friend told her.

"A cop? I don't want anything to do with a cop."

"Well, he's also a helicopter pilot in the military."

"I don't want anything to do with someone in the military."

Diane was an intellectual, a bookworm, and she figured she'd end up with a college professor. She didn't know anyone in the military and didn't really care to.

When Ray came swaggering uninvited up her driveway in his uniform a few days later, she could only wonder, What in the world does this police officer want? Her two-year-old, Sara, had red Popsicle stains all over her face and had just wet her pants. Diane was chasing her around the yard, trying to get her upstairs and into the tub.

"Are you Diane?" the officer asked. When she didn't say anything, he offered, "I'm Ray."

Only then did it hit her: This was the guy her friend had told her about. They chatted for a bit, but Sara was now hanging upside down on the fence, her sundress over her head, her bare bottom exposed. This wasn't the best time to get to know each other.

"I'll call you later," Ray said.

Yeah right, Diane thought.

A few hours later he did call. And as they got to know each other over the next few months, the army stereotype began to fade. He seemed too gentle to be a soldier or a police officer or anyone for whom carrying a weapon was as common as wearing a belt. He was polite, had manners, looked her in the eye—someone obviously had raised this man right, she thought. Plus, he had a smile that projected trust and warmth. This, she decided, was no shoot-'em-up grunt.

Not that he was a romantic interest. She didn't need a lover, she needed a friend. Her husband had up and left her less than a year before, leaving her alone with two children, no alimony, and very little child support. Money was tight. She stayed up nights worrying about how she was going to raise her children alone on a librarian's salary. She was part of a support group for divorced men and women, and she was still too unsure of herself, and of men, to start dating again.

"I knew I wasn't interested in Ray," she said. "I never looked at him as a romantic interest."

Over the following weeks and months, he dutifully played the role of good friend. They talked on the phone, had coffee together, went for walks. But they never dated, and he never pushed it. Instead, they talked, and he listened to her in a way that no one ever had. "Men are always wanting to fix things for you," she said. "But I could tell him all my problems and he would listen, really listen."

Soon she was telling him everything, opening up as she hadn't to anyone, not even her ex-husband. She felt safe around Ray, and she trusted him enough to talk about her mother's battle with depression, her own messy divorce, the loneliness she felt in trying to raise two children alone. He charmed her, not with money or flash but with a gentleman's sincerity and the selflessness that comes with love.

He didn't want to admit it, but Ray had fallen for her—desperately. He hadn't told Diane, but he had been engaged to someone else when they'd first met. Now, after spending time with Diane, he knew that relationship was doomed, and he'd called off the wedding. In his mind, no one compared to Diane, this quiet, strong woman who was now making it as a single mom. Plus, she was simply beautiful—a classic midwestern girl from Youngstown, Ohio, with green eyes, chestnut hair, and a shy smile.

Even before they'd met, Ray had known he was going to be moving from North Carolina to Maryland to work for the state police. Now, just a few months after meeting Diane, the day he was scheduled to leave was fast approaching, and he realized there was no way he'd be able to move there without her. Unable to stand it any longer, he stopped by her house one morning before going to work. Immediately, she wanted to know what was wrong. By the long look on his face, she thought someone had died.

"I think I love you," he blurted out.

There. It was out. He had said it. But he wasn't sure she felt the same way. He hadn't thought that far ahead. Suddenly it dawned on him that she might not reciprocate. And so, fearing rejection, he bolted before she could respond.

Diane was so stunned that she couldn't run after him. She just stood in her kitchen, speechless. Did she love him, too? She wasn't sure. This had all snuck up on her so quickly. But as she thought about it over the next few weeks, which were agonizing for Ray, she knew that she did love him. His bold, almost juvenile declaration had suddenly stirred something in her. The more she reflected on it, the more she saw the gesture as a genuine extension of the sweet and sincere man she had come to care for over these past months. She now had to decide how much she cared for him and to what degree. But once she focused on the question, she was soon awakened to that fact that her love had been building up in her quietly, slowly in lockstep with her trust in him.

Her newfound affection for Ray didn't take only Diane by surprise. When she told her aunt she was seeing a Vietnam vet, the aunt wondered aloud whether he had any psychological issues from the war. Given everything Ray had seen and been through in Southeast Asia, a lot of people had worried he'd come home scarred and shell-shocked, unable to function like so many other veterans. The truth was, the war made him stronger, more mature and confident. Time and time again, he had flown straight into the fire and emerged unscathed—which didn't make him feel invincible as much as lucky. For whatever reason, he had been spared. He had watched his friends die, and he feared death himself. But when it was all finally over, he realized that during those months he had grown into a better version of himself, ready to tackle whatever was next. It was the antithesis of the stereotypical portrayal of Vietnam veterans—bereft and homeless, trying to chase away their ghosts with booze and drugs. But that was not Ray.

A few months later, Ray and Diane married. And during a trip to Florida that served as both a honeymoon and a vacation with the kids, Diane leaned back in her lounge chair and nestled her toes in the sand. The waves were lapping gently, the sun was warm on her face and arms, and she watched Ray build a sandcastle by the shore with her kids. She could feel years' worth of tension and worry dissipate.

For the first time in her life, she felt, she could truly relax.

Years later, as the country geared up for the first Gulf war in 1991, a friend asked Diane if Ray was going to be deployed.

"For what?" Diane wondered. It never even occurred to her that Ray could end up going to war. He was in the National Guard, not the active army, and the Guard didn't go to war. If there was a tornado, or a hurricane, or a riot, she knew he'd be called. That's what, in her mind, the Guard was for: a sort of glorified police force called up to protect the home front. "If he were an active-duty soldier I never would have married him," she said.

But now in the Iraq War, more than a decade later, thousands upon thousands of Guardsmen and reservists were being mobilized. "Are you going to go?" she asked her husband again and again. Each time the answer was the same, No. He was too old, he said. His rank prevented deployment. Plus, the army needed him at home to train the young pilots who were going.

What he didn't tell her was that increasingly he wanted to go. Like so many others, he had come to view the Vietnam War as a sad chapter in U.S. history. Ray was proud of his service, but not of the way politicians had handled the war, and he would have liked to serve in a conflict that the whole country supported. Somehow, he felt, that could make up for Vietnam. He was also getting tired of training all those kids. They reminded him of himself before Vietnam, eager and scared at the same time. It didn't seem right to keep sending them off to fly in combat while he stayed home. I may be old, he thought, but I can still fly. He did so almost every day with the Maryland State Police, tracking bad guys and transporting the injured to the hospital. He could do some good in Iraq, he thought, maybe save some of these younger pilots from getting killed.

He got the message the day he and Diane returned from a European vacation, September 11, 2005: A Black Hawk Guard unit in Virginia, the 2-224th, needed all the pilots it could get, and Ray's name was on the list. He waited until he and Diane were getting ready for bed to break the news. It had been a hectic day of traveling, and now Diane just wanted get everything unpacked and straightened up. Ray pulled her toward the bed, lay down next to her, and pulled her close.

"Honey, I've got something to tell you," he said. Immediately she feared the worst.

He's leaving me, she thought. There could be no other explanation for the paralyzing dread she was feeling. They had just spent three blissful weeks in Europe. But she still bore the scars from her first marriage, and something in his tone made her realize that whatever he was about to say was serious. Maybe he had lost his job, she thought.

"I'm being sent to Iraq," he said.

She had been ready to believe that he wanted a divorce, or that he had been fired, or any other manner of catastrophic news. But this she was not prepared for. He was a fifty-eight-year-old grandfather. Grandfathers don't go to war. He hadn't been deployed when his home unit in the Maryland National Guard was sent to Iraq. Why would he be going now? This had to be some sort of mistake.

"I don't understand," she said. "How can this be?"

The Guard is hard up for Black Hawk pilots—it's my turn. Orders are orders, he told her. He didn't want to go, but he didn't have a choice. A unit from Virginia badly needed pilots, and it would grant him a waiver so that he could deploy with the unit.

She was dumbfounded. How dangerous would it be? Where in Iraq would he be stationed? Would they be able to talk? Ray tried to keep her calm, but she was frantic. He was supposed to retire soon. How would this affect his job with the state police? And how would she handle everything at home all by herself? A massive tornado had come within a quarter mile of their home three years before. What if there was another one while he was gone?

But no matter how many questions she asked, she could not comprehend how this could happen. It just didn't make sense. "I don't understand," she said again and again.

There had to be something else, something he was not telling her.

Initially, Ray was supposed to report within a month. But the army had not yet cut his orders, which he would need to travel.

And so he waited. And waited. The 2-224th, the unit to which
he had been assigned, was in the Arizona desert training with the
Marine Corps, and Ray was still at home while the army bureaucracy worked on the proper paperwork needed to get him there.

Ray told his bosses at the state police that he'd be shipping out
soon. He and Diane girded themselves for the day he'd finally
leave. And Ray got himself readied for war. But the orders didn't
come. Weeks passed, and still nothing. Diane allowed herself to
believe that maybe he wasn't going after all, that it had all been a
bad dream. But getting her hopes up, she knew, was dangerous.
She needed to prepare herself for the deployment.

Ray, meanwhile, was growing angry. He could see that the waiting anguished Diane, and it was downright unfair to his employer,
who justifiably wanted to know if they were going to have to find
someone to cover his shifts or not. After thirty-eight years in the
military, he knew all too well that the army was a massive bureaucracy whose unofficial motto was "Hurry up and wait." But this was
ridiculous. His life was on hold.

By the time the orders finally came, three months had passed. It
was now January. The training in the Arizona desert was over. Ray
would make a short stop at Fort Bliss, Texas, then head straight
for Iraq. By now Diane was just as livid with the army as Ray was:
This is how the government treats its soldiers?

CNN had heard about the Vietnam vet about to ship off to Iraq
and asked if they could do a story on Ray. Before the cameras they
were every bit the model American family, patriots with stiff upper
lips, sound bites at the ready. "My number's come up so I feel that
I must serve," Ray said. "As long as I signed up and received the
benefits I felt that whenever they need me where they need me
I had to pay back."

The cameras rolled as Diane hugged him good-bye and wished
him luck.

They didn't for a moment let on about how angry they were at
the army.

3

Kate

Be All You Can Be

"Mom, I have to talk to you."

What had her daughter done now, Nancy Broome thought. Was she in trouble? Sick? Did she need money? Kate was a great kid, did well in high school, and never had a curfew because she didn't need one. But recently she'd been running a little wild—drinking, smoking pot. A few months before, she had dropped out of college. Not that Kate bothered to actually stop by the registrar's office and disenroll; she simply stopped going. A semester's tuition down the drain. Then Nancy remembered the mother-daughter conversation they'd had in the car three months before, when Kate matter-of-factly informed her that she'd lost her virginity.

Nancy had responded in her typical fashion, dissolving the tension with sarcasm: "Didn't I tell you, you couldn't until I did?" She had that kind of open relationship with both Kate and Kate's twin

35

sister, Becky. She'd raised them as best she could, considering her husband had died when the kids were three. But now Kate was telling her mother to sit down, and was nervously fiddling with her cigarette.

"You're pregnant," Nancy Broome said. It wasn't a question so much as an educated guess.

Kate's having a baby would have been bad, yes. She was just eighteen years old and didn't seem capable of taking care of herself, let alone another human being. Who knew who the father was, and if he'd want any part of the baby. Nancy doubted Kate would marry the guy. No, she could take them in, baby and all. They'd deal with it as a family. Things could be a lot worse than a pregnancy. A baby would bring some stability to her daughter's life, force her to finally grow up, take on some responsibility.

"No, Mom. I'm not pregnant," Kate said.

Well, then what? Nancy wondered. What was the worst thing her daughter could say right now? That she had cancer? She was running away? Joining the circus? The army?

Oh, no, she thought. Not that. Anything but that.

Nancy Broome graduated from high school in 1966 and saw her classmates drafted in droves. For her, the military was inextricably linked to the Vietnam conflict, an unjust and ugly war that took so many of her generation. The military was the blond-haired boy ahead of her in school who came back from the Southeast Asian jungle so disfigured, she could only think, "His mother is going to have to change his diaper for the rest of his life." Years later, as the last of the troops were finally coming home from Vietnam, she went to her best friend's house to watch the coverage on her TV. She watched those soldiers get off the plane and couldn't help but think, "Where are the parades? Why aren't the businesses closing down? Why isn't this a national holiday?"

Now it was 1999, and although there was no war in sight, still the very thought of her daughter joining the military was one of her greatest fears.

"You didn't join the army," she said.

Kate was shocked that her mother guessed correctly. Never had Kate shown even the slightest interest in the armed services. She knew only one person who had joined, an acquaintance from high school. To her and virtually every one of her friends, the military simply was never an option. Everyone went to college, or worked, and that was that. But her mother knew her better than she thought.

"Yes, I did," Kate said finally.

"Well, wouldn't you rather be pregnant?" Nancy blurted out.

It was yet more of her usual sarcasm. Kate let out a rolling laugh so similar to her mother's it was as if she had inherited it along with her curly hair and brown eyes. But Nancy was at least partly serious: She'd almost rather Kate were pregnant than enlisted. And though they were laughing, there was nothing funny about joining the army, and Nancy wanted to make that clear. This was a serious commitment. Once you signed, you were in, she lectured her daughter.

But Kate knew she had to make it work. She had no other options. Her life was stalled. She hadn't lasted more than two months at Pellissippi State Technical Community College in Knoxville. Before midterms, she had simply stopped going to class and was instead partying almost every night, all night—bong hits and bars. She played a particularly pernicious drinking game called King's Cup in which each player had to pour some of their drink (no matter if it was beer, wine, or booze) into a bowl whenever they pulled a king from a deck of cards. When the fourth king was pulled, the person who drew it would have to down the whole noxious brew.

For money, Kate was delivering pizza in an eleven-year-old Ford Tempo that she had bought for $2,000 with her sister. They'd saved up for months because the rule in their mother's house was that you were responsible enough to get a driver's license only when you could afford to buy a car on your own. Nancy's daughters were going to learn the value of work. But the girls didn't take care of their car, never changed the oil, and when it died less than a year after they bought it, Kate left it to rust on the side of the road. No car meant no job. No job, no money. And so Kate moved back home.

She'd been an honor student in high school, the kind of kid you didn't worry about. But now, a year after graduation, Kate felt as if she had screwed everything up, including college, which was going to be her ticket out of Knoxville, and she had no way to make it right. She was working a crappy minimum-wage job at a Chuck E. Cheese–like facility for kids, realizing what a mistake she had made by dropping out and wondering where she could scrape together the money to get back into college.

At first she didn't even notice the army recruiting office two doors down from her job. But eventually she found herself taking smoke breaks in front of the office, studying the recruiting posters. The army offered a life of travel and adventure and, most important, an escape, a chance to "Be All You Can Be." Normally she would have seen that phrase as a corny marketing ploy. But in her current state it called out to her. She so clearly was not being all she could be, and it bothered her. The recruiters who went in and out of the office were fit and cute. Slick salesmen all, who'd been trained not only to be warriors, but to be charming and confident—the military's ambassadors to the civilian world.

It wasn't long until she was in front of the office again, puffing on a Camel Light, her mind made up. The recruiter whom she'd gotten to know a little bit during her smoke breaks came out and lit a cigarette of his own.

"So when are you going to come in and talk to me about joining the army?" he said.

Kate blew a breath of smoke. "Right after I finish this cigarette," she said.

The recruiter's eyes bulged. "Let's hurry up and finish these cigarettes," he said, sucking his down in huge tokes. He started immediately screening her to see if she'd qualify. Did she have a high school diploma? Had she ever been arrested? He asked her not if she used drugs, but "Could you pass a drug test?"

"Not if you gave me one today," Kate admitted.

"You smoked pot once and didn't like it," he suggested.

She looked at him, dumbfounded, not knowing what to say.

"You smoked pot once and didn't like it," the recruiter said again, and Kate got it: He wasn't asking her. He was coaching her about how to handle questions about her past drug use.

"Right," she said.

Not a problem, the recruiter said. Stay clean for three weeks and we'll test you then.

She passed the test, and soon she was shipped off to basic training, where for the first few weeks she thought of quitting every day. But eventually she fell into a rhythm, finding the structure even comforting. She kept her bunk clean, her boots polished. All the running and push-ups were soon toning her body, giving her a confidence she'd never had. Eventually, she even came to like the drill instructors, who had in the beginning lambasted her for her inability to keep her unruly curly hair at the regulation above-the-shoulders length.

By the time she completed, she'd lost enough weight, some fifteen pounds, that she didn't fit into any of her old clothes. So Kate asked her mom if she'd take her to the mall to buy her some new jeans. They found a two-for-one special, but when they got to the register they realized that neither pair had a price tag. So Kate ran back and got a third pair with the price attached, and didn't realize until she got home later that the cashier had mistakenly included them in the bag as well.

"Mom, you need to take me back to the mall," she said.

"Why?" Nancy Broome demanded. "I don't go to the mall twice in a year, why would I go there twice in a day?"

"Because they gave me three jeans by mistake, and I need to return one of them," Kate said.

"Well, what do you want to do that for? You got a free pair," said a friend who happened to be visiting.

"Haven't you heard of the word 'integrity'? Does that word mean anything to you?" Kate said.

Her mother beamed: That's my daughter.

Kate shipped out to Fort Lewis, Washington, because out of the choices the army offered, it was the farthest away from home—and her past life—as she could get. The military entrance exam, which the army uses to determine what sort of soldier you'll be, found her best suited for military intelligence, military police, or work as a medic. She figured her past drug use would disqualify her for intelligence work, and there was no way she'd become a cop. That left medicine, and the irony was that as she was struggling to get her own life together, she'd be learning how to save others'.

The medics at Fort Lewis were a tight bunch. They pulled long shifts together; trained together; lived, ate, and socialized together, almost as a breed apart from the other soldiers. So it was no surprise that eventually she started dating one of them. At first it was strictly a working relationship. But soon they realized they had a lot in common, and they made fast friends. He was married with three kids, but about to begin a messy divorce. She was there for him. They started hanging out constantly, so much so that their commanders wrote them up for it. Then they were in love. It just happened. There were no grand romantic overtures, just a natural evolution from acquaintance, to friend, to lover. It seemed like the most normal thing in the world.

When their enlistments were up, they decided to move to Virginia because it was halfway between her hometown (Knoxville) and his (Philadelphia). Kate had decided she was finally ready to give college another shot, and Virginia had some great state schools. She'd be more disciplined this time—the army had taught her that. She'd study hard and go to class, and maybe one day she'd even become a teacher. The only way to pay for school was to stay in the military, which didn't bother her. She'd gotten used to the lifestyle, and she thought her newfound discipline would help her get through classes. So she transferred to the National Guard, figuring the one-weekend-a-month training would fit her college schedule.

By now it was 2004, and already the rumors of her new unit, the 2-224th, going to war were spreading through the ranks. But Kate knew that soldiers gossip every bit as much schoolgirls, and she didn't believe a word of it. The battalion had returned in 2001 from a six-month tour in Bosnia. There was no way the army would deploy them again so soon. She enrolled in Virginia Commonwealth University, a twenty-five-year-old sophomore in classes with kids who were no older than the privates she used to boss around as a section sergeant. Old as she felt, she was thrilled to be back in school. She and her boyfriend rented a cute apartment in a trendy neighborhood of bars and coffee shops known as the Fan, the closest thing Richmond had to Greenwich Village.

Then on a cold, rainy morning, the phone rang at six thirty. Kate answered in a state of half sleep. She had her final sociology exam in two hours and had been up late studying.

"You better have your shit together," the voice on the line was saying. It was her sergeant. "We're going to Iraq."

It wasn't yet clear when, or for how long, but the long-whispered rumor had now officially become fact. By now her boyfriend had sleepily followed her into the living room, and as soon as she told him, she broke down into sobs. She wasn't ready to pick up and leave, not after she had gotten her life back together. The thought of having to ship to Iraq where who knows what sort of horror awaited didn't shake her; Iraq was still very much an abstraction. Though she didn't know it at the time, the 2-224th wouldn't deploy for another ten months. What scared her more was that with a single phone call, her life had been completely upended. Not that she was surprised. She knew the drill. But she had a boyfriend and a cozy apartment and was getting good grades. Things were perfect as they were. Now it felt as if the once-solid ground she stood on was shifting like quicksand, and she needed something solid to hold on to.

A week later they were married in a rundown chapel they found in the phone book. The pastor, whose congregation consisted mostly of the homeless, showed up in jeans and a flannel shirt. Kate wore a white linen dress, but she'd forgotten the bouquet of white roses her coworkers had given her. So the pastor handed her the most hideous arrangement of orange, blue, and red fake roses, which Kate held only because she didn't want to insult him.

They had invited no one, and had told only a few people that they were actually going through with their plans. There was no photographer, no best man, no maid of honor. A framed hologram of Jesus seemed to mock her from a nearby wall. The ceremony was brief. And when the pastor got to the part about "standing before these witnesses," he quickly added that consisted of God because the folding chairs scattered around the room were empty.

"It was not the wedding I wanted," Kate said.

Still, she was thrilled to have taken the step. It would get her through the year in Iraq. He was her rock, and now that they were married, she'd have something to look forward to at home, something to sustain her. Shortly before she left for Iraq, she wrote in her online journal:

> sometimes i think there must be a way out of this . . . but i know i have to go . . . i have to leave my family . . . my husband . . . my friends . . . my dogs . . . i heard my sister cry last night when i left her house. it was so hard to walk away, and i know she thinks i didn't hear her. But i did, becky. i love you and want you to know i am going to be okay . . .
>
> and last night my husband and i held each other all night long. i needed that so much. you know, he is my home. wherever ken is, that is the most wonderful place in the whole world to me. leaving him for a year means i will be emotionally homeless for a very long time.

4

Mark

Sir, I'm a Citizen-Soldier

Mark was by far the wildest of her three children, so hard to control that Elaine Baush used to say that if Mark had been the firstborn he would have been an only child. Shortly after he learned to walk, he jumped into the deep end of a motel pool during a family vacation and sank right to the bottom, forcing his then eleven-year-old sister to jump in fully clothed and pull him out. In high school, he snuck out his second-floor bedroom window to meet his buddies and sometimes play a reckless game called "roof-top surfing," where Mark would cling to a car roof while it sped as fast as seventy miles per hour through the twisting country roads of northern Virginia, where he grew up.

Other families had family pediatricians; the Baushes, thanks to Mark's numerous injuries, had a family surgeon, whom his mother "begged not to retire until Mark was grown." And when Mark announced he was going to attend the all-male Virginia Military Institute for college, Elaine knew there would be no point in protesting, even if the school's Spartan ethos clashed with her liberal sensibilities.

His interest in VMI had come as a surprise. But given the way her father regaled Mark and his other grandchildren with stories about his naval service during World War II, perhaps it shouldn't have. Elaine mounted a protest she knew would not dissuade her obstinate son, and she tried to enlist her husband, who had served in the air force and flown missions into French Indochina before the Vietnam War. But he said Mark was old enough to make his own decisions, and he assured her that the rigors of VMI would be good for their son.

Located in the Blue Ridge Mountains, in Lexington, Virginia, VMI aimed to create citizen-soldiers of the highest caliber. "There may be no other college experience in America so proud of its product: citizen-soldiers prepared both for civilian and military leadership and service to their nation in times of need," the brochure boasted. Founded in 1839 by the Commonwealth of Virginia, VMI was a reaction to the creation of the U.S. Military Academy at West Point thirty-seven years earlier. While that august institution trained officers for the country's army, several states, including Virginia, felt they needed military institutions of their own to supply their militias with quality leadership.

Like all incoming classes, the members of Mark's class were bused to the New Market battlefield, where during the Civil War in 1864 more than 250 cadets fought and 10 were killed. On that ground, before taking their oath, the new cadets would learn they were part of a long American tradition, stretching back generations, of citizen-soldiers. It was a tradition that was alive and well at New Market, and before then, when the Massachusetts General Court directed various militia companies to organize into three regiments on December 13, 1636, now considered the birthday of the National Guard. The young men standing in an old Civil War battlefield were part of a tradition that was enshrined in the Bill of

Rights and seen as a central tenet of American democracy, which has always looked suspiciously at large standing armies. On his midnight ride, Paul Revere never said, "The British are coming." Instead, he warned that the "Regulars are coming out." In other words, the Red Coats of the king's professional army, seen then as the arm of tyranny and the antithesis of the Colonies' democratic citizen-based militias. The militia, John Adams wrote, was one of the pillars of American society because it was rooted in the civilian world and therefore "comprehends the whole people."

Taking their oath on a Civil War battlefield, Mark and his classmates were indeed part of that continuum. But like the military as a whole, VMI had become to outsiders another, insular world, wholly removed from the civilian realm. At the center of campus was a tall, castlelike fortress that to Elaine seemed better suited to repelling invasions than enlightening young minds. Taps signaled bedtime at 2300. Reveille at 0700. The students slept in barracks, not dorms. And the students weren't even students. They were cadets. First-year students, like her son, were not even that. They were "Rats" who had to survive a grueling Hell Week, and a ritual called "the Ratline," which lasts about six months and according to the institute was to "assemble a class imbued with honor, discipline, pride and respect." But to Elaine it all seemed a perverse, even medieval, way to break down young men, who she thought were no more than baby-faced boys.

Upperclassmen meted out discipline through testosterone-fueled "sweat parties," which mainly consisted of working the Rats to the point of exhaustion with countless push-ups and long runs at all hours. Around the barracks Rats had to maintain a "strain" position—shoulders rolled back as far as possible with their chins pulled back into their necks. In the cafeteria, Rats had to sit on the most forward four inches of their chairs, their backs straight, and eat square meals, and failure to comply with any part of the exercise could lead to more push-ups, more running, more yelling, less eating. The Honor Code was strict; Rats were warned that even pocketing a lost penny was tantamount to stealing. Violation of the code could quickly lead to expulsion. And whenever anyone was kicked out, the cadets learned about it in a somber dead-of-night ceremony, with drums rousing them out of bed to hear the Honor Court President in full dress uniform say of the condemned, "He has placed personal gain above personal honor and has left the Institute in shame. His name will never be mentioned in these four walls of Barracks again." By the end of each year, about 20 percent of each incoming class would quit of their own accord, which is exactly what the administration wanted: to weed out the weak.

Elaine thought the school's traditions were silly at best and ghastly at worst. The sight of young men marching about in uniform was stunning for a woman who'd come of age in the 1960s, attended Mary Washington College, and believed college was a time for self-expression, experimentation, and discovery, not strictly enforced conformity. When she saw Mark during her first parents' weekend visit, her impression of VMI worsened exponentially. The strain of Hell Week and the Ratline had left Mark laid up in the infirmary with pneumonia. He was so gaunt in his striped robe that Elaine thought he must have lost twenty-five pounds. With his hollow cheeks and shaved head, "he looked like a prisoner of war," she later recalled. "I just wanted to snatch my baby out of there." But despite her pleading, he refused to go home.

One of the school administrators had told a group of parents that most people either loved or hated the place, and Elaine knew exactly to which camp she belonged. She felt even more strongly when, during Mark's sophomore year, the Justice Department sued the institute, arguing that as a publicly funded college it could not exclude women. Women would do this place some good, she thought. The Supreme Court eventually agreed, ruling in 1996 that VMI had to admit women. The following year it did.

But despite his mother's misgivings, Mark had found his calling. During his four years there, he had, as the brochures promised, become a man. He studied harder than he ever had, learned to keep his room neat, tuck in his shirt, look people in the eye. VMI had harnessed his feckless energy and transformed him into a young man who arranged his socks in neat rows, each with a matching upturned smile crease in the fold. Elaine couldn't help but notice how passionate he was about the place—even if his mischief kept him perilously close to getting kicked out himself.

A short, skinny kid who had had a shock of brown hair prior to its being shaved, Mark looked, and acted, like Ferris Bueller, which soon became his nickname. As if VMI didn't heap on enough sleep-deprived stress, Mark went out looking for adventure on his own, often sneaking out of the barracks at night. Escaping the tightly secured campus, known as "running the block," was a feat in itself that required Mark to slip by two sets of guards and lower himself out of a second-story window using two sets of bed sheets tied together.

One night, he and some friends snuck out and got drunk on Mad Dog, and Mark didn't stumble back to the barracks until just before dawn. At Reveille, an hour or so later, his roommates, disgusted that Mark had snuck out to party yet again, dragged him out of bed and left him to get dressed and ready by himself. He threw on his uniform blouse, his black socks, black shoes, and his hat, but he forgot to change out of the fluorescent pink and purple "Jams" shorts he had been wearing the night before. Still drunk, he stumbled out into formation just in time.

Mark's fellow cadets tried to hide him in the back of formation before anyone saw him. But it was too late. This morning a special delegation of ROTC cadets from other colleges had come for an award that VMI bestowed on the best ROTC programs in the country. Mark's ROTC instructor, who had the reputation of being a real hard-ass, no small distinction at VMI, took one look at Mark and went straight to him.

"MR. BAUSH," he thundered, "WHAT IS THE MEANING OF THIS?"

"Of what, sir?" Mark was drunk enough to have forgotten his pants, but no VMI cadet ever forgot to use the word "Sir" when addressing a senior officer.

"Of these pants?" The instructor's face was bright red now.

Mark glanced down at his shorts, smiled, and said, "Sir, I'm a citizen-soldier."

He pointed to his shorts and said, "Citizen."

Then he pointed to his uniform. "Soldier."

The other cadets in formation were too shocked to laugh, and they knew Mark was about to get reamed.

"Well, Mr. Baush, citizen or not, you are FUCKED."

The punishment was severe. Mark, who was already on probation for various infractions, was nearly kicked out. But it was worth it, every last demerit. He was, in one fell swoop, a near-mythological hero on campus. For weeks, cadets whom Mark didn't even know came up and congratulated him for the crazy stunt and marveled how he had managed not getting expelled. They'll be telling that story for years, other cadets said. And they did. Emboldened by the glory his mischief had brought, Mark was awakened to a lesson he had perhaps known all along and, ironically, VMI had been trying to instill in him ever since he arrived, which was this: The greater risk you took, the more pain you endured, but the higher the stakes, the bigger the reward.

At VMI, as in the military as a whole, the ratio of courage to glory, of pain to triumph, was the fundamental calculus that fed the ambitions of people like Mark and transformed them into self-sacrificing soldiers, capable of inexplicable acts and heroism, even if it meant breaking the occasional rule. This was what drove him. The whispers in the chow hall. The younger cadets pointing at him. He fed off it like a drug.

VMI not only taught him how to become a man, and a gentleman—and to know the difference—but it also helped him discover something about himself that the school didn't advertise in its brochures. Somewhere in the Ratline and Hell Week, in the pre-dawn push-ups and the moonlit runs, he had stumbled upon a switch inside him that allowed him to tap an atavistic toughness. Flick the switch and he was on a wide-eyed, adrenaline-fueled, hyperfocused high, immune to pain and infused with the ability to keep a blank expression as an upperclassman sprayed spittle-laced derision all over his face, to run the extra mile when his legs seized, to smile and remember his "Yes, Sir" etiquette, even when blindingly drunk, when the ROTC officer called him out in front of the entire corps of cadets.

In short, the ability to stay cool under fire.

When he graduated, he did not go straight into the National Guard like so many of his classmates, a decision that pleased his mother immensely. Four years of VMI was enough military for now. As good a soldier as he was, there was still too much juvenile Ferris Bueller in him to make a good officer and have other soldiers depend on him. Instead, Mark set his sights on the business world and making his first million. Within three years of graduation, he was well on his way. He had bought a farmhouse on fifty-five acres in the Shenandoah Valley and was commuting into the Washington, D.C., suburbs, where he worked as an assistant manager of a financial services branch, pulling in nearly six figures processing loans. This was the life his mother had wished for him, and by every objective measure, Mark was thriving. Good job. Good car. Good house.

Except that he was miserable. He hated everything about it: wearing a tie, working nine to five, being tethered to a desk, the fluorescent lighting, the traffic on his hour-plus commute. He hated his office, his boss, and the stale air, and he especially hated that every once in a while he caught disturbing glimpses of himself thirty years hence caught in the same stifling trap. At twenty-five, he was having a midlife crisis.

He missed the camaraderie of VMI, the adventure, even the pain the place inflicted on its cadets. At least that was real. He missed flicking the switch, and every once in a while he tested himself, just to see if he still had it. "It," of course, was the hard-to-define, wild, masochistic, never-say-die reckless abandon that had been his lifeline at VMI but had since his leaving begun to fade—or so he feared. Once, at a party two years after graduation, Mark stepped on a piece of broken glass and sliced open the instep of his left foot. Instead of going to the emergency room, he sterilized a needle with Bacardi and closed the inch-long gash with three stitches of dental floss while stone sober. Yeah, he thought while rejoining the party, I still got it.

Life in the civilian world had become a numbing bore. Mark needed a challenge. So when one of his VMI friends, who had gone straight into the Guard, announced he was running the Richmond marathon, Mark said he'd run half of it with him even though he had not trained at all. When his friend left him at the second-mile marker, Mark felt like an out-of-shape civilian fool, whose soldier friend had literally passed him by—in the race and, Mark thought, in life. His friends who had gone straight into the Guard were rising up through the ranks, flying Hueys and Black Hawks and prancing about in flight suits while Mark was spinning his wheels in corporate America.

As he lagged behind his buddy in the race, Mark suddenly decided he would run the whole 26.2 miles. It was an impulsive, crazy decision—and completely typical—spawned subconsciously by the belief that finishing the marathon was a way of making up for his boring civilian life. At mile 10, his legs were cramping and his breath escaped him. At mile 15, he had to start walking. By mile 20, his walk deteriorated into a limp. His feet, covered in blisters, throbbed. Blood trickled through his shoes, and he figured he had lost at least three or four toenails. Hours passed. Streetlights guided the way, and the course was empty. Eventually, a work crew came by in a truck picking up the traffic cones and opening the street to traffic. They offered him a ride, which he refused. But he did take the map they handed him so that he could find the finish line. He had flicked the switch, could taste the bitterness of the adrenaline in the back of his throat, and could feel the pain enveloping every part of his weary body, as he kept going.

Later, when he told people he had run a marathon on a whim, they would think he was crazy or stupid or both. But the long, painful journey of the marathon was the anodyne to a boring life, a cleansing, refreshing rite that reminded him what he'd been taught at VMI, which was, simply put: You can accomplish more than you think. Trite as it sounded, Mark had always believed it. And now, willing himself toward the finish line, hobbled and bloodied but not defeated, he believed it all the more. It wasn't just pushing his limits that he missed. He longed for VMI's ethos and wanted to again live by its code, which was absent in the "Me first" civilian world. VMI had changed him, perhaps forever, in some fundamental ways, and it wasn't just in developing a tolerance for pain. There was a profound emotional component in making himself a better person, a better soldier, sacrificing for the greater good. Stripped by exhaustion of pretense, he found his race-course epiphany as powerful as a baptism. He knew now where he belonged, and it was not working in a cubicle at a job he hated. He needed to get back into uniform.

Finally, after nearly seven hours, Mark completed his marathon. The streets were empty. The finish line had been taken down. And he was in so much pain, he could barely walk. His friends, who thought he'd quit the race and gone home, were surprised when Mark called.

"Never say die, motherfuckers," Mark bellowed into the receiver. "Now come pick me up."

Within a week, he had talked to a recruiter. Within a few months he had enlisted in the Virginia Army National Guard. It felt good to be back, and he dedicated himself to it in a way he never had to anything else. Basic training was a breeze; Mark graduated as his battalion's Honor Graduate. A few months later, he was off to Officer Candidate School. After that, he was one of the few Guardsmen to go to the elite Army Ranger School, which he completed despite developing a stress fracture in his left foot with three grueling weeks left to go. Later came flight school, because that's where his VMI buddies had gone. (Because pilots, the joke went, were automatically issued a big watch, a fast car, and a hot girlfriend.)

Mark moved up through the ranks, from lieutenant to captain, and soon enough he was flying missions. In 2001, he deployed with the 2-224th to Bosnia, where he first discovered that he felt at home in war. When it came time to go to Iraq, he was eager to deploy again, even if it came at great personal sacrifice.

PART TWO

IRAQ

5

Miranda

The Terrorists Ate My Homework

The sign-up sheet for door gunners was posted in the hallway much as if the 2-224th were looking for volunteers for a battalion softball team. The first time Miranda saw it, the sheet was empty, and she passed by without adding her name. Not that she wasn't interested—in fact, she found herself intrigued by the prospect of riding shotgun in a Black Hawk. She just thought that as a woman she wasn't allowed to be a door gunner. Female soldiers were strictly forbidden from combat roles in the armed forces, and Miranda figured all the slots would be filled by the young gung-ho guys in the unit, eager to get up in the air.

Like that of many aviation units, the hierarchy of the 2-224th was marked not just by rank but also by those who flew and those who did not. The cool kids were pilots, door gunners, and crew chiefs, who served not only as door gunners but as onboard mechanics as well. The lower caste consisted of everyone else who worked to keep the birds in the air: the technicians, the supply clerks, the electricians. There were even different uniforms: one-piece flight suits versus the run-of-the-mill army blouse and pants for everyone else.

When Miranda passed the sign-up sheet again a couple days later, it was chock-full of names, and to her surprise many of them belonged to her fellow female soldiers. As she studied the list, she couldn't help but feel proud that so many women had volunteered for one of the most dangerous jobs the unit had to offer—so dangerous, in fact, that a few months earlier she had tried to talk one of her male friends out of volunteering.

"The bullets will be flying both ways," she'd told him. Not only could you get hurt, she lectured, but "you could actually be killing people." Like Miranda, he had a safe rear-echelon job, and she urged him to keep it. But he'd signed up anyway. And now, staring at the list, she could hear herself reciting all the reasons against signing up. But she also couldn't help but think, If he can do it, why can't I?

It was December 2005, and the 2-224th was stationed at Fort Dix, New Jersey, for predeployment training. Soon the battalion would be in Iraq, a prospect that for Miranda was both terrifying and awesome. She was going to war, which meant that someday she would be able to tell her grandchildren she was part of history. And when they asked what the war was like, she didn't want to have to say, Well, I spent most of it in a dank supply office, ordering socks and T-shirts. She'd enlisted in the army in part because after 9/11 she didn't want other people to have to do her fighting for her. But if she were tethered to a desk, even deep in the Iraq desert, wouldn't she still feel as if she were on the sidelines? While part of her was scared out of her mind, another part was, she had to admit, at least a little excited by the prospect of actually getting to see some action. "Somehow, a week of crawling through sand and blowing things up has started to make me feel like I'm really a soldier," she wrote in her journal about the Fort Dix training. "I can really blow things up, take people out, and maybe, just maybe, I could be brave."

She wanted to play a part. But perhaps more important, she believed it was her duty as a woman to make a statement. The army, though by no means perfect, had come a long way in integrating women into the forces, in large part because other female soldiers had stepped up. The 2-224th had three female pilots and a handful of crew chiefs, and the unit's sergeant major, the highest-ranking enlisted soldier, was a woman (and the mother of a young girl) who was almost universally well liked—and respected. Now, Miranda felt, it was her turn. So she pulled a pen from her pocket and added her name to the list.

"I just keep feeling like I can't let this opportunity pass me by," she wrote in her journal "Door gunning is about the closest that a female can get to combat in the Army. There are very few female door gunners in the Army. . . . People keep acting surprised that I'm even allowed to do it. 'Isn't that combat?' they say. Well, yes, it is, but as far as combat goes, it's pretty safe. I'm going to be the one behind the machine gun, not in front of it. I'm going to be the one thousands of feet above the ground, not on the ground. So really, it's combat lite."

But still combat.

The leaders of the 2-224th had a problem that many other units would have envied: too many soldiers signing up for door gunner duty. So many, in fact, that Miranda figured she wouldn't be chosen. That belief was solidified as some of the adrenaline junkies she figured would get the duty started bragging that they had been chosen, and she hadn't heard a word. Miranda wasn't surprised that she hadn't made the cut. She'd been in a helicopter only one time before. And while she was an excellent shot with her M4 rifle, qualifying as a "sharp shooter," she had never squeezed a single round from a door gunner's M240 machine gun, which, at twenty-five pounds and the capacity to fire up to 950 rounds a minute, was another beast entirely. It took courage to sign up, and Miranda felt proud she had done at least that.

Unbeknownst to her, however, her commander, Captain Mark Baush, had in fact chosen her for the duty. It wasn't even a hard decision, he said later. Miranda was clearly more qualified than many of the men. She was a great shot, garnered virtually unanimous kudos about her leadership and judgment, and despite her small stature was quite strong and in great shape. The fact that she was a woman didn't even enter into the equation, Baush said. As a pilot himself, he had a personal stake in choosing door gunners who wouldn't crack under pressure. At formation a few days later when her first sergeant read her name from the official list of door gunners, Miranda was floored. Only one other woman had been chosen. While she stood at attention, trying not to look shocked, she could feel the silent stares of those around her, and could tell what they were thinking: She'll never be able to do it.

The taunting began almost immediately. Not by many soldiers; in fact, most had no problem with Miranda's having been chosen. But one soldier in particular apparently had to make a comment every time he saw Miranda. "You know if the bird goes down you're going to have to carry the weapon—and ammo," he'd say. "You sure you can do that?" When he saw her in the gym, he'd tell her it was a good thing she was working out because she was going to have to get a lot stronger if she was going to be a door gunner. Others chimed in. "We've never had a female crew chief who stuck around," they said. "You sure you don't just want to go back to your desk job?"

Everything was moving so fast. A few shorts weeks before, she had been a student at William and Mary in the middle of rush week. Now she was getting a quick course in the rules of engagement—when and how to fire—and emergency evacuation procedures in the event that a helicopter went down. At the firing range she learned how to lead targets by taking into account the path and speed of the helicopter. She shuddered to think about having to do this for real, when the target wasn't some black-and-white cutout but a live person who in all likelihood would be firing back. Was she really expected to take this all in just weeks before deploying?

As Miranda and her fellow soldiers learned about the difference between a mortar and a rocket, and how the terrorists concocted roadside bombs out of whatever they could get their hands on and planted them in the most unlikely places—litter, dog carcasses, or buried in the ground—she realized she was slowly morphing from being a sorority girl citizen-soldier to being a soldier. Period. At William and Mary, she could live comfortably in denial about the war. But now that the 2-224th was training for combat at Fort Dix, there was no escaping that she was going into combat. But was she ready to be a door gunner? Were the other soldiers right about her? Doubts started to creep in. Maybe I should just stay at my desk job, she thought.

"I've taken a lot of flak for trying to be a female door gunner," she wrote in her journal. "For some reason, even though we've had female flight crews before, apparently females are not strong enough to shoot a mounted weapon. As much as I am filled with the burning desire to prove them wrong, there is the part of me wondering if they are right."

The night before she was to go up in a Black Hawk to test her accuracy with the weapon, she could barely sleep wondering what Iraq would be like. For all the training, she had no real idea how dangerous it would be. Would the base be pummeled regularly with mortars and rockets? Would their flights weave through storms of gunfire that she would be required to return? She kept thinking of the scene in *Apocalypse Now* in which a swarm of helicopters lays waste to an entire Vietnamese village while Wagner's "Ride of the Valkyries" blasts in the background.

She called one of her best childhood friends because she needed someone outside the army to talk to. She would have never admitted this to anyone in the 2-224th, but she was freaking out about the upcoming firing test.

"Why?" her friend asked. "Because you're afraid you might fail?"

"No," Miranda said. "I'm afraid because I might pass, and then I'll have to do this."

"You can always back out," her friend insisted. "You volunteered, remember?"

But she couldn't back out now. The other female soldier who'd been chosen was forging ahead, and so would she. So, as her classmates back at William and Mary were busy with final exams and looking forward to Christmas break, Miranda was wrestling with a troubling question: Would she be able to pull the trigger when a human being was in her sights?

Nearly two hundred miles west of Baghdad, past Ramadi and Fallujah, out in the vast desert of Anbar province, Al Asad Airbase was as different as it could be from a college campus. But in some respects being there reminded Miranda of college life—and not just because she still had homework in the three independent studies her professors consented to so that she could graduate on time.

Just as in college, everyone ate together in a cafeteria, only at Al Asad it was called a "chow hall." Like college students, soldiers complained about the food, deeming it "Geneva Convention–violation bad." But the truth was it just got repetitive after a while. Thanks to the magic of the defense contractors who supplied the food and were no doubt making a bundle doing so, there were burgers, steak, chicken fingers, pizza, pasta, Alaskan crab legs served on seafood night, a salad bar, an ice cream bar, and a rich chocolate cheesecake that was, in the words of one pilot, "as addictive as caffeinated heroin." Outside the chow hall, there was a Burger King, a Subway, and a Green Beans coffee shop that served chai lattes. Other soldiers may have returned home from their tours gaunt, but those who served at Al Asad usually came home having gained weight—their own version of the freshman fifteen.

Except for the mystery novels in place of the textbooks, the base's Post Exchange had everything the college bookstore did. The PX even sold DVD players, televisions, and mountain bikes. To Miranda's chagrin, though, it carried only one brand of female deodorant, while the men had several choices. The Al Asad gym was not nearly as fancy as the one at William and Mary, but it did hold classes, including one called "abs hour." The main difference, as Miranda observed, was that instead of spending equal amounts of time "lifting, flirting, and hanging out at the water fountain, this is the kind of gym where extremely large Marines come to inflict at least two hours of pain upon themselves. . . . I have the feeling that most of the guys here—and the gals—could pick me up, break me in half, and do curls with each half of me without breaking a sweat."

The base had been used by Iraqis as an athletic training facility. Next to the soccer pitch, which was ringed by a track, were the swimming pools and the high dives. Some of the soldiers lived in the old athlete housing, Spartan accommodations they dubbed the R.I.B. ("Rat Infested Barracks") and that had Turkish toilets— holes in the ground—they had to fill with dirt in order to keep the scorpions from crawling up. Soldiers brought their own water to the bathroom to brush their teeth because what came out of the faucet was nearly the color of chocolate milk. And to save water they had to turn off the shower while they lathered up.

Those who were lucky, like Miranda, lived on the other side of the base in "cans," trailers roughly the size and feel of a shipping container. They had it much better: Internet access for $200 every three months, air conditioning, television that showed reruns of American programs such as *House*, *CSI*, and *Law & Order*. In the center of the base was the recreation center, which had phone banks so that service members could call home, Internet access, and pool tables. The hip-hop dances were on Friday nights, salsa on Saturdays, country and western on Sundays. Those who never left the base were known as Fobbits (F.O.B. means "Forward Operating Base"), and for them it was easy to forget there was a war raging outside the wire.

Even though the base was nicknamed "Camp Cupcake" for its relative comforts, it was occasionally pounded by mortars and rock-ets that would trigger the base's screeching alarm system and send soldiers ducking for cover. Virtually every building was protected by towering twelve-foot-high concrete blast walls, and U-shaped bunkers designed to provide protection against mortar attacks sat on corners. But unlike those at many military bases, the service members stationed at Al Asad were not required to keep their body armor and helmets on at all times.

But perhaps what made Al Asad seem like college the most to Miranda were the bonds she formed with her fellow soldiers, which were not unlike those she'd formed with her sorority sisters. In Iraq, she shared a trailer with three other female soldiers, and they soon became close. They stayed up nights talking about everything from politics to relationships, and during those moments she could very well have been back on campus, gossiping with her college friends. One night a couple of months into the deployment, Miranda and one of her roommates had a particularly intense conversation about commitment and marriage that made them forget where they were, which Miranda described to her stateside civilian friends in a detailed e-mail. "We sat on the edge of her bed, talking all night, hugging pillows and stuffed animals, getting teary and hugging each other at the especially hard parts," she wrote. It was a long missive designed in part to demonstrate that even though she was now a soldier in Iraq, "things were really no different than they were in the academy dorms or the Kappa Delta house.

"This is who is fighting for you," she continued. "We are not fearless, we are not strong. We are scared of growing up and we cry over boys. We hug stuffed animals and get scared to walk to the latrine tents alone. We get mad at our bosses and sick of carrying our rifles and rank our junior officers by how cute their butts are. We cry and we get homesick. This is my Iraq."

Which was in part true. There were many moments when Miranda sat on the edge of her bed in her pajamas, holding a stuffed animal, and could have very well been back on campus. Those moments were important not just for their escapism value but for maintaining a sense of normalcy in what had become a very abnormal situation. After death or injury, what she feared most about Iraq was that it would eventually change her in some funda-mental and permanent way, as if she were going to get something hideous tattooed on her psyche. She held on to the rituals of her past life, but no matter how many times she painted her toenails pink or gossiped with girlfriends, she could not help but notice that the more time passed, the more she was becoming a different person. From time to time, she hinted at it in her e-mails home, but she masked the danger and her own fear with humor and a breezy "What, me worry?" tone.

She wrote home about the time the base was hit again with mortars, sending Miranda and her roommates diving for cover. "The indirect fire alarm starts going off," she wrote. "Everything is quiet. All I can hear is my heart pounding as I crawl towards my body armor."

And then while trying to put her body armor on, one of her roommates accidentally hit the play button of her MP3 player, letting loose a Kenny Chesney country song at full volume.

"Aren't you from Brooklyn? And black?" another of Miranda's roommates yelled to the one whose music was now filling the room. "What the hell is that doing on your playlist?" They all dis-solved into hysterical laughter "so that the last thing on our minds was indirect fire," Miranda explained in her e-mail home.

It comforted her friends back home to know that Miranda was taking combat in stride and could slough off a mortar attack with a joke. It comforted Miranda as well to paint the war bright and rosy, like her pink toenails. But there was much she wasn't telling them.

Nighttime in the desert was almost pure black, like a far corner of the galaxy light-years from the nearest star. When the sun went down, soldiers and marines on base were required to wear reflective sashes across their chests, Miss America–style, so they wouldn't get run over. The darkness swallowed nearly everything—even Black Hawks, which flying with their lights off were rendered nearly invisible to those on the ground. The wee hours were the safest time to fly. Pilots could see the flashes of gunfire and the arc of their path lit by tracers and act accordingly, while the insurgents on the ground had only a distant and disembodied sound of the helicopter's rotors as a target.

Early on in the deployment, there had been a couple of near-midair collisions, but most pilots still preferred to fly at night than in the middle of the day, when a helicopter stood out as an easy target against the nearly monochromatic desert. Miranda, though, had not spent enough time training with night vision goggles, which turned everything hazy green and distorted depth perception, to qualify for night missions. And so she was allowed to fly only in the middle of the day, and at first only with an instructor. That greatly limited the number of times she could fly, as did her day job as a supply clerk. And the more experienced soldiers went out for missions, the more frustrated she became.

But here she was flying over the barren desert. She was supposed to be on the lookout for terrorists but at first seemed to see anything but. There were camels and Bedouins and the occasional palm tree and miles of miles of peaceful nothing, which at times made it hard to believe there was a war going on. Flying a few hundred feet above ground, lulled by the beat of the rotor blades, she found the desert beautiful and hypnotic, with wind-shaped ripples that made the sand look as vast and as deep as the ocean.

She was admiring the stark beauty of the desert one April afternoon when the voice of the pilot crackled over her headset. There was a report of a couple of suspicious characters up to no good—possibly burying a makeshift bomb known as an improvised explosive device (IED) along a heavily traveled supply route—and Miranda's chopper was assigned to go check it out.

Soon she saw them: two men, both dressed in long black robes with black-and-white Arab keffiyeh, hunched over. For a split second, she wanted to call out that everything was fine, that these two guys weren't doing anything to be worried about. She wanted to tell the pilot to keep on his merry way and forget this ever happened. But she knew this was indeed something.

The men appeared to be digging. From her perch on the left side of the helicopter, Miranda could even see the pick they were using to claw away at the sand. She fingered the trigger. Left low, she thought, remembering that she would have to aim behind the men to compensate for the speed of the helicopter. Left low.

Miranda reported that the two men appeared to be digging. "One has, what do you call it?" For the life of her she couldn't think of the word for pick or shovel, and her mind shifted back in time to one of her early-American-history classes at William and Mary. "They're digging on the side of the road with a pioneer tool," which she knew sounded ridiculous. A pioneer tool? Door gunners were supposed to relay what they were seeing to the pilots as clearly and with as few words as possible, but Miranda found herself rambling, all the while repeating to herself, Left low. Left low. The pilot had seen the men as well, and they brought the helicopter in so close to the ground that Miranda could see the face of one of the men when he looked up. He appeared to be middle-aged, with a dark beard and dark eyebrows. For a moment, they made eye contact. Miranda aimed, waiting for the order to fire. Left low, she repeated. Left low.

The men were definitely digging a hole. But for what? The pilot couldn't call out the order to fire unless he was sure they were burying an IED. So he banked hard and circled back around for another look. But this time he approached the men so that the door gunner on the right side of the helicopter would have the shot. As the helicopter swooped in, Miranda couldn't help feeling ashamed, even though the crew chief was older and had flown many more missions. Again, they couldn't tell what the guys were doing, and so they reported their locations to base so that a ground patrol could check them out.

As the helicopter peeled away, Miranda was relieved it was finally over and that she hadn't had to fire her weapon. It had happened so quickly that she hadn't had time to think, only to react as she had been trained. She'd had the men in her sights, and she had been ready to fire—left low, left low—and with the order, they would have been goners. Of that she was certain. If once she doubted whether she would be able to pull the trigger, now she knew.

As soon as it was over, she refused to embellish the incident with any real emotional significance. Instead, she kept it tucked neatly in the recesses of the back of her mind as an ambiguous event of which she was both proud and ashamed. How she felt about it depended on whether she was feeling more soldier than citizen, or more citizen than soldier.

The problem was, the line between the two was beginning to blur.

She was nothing like the badass marines who went out on foot, confronted the enemy face to face, and returned to Al Asad exhausted from harrowing days without sleep. They were an entirely different species of warrior, who not only fired their weapons but were routinely fired upon. And even if the marines looked at her and the National Guard as only slightly more ready for combat than the Salvation Army, there was no denying that Miranda was now a full-fledged soldier. Not a weekend warrior, not a citizen-soldier, but a card-carrying member of the United States Armed Forces. Miranda was starting to sense the change; she was developing a soldier's carapace, a tougher edge that allowed her to go out on missions without fear. She was more like her fellow soldiers in Iraq than civilians back home—or even her old self. All of which made doing her homework more difficult, as did the mortars.

When Al Asad came under fire two months into the deployment, the base lost power, making her lose several pages of the paper she had been working on for school. "Crawling around in body armor, sitting in a bunker and thinking about how people want to kill me ruins my chain of thought," she wrote. "How do you write your professors and tell them that the terrorists ate your homework?"

She still had work to do before she would be eligible to graduate. Three of her William and Mary professors had agreed to let her finish her studies with them online, and as much as she was exhausted after long flights and days in the supply room, she forced herself to do her reading for her final papers, even though William and Mary felt as if it belonged to a past life.

"Nothing like getting home from an eight-hour flight at 8 P.M. and study[ing] until midnight to get up at 4:30 [A.M.] to make the next flight," she wrote to her father and stepmother after one particularly tough day. "Somehow, through the mercy of God, I am actually managing to turn out work. Each paper feels like the 50th pushup. I don't know where it comes from, but suddenly I struggle a little and it slips out. Usually at this point in the year I would be super worried about grades and graduate-school applications, but now I find myself more concerned about graduating and not falling asleep on a flight and falling out the door."

It was she added, the "worst finals week ever."

As she struggled to finish her schoolwork, she also debated whether to return to William and Mary to walk with her class at graduation. All soldiers were granted two weeks' leave, and Miranda arranged hers so that she could walk with her class in May. But now she was torn. A visit home would only make going back to the war more difficult. She could already sense the gulf growing between her and her friends back home, who were busy planning the annual post-graduation "beach week" vacation on the North Carolina shore. They had included Miranda in the e-mails arranging rental houses, and Miranda had read all the messages back and forth about who would be rooming with whom, knowing she'd be back in Iraq while they were all partying on the beach.

Maybe, she thought, instead of going home she should travel around Europe for a couple of weeks. When she floated this idea past her father, he was insistent she come to graduation. Not only because she should be with her family, but because graduating was important—for her and for the people, her professors, her family, who had helped her. Plus, when she'd left campus in the fall, she had promised her sorority sisters she'd see them again when she came home on leave.

The flight home was grueling, a two-day marathon with stops in Kuwait and Ireland and Atlanta. During her layover in Atlanta she couldn't get over how spic-and-span clean the airport was. Everything shone in an intense, almost blinding way from the sunlight glancing off the floors to the multicolor arrival/departure monitors. Outside, the landscape was so lush and colorful it was overwhelming after months of the bland tan desert. She'd been gone just a few months, but she already felt out of place and stayed close to the other soldiers traveling with her. Even though they were strangers from other units, they all wore their uniforms, as required, and moved together like a school of tan fish through this now strange civilian world.

On one level, Miranda knew that what she was seeing during her layover at the Atlanta airport was completely normal: travelers bustling back and forth, people waiting for their flights at the airport bar, watching the sports highlights on television, reading newspapers and books, stuffing their faces with fast food. But part of her found it completely jarring. One minute she had been in Iraq, and then she wasn't. The whole experience had a surreal, *Wizard of Oz*, click-your-heels-three-times feel that made the war seem like a distant dream. Here in the hustle and bustle of the brightly lit Atlanta airport, there was no war. Iraq did not exist.

Waiting for the last leg of her flight home, Miranda was jet-lagged and lonely. Around all these civilians, she suddenly felt unclean, contaminated by war. She longed for a hot shower but had to settle for the next best thing, a sink bath in the women's restroom. She wet some paper towels and was wiping the grime off her arms and neck when she noticed a woman and her daughter staring at her as if she were a homeless vagrant. The mother wore more makeup than Miranda had seen in months, blond highlights, and pearls, and next to her Miranda couldn't help but feel homely.

Suddenly embarrassed at bathing in public, she started to pick up her army duffel bag, when she heard one woman whisper to her daughter, "Can you believe what she's doing? At least I raised you right."

Miranda wasn't even home yet, and already she missed Iraq.

6

Ray and Diane

Keeping Up Appearances

The enemy was waiting. They had to be. There was simply no way there could be this much gunfire, this much hell raining down, if they weren't sitting hidden in the dense trees, waiting for the helicopters to arrive.

They were tough bastards, too. Two U.S. Cobra helicopters had led the way into the landing zone like blockers clearing the field for a running back, blasting the forest with rockets and violent spasms of gunfire that made Ray Johnson wonder how anyone could have survived. But when he nudged his Huey to the ground, allowing the grunts on board to hop off, the firefight broke out. His crew chief started screaming, "We're taking fire! We're taking fire!" And Ray could see the muzzle flashes coming from the forest, while his door gunner was emptying his 7.62-caliber machine gun into the tree line.

At any moment, Ray could be a goner. Any of them could. All it took was one shot. A bullet to the brain, or a vital organ, or if one clipped an artery, and yet another flag-draped casket. One of tens of thousands of dead and injured. By now, April 1969, five months into his Vietnam deployment, Ray, an active-duty pilot with the 117th Assault Helicopter Company, had seen more than his share of death. At twenty-one, he had already accepted the near-suicidal nature of the mission—transporting long-range reconnaissance patrol soldiers deep into enemy territory—and had come to terms with the fact that he almost certainly was going to die.

He often had a great view of these spectacular battles, as he did today: trees shuddering in the torrent of fire, orange-red explosions, dense black smoke, the syncopated ping, ping, ping of bullets that sounded like a child drumming two spoons together. He could see all of it out the side of his doorless helicopter. Not that a door would stop a bullet anyway. Bullets ripped right through the helicopter as if moving through flesh. At first, it scared him frozen. But after a while, he just got used to it. Either you were going to get hit, or you weren't. Ray told himself it was in God's hands. There was nothing he could do about it. You had to sit there, wait for the grunts to get off or on the bird, then take off and do it again. You could hope you didn't get hit. Hope the bullets stayed clear of the engine and organs. And you could stuff your pistol between your legs, as Ray and the other pilots did, and hope it would keep your nuts from getting shot off. But it was only hope.

Today's gunfire was particularly intense, and Ray was getting nervous in the few seconds it took the grunts to exit the chopper. If it weren't for his screaming crew chief, Ray would have had no idea they were getting hit. He couldn't hear a damn thing. The roar of rockets, the angry rat-tat-tat of machine gun against machine gun, wiped out all other noise. When finally he got the signal to take off, he was once again thankful that today wasn't his day to die.

As they made their way above the tree line back to the base, Ray started to relax. Another mission in the books. In the distance he could see the base tower. But then he glanced down at his controls and saw that the oil pressure was dropping fast. He checked the exhaust gauge. It was running in the red. And suddenly, about a half mile from the base's concertina wire perimeter, the helicopter lost power. As if by instinct, Ray's training kicked in—he'd have to hold the helicopter steady and make a crash landing. He told everyone on board to hang on and hoped he could make it to the other side of the fence where the ground was flat. The helicopter was dropping fast. The base's fence was getting closer. They were headed right for it. Ray braced himself.

The Huey hit so hard it bounced. Ray's head whiplashed on impact, and when the chopper hit again, it did so on its side. Ray and his entire seat were ejected out the side window into a ditch. The helicopter's rotor blades chewed into the ground, snapping off one at a time, getting closer and closer until one of them came crashing down on Ray's left thigh like a guillotine. He howled in pain, amazed that his leg wasn't completely severed. But he had another worry.

I don't have my Nomex flight suit, he thought. His leg may or may not have been broken. The helicopter was wrecked; the other passengers might very well be dead. And if the helicopter caught fire, which could happen at any moment, he would too, because he had forgotten to wear his fire-resistant Nomex suit. Lying in the ditch a few feet from the fallen chopper, his leg pinned under the rotor blade, waiting for the helicopter to blow, he started shaking uncontrollably, thinking, I'm dead. I'm dead. I'm dead. I'm going to burn.

He had no idea where everyone else was, or if they were okay. He just knew that if help didn't arrive quickly, he wasn't going to make it. Finally, in the distance, he could hear the sirens approaching, and soon he was pried from underneath the helicopter blade. Everyone on board was okay.

After a week in the hospital, where he was treated for cuts and bumps and a severe bruise on his thigh, he was back in the air flying, taking fire deep in the jungle. It was 1969, Woodstock and 250,000 protestors converging on the Mall in Washington. But

Ray was a soldier with a war to fight. He didn't think his injury qualified him for a medical discharge and a plane ticket home, and he didn't ask to be relieved, either. And so after a week, he left the hospital, walking gingerly on his bruised but intact leg, and got back in the cockpit.

Thirty-seven years later, Ray was back at the controls. He was fifty-eight, not twenty-one, a National Guardsman, not an active-duty soldier. The chopper was a Black Hawk, not a Huey. The war was Iraq. It was, he thought, a chance at redemption after Vietnam, for him and his country—the opportunity to fight an admirable war. Not that in the years after Vietnam he had turned into an anti-war protestor. Not by any stretch. He was proud of his service, and it showed. He'd decorated his house with mementos from the war: Vietnamese currency, a large framed map of the country in the hallway, black-and-white photos of him and his fellow soldiers smiling in the jungle. Though he rarely talked of Vietnam, he didn't bury it into the recesses of disgrace; he had fought alongside too many good men for that. Rather, he embraced the parts of it that were admirable—the bonds, forged by combat, he felt with fellow soldiers—while passing over that which he, like the nation, had come to view as a debacle.

He was not angry about the war as much as he was sad. So many lives lost. So much damage. How could the politicians make such a mess of things? He had hoped modern leaders would learn from the experience, and by the time the United States invaded Iraq, he was again ready to serve his country. Yellow ribbons and flag waving was one thing. But Ray was a soldier—an older soldier, yes, one of the oldest around. But he was fit and flew the medevac helicopter for the Maryland State Police, and he wanted to serve one last time before retiring for good.

Upset as she was, Diane had supported him, even if she thought he was crazy to be shipping off to war at such an age. What she didn't understand was why the Guard was involved so heavily in the war at all. During Vietnam it wasn't only the draft dodgers and the college kids who avoided combat. The reserves were also, for the most part, left at home to respond to riots and protests, like at Kent State, where Diane studied for her graduate degree in library science a few years after the shooting there. But the truth was that Vietnam was the anomaly for the Guard, which had been called for virtually every other American conflict, and whose leadership was upset that their ranks became a haven for those looking to get out of going to Vietnam.

Mobilizing the country's citizen-soldiers only made sense. They were well trained and experienced, and perhaps best of all they had volunteered to join the army, which could not be said of the thousands of conscripted civilians the military was struggling to mold into soldiers. Leaving Guardsmen behind was not only unprecedented but a dangerous abandonment of three centuries' worth of military policy that General Hal Nelson, the Army's Chief of Military History, would later refer to as a "watershed in American military history."

The Joint Chiefs of Staff urged President Lyndon Johnson to call up the reserves. So did Secretary of Defense Robert McNamara, who told the president it "would be a vehicle for joining together support." General Harold K. Johnson, the Army Chief of Staff, threatened to resign in protest, and would later say that the failure to call out the county's citizen-soldiers "was, I think, the greatest single mistake that was made."

But LBJ was content to send a steady stream of draftees, who were by and large from lower classes and without much political influence. By contrast, Guardsmen and Reservists were, according to one study, "better connected, better educated, more affluent, and whiter than their peers in the active forces, and the administration feared that mobilizing them would heighten public opposition to the war."

After the war, the new army chief of staff, General Creighton Abrams, revised the army's structure in a way that, although it was little understood at the time, would make the reserves an integral part of the country's combat force. As he repeatedly told his confidants in the Pentagon, "They're not taking us to war again without calling up the reserves." Later, Secretaries of Defense James Schlesinger and Melvin Laird institutionalized this restructuring of all military forces, calling it the "Total Force Policy."

As Ray prepared to deploy to Iraq, Abrams's vision had been fulfilled. The reserves were once again a crucial component of the force—so crucial, in fact, they were being stretched thin enough that fifty-eight-year-old grandfathers were being mobilized. Diane was worried sick that Ray might not be up for this. She told him she feared he would come home a changed man. But he laughed at the notion. He could nearly qualify for the senior citizen discounts at the movie theater; nothing was going to change him now. If any war would shape his outlook on life, it was Vietnam.

So he assured Diane there was nothing Iraq could throw at him that he hadn't already been through. "I'll always be the same old Ray," he would say with a confidence that convinced her.

But what he didn't tell her was how much he worried about how she would fare on her own. A year was a long time to be away. While he knew that Diane supported him, there was no way he'd be going if it were up to her. He was dedicated to his country and his army and felt he could help some of the younger, less experienced soldiers survive the rigors of combat. It pained him as a seasoned flight instructor to train all of these kids, as young and eager as he had been at their age, to fly into combat while he stayed behind.

He also felt as if he were abandoning his wife. And he knew from personal experience how absence could harm a marriage.

Diane kept insisting that everything was fine. She was just having a bad day, she told Ray. They had termites, that was all. She could handle it. She'd call the exterminator. No big deal. You've got bigger things to worry about over there, she told him. Don't worry about me.

But Ray did worry. He'd been in Iraq six months, and now he could tell that the separation was taking its toll. The international phone connection was a tad fuzzy, but he could clearly hear the distress in Diane's voice and knew that the long silences meant she was probably crying, even as she tried to assure him that she was okay. He wanted to fly home and immediately hug her, and he felt helpless and guilty that he had done this to her. He was the one in a combat zone, but it was obvious that Diane was having the tougher time.

After he hung up with an "I love you" that he tried to make as strong and as reassuring as possible, he immediately dialed his best friend at home.

"Mike, you'd better go out and see Diane," Ray said. "I think she's having a nervous breakdown."

Diane wished she could tell Ray about what really was happening. The war had robbed her not only of her husband but also of her best friend, the man who'd rescued her from a miserable divorce and had in the years since become her closest confidant. Life without him even in the best of times was difficult. But now she was indeed on the verge of collapse. Only she couldn't unburden herself to the one person she needed most.

Ray had missions to fly, and she didn't want him distracted by her problems at home. Even if she did tell him, what had transpired in the past few weeks had been so surreal, her own tragicomedy, that he wouldn't have believed it. She hardly did herself. Maybe at some point, when he was home, they would look back on this time and laugh. But now it was all she could do to stay afloat.

Refinishing the basement was one of those home improvement projects that had near-permanent status on Ray and Diane's to-do list, along with painting the garage and trimming the shrubs.

When Ray got the call for Iraq, he suddenly decided to tackle the basement before he left. Diane thought he was out of his mind. They had other things to worry about. And the basement would be no small job. It needed carpet to cover the bare cement floor, drywall over the exposed insulation, and a ceiling to seal off the rafters. They'd have to hire an electrician to do the wiring. Then there was the shopping: new furniture and weights for the exercise room they were putting in. Diane didn't see the point of rushing through such a cumbersome renovation when they had precious little time left together.

But Ray was insistent—it would be nice to come home to after Iraq, he'd say—and as mad as she was, Diane didn't feel she could argue with a man who was about to be sent to war. So she didn't protest about the workers trudging through the house during Ray's last months home. And she didn't complain about the electricians who burst a pipe, letting loose a geyser in the basement. She just wanted everything done and the contractors gone—even though when they had finished there was evidence that they had done a rush job. (The light switches for the den were two rooms away, and the den, home to the entertainment center, had just one electrical outlet.) But Diane was too preoccupied with Ray's pending departure to make a stink.

For his part, Ray was relieved that the renovation had been completed on schedule so that Diane wouldn't have to worry about it while he was in Iraq. He wanted everything to go as smoothly as possible for her, which is why he had asked his best friend, Mike, to check in on her from time to time. Mike did. And so did the neighbors. And her coworkers at the library were constantly asking her if there was anything they could do. But the fact was that none of them could really understand what Diane was going through. Like other Guard units, the 2-224th had a family support group made up of the soldiers' spouses. But Ray had been transferred into the 2-224th at the last minute, and no one from the group had contacted her. Even if they had, she probably wouldn't have felt comfortable around a bunch of strangers, most of whom were from Richmond, Virginia, the unit's headquarters, more than an hour from Diane's Maryland home.

What she wanted was a friend who knew what it was like to go to sleep worrying if your husband might be shot down over Baghdad. But none of her friends or even acquaintances had loved ones in Iraq. No one else froze every time the news talked about combat casualties. No one else, it seemed, was affected by the war. And so even though Diane was surrounded by friends and neighbors, she still felt very much alone.

At first, she was able to push the negative thoughts from her mind, and she felt guilty every time she felt the slightest bit victimized. I don't have it so bad, she thought. There were military wives out there with young children. She stayed busy at work, then came home and curled up in bed with her cat, Sugar Baby, and read the biography of Martha Washington. Now there was a woman who knew what it was like to have a husband off at war.

But no matter how much solace she took in the company of the first First Lady, the war was always there. At night, especially when the day had passed without word from Ray, and the news was full of casualty reports, the what-ifs mounted, making it hard to think of anything else, let alone sleep. What if he was injured? What if he was shot down? What if the worst happened? Her coworkers at the library got used to seeing Diane drag herself in after yet another sleepless night. Most of them assumed it was the migraines they knew she suffered from. Diane did her best to try "to remain professional at work," she would later say. "But it was getting harder and harder to put on that calm I'm-okay face."

Prepare for the worst and it won't be so bad when it happens, she thought. Which was why she needed to renew her recently expired military ID. When Ray was at home, she didn't feel as if she even needed one. Unlike the spouses of active-duty soldiers, who used their IDs to shop at the base's commissary and Post Exchange, Diane wanted one only in case of emergency. If something happened to Ray in Iraq, she figured a military ID would allow her in to see him at the army hospitals.

By the time she drove to Andrews Air Force Base, a few months after Ray had left, she was just plain mad. Mad that she had to take a day off work to perform this macabre exercise of renewing her ID just in case. Mad that Ray had been sent to war at the time in their lives when they were supposed to be thinking about retirement.

Mad at the army for taking him, while she saw some active-duty service members staying home. Was the army that hard up that it would subject even fifty-eight-year-old grandfathers to combat? And wasn't the National Guard just that: a National Guard that was supposed to protect the homeland in times of domestic crisis? What was it doing in Iraq?

Finally, she was mad at the way he'd been called up—the endless delays in getting his paperwork, the back and forth—which had allowed her to hope, if for a short while, that he might not be going after all.

Soldiers quickly get hardened to the bureaucratic "hurry up and wait" mentality of the army and aren't surprised when everything goes haywire. It's part of military life, and over the years soldiers have even developed their own crass lexicon to describe it: SNAFU (Situation Normal: All Fucked Up) was coined by World War II soldiers. By Iraq there was a new favorite phrase: BOHICA (Bend Over, Here It Comes Again). But up until her husband was deployed, Diane had never fully understood why her husband would get so frustrated with the army.

When she arrived at Andrews with her nineteen-year-old daughter, Sara, in tow, she pulled up to the security gate and showed the guard her ID.

"It's expired," he said.

"I know," she said. "That's why I'm here. To get a new one."

"Too late," he explained coldly. "This one is expired, and I've got to take it." He handed her a temporary day pass instead and waved her through.

At the ID office, the clerk told Diane she had to have her old ID in order to receive a new one.

The guard took it, Diane tried to explain.

But the clerk said it didn't matter. The computers were down. She wouldn't be able to help her anyway.

"How long are your computers going to be down?" Diane asked.

"I don't know," the clerk said. "Why don't you just come back tomorrow?"

"I can't," Diane said. She wasn't about take another day off work and make the hour drive. "I'll wait."

She and Sara killed a few hours in the library and eating lunch. By the time they got back to the ID office it was almost four in the afternoon, and a new clerk was manning the desk.

"Are the computers back up?" Diane asked.

"What?" the man said. "The computers weren't down."

Diane explained that they were down earlier, which is why she hadn't been able to get a new ID.

"Sorry," the man explained. "They probably just told you that because I wasn't here."

Diane was furious, but she kept her emotions in check. She just wanted to get this over with.

"I'm here to get a new ID," she explained.

"Your husband needs to be here for me to issue you a new ID," he replied.

"He can't be here," said Diane, growing agitated. "He's in Iraq. But I had him sign the form before he left."

"Well, I'm sorry," the clerk said. "I can't help you. The form has expired. Your husband has to fill out a new form and mail it in."

"He's in Iraq," Diane said again.

"Well, then he needs to send it in from Iraq, and before we can do anything I need to see your old ID."

"The guard took it," Diane said again.

"Well, I need the old one in order to give you a new one," he said. "You'll have to go back out to the guard station to get it."

Walking to her car outside, she was furious.

"I don't fucking believe this," she said. "This is how they treat the families of soldiers who are off fighting in Iraq."

"Mom!" Sara gasped. She had never heard her mother curse before. Diane had never dared use the F-word. Not once. She was a churchgoing librarian and mother of two from Ohio who considered *damn* an un-utterable vulgarity. But passing through her lips, the F-word, she had to admit, felt good, empowering, even if she felt guilty later. She had used it like a pro, too. No hesitation.

The right emphasis. She rolled right through the word—*fuckin'*—
rather than pronounce the whole thing like some novice: *fuck-ing.*
She even used it as an adverb. "I can't fucking believe it."

She hadn't complained when Ray left for Iraq. And she kept
quiet when the army jerked him around during the weeks before he
deployed. She sent him off as a good army wife, even though that was
the last thing in the world she wanted to be. But this was too much.

When she returned with the ID that had been taken from her
and the clerk once again told her, "Sorry, but you need the form,"
she exploded: "We've done everything we were supposed to do.
You know what? Screw it. I don't need the ID. Forget it. This is
ridiculous. No wonder no one wants to join the military."

"Hold on. Hold on."

It was a supervisor, rushing out from a back room. "We'll do it.
We'll do it."

A few minutes later Diane had her new ID. In the photo, her
brow was still tilted at a menacing angle, her mouth taut, her eyes
like stones. It bore no resemblance to Diane's normal, sweet get-
along demeanor. The woman in the photo had a harder edge.
Diane barely recognized herself.

Sugar Baby was sick. The poor cat was curled up in the corner,
facing the wall and refusing to eat. It was if she were saying,
Please just let me die in peace. Diane needed to get her to the vet
ASAP. But the electrician had just arrived, and she didn't know if
she could trust him in the house alone on his first day of work. She
picked up Sugar Baby, who weighed nearly nothing, and thought
she had no choice. Her dear cat, the first pet that had comforted
her since Ray had left a few months earlier, was dying.

Then again, she had met Matt, the electrician, at a Bible study.
How bad could he be? He had mentioned he was an electrician,
and Diane told him about the screwy switches in the basement.
Now he was here to check it out. Diane apologized for leaving him
alone as she rushed out the door to the vet.

With Ray gone, she couldn't bear the thought of losing Sugar Baby. But the vet took one look at her precious pet and told her Sugar Baby was not going to make it. A few moments later, Sugar Baby was dead. Diane cried all the way home with her cat in a box on the passenger seat. There was no way she could leave her behind. She'd take her home and bury her in the backyard.

As soon as Diane had left for the vet, Matt went to work in the basement and was soon dumbfounded. It was an absolute mess. There was only one outlet for the entire den, several wires seemed to lead to nowhere, others were stripped down—a clear fire hazard that would never pass inspection. This was not merely a matter of fixing a couple of switches as Diane had told him. It was going to take days just to figure out the extent of the problem, and then probably weeks to straighten out.

When Diane returned home from the vet, Matt could tell she was upset by having to bury her cat in the backyard, which given the hard-packed soil was a much more difficult job than she had imagined. By evening, Diane was emotionally drained and physically exhausted and just wanted a quiet moment to herself. Matt came upstairs and broke the news: it was bad, worse than he feared. She didn't understand all the technical terms he was using, but the words "fire hazard" made her heart race, and she told him to please just fix it.

At least they had caught the problem before there was any real trouble, she thought as she plopped herself down on the sun porch, trying for the first time in this hectic day to relax. But within moments, Beau, her normally staid bichon frise, started barking. She yelled at him to be quiet, but he was going nuts, barking. Then she saw what was agitating him, a big hornet buzzing around the skylight. Then she saw another. And another. There was a swarm.

Diane frantically backed away and called out to Sara, who had been up in her room. "Where are they coming from?" Diane's father was so allergic to stings he had to carry an epinephrine pen. It had been years since Diane had been stung, but she was allergic too and feared that a sting would send her to the hospital.

Sara grabbed a shoe and went after a hornet, and Matt, hearing the commotion, came up from the basement.

He got his electric tape and sealed off the hole that appeared to be their entry point. They sprayed some insect killer. But by the next day the hornets were back, lurking like an ominous portent in a malevolent pack near the ceiling.

Normally, Matt would not have taken the job. He thought he was just coming over to help an acquaintance from Bible study with a small switch problem—not a massive basement rewiring. With all his other work, he really didn't have the time for it. But Diane was so sweet and clearly desperate that he couldn't say no to her. He would only be able to fit her in on nights and weekends, he said, which was fine with Diane, who told him he could even invite his wife over to the house while he worked.

Matt showed up a week later, and Diane entertained his wife in the living room. But soon after he got to the basement, Matt called up. "You better come down here," he said. There was dread in his voice.

The brand-new carpet in the hallway was soaking wet. "Where did all this water come from?" Diane asked. Matt showed her. The house's central air conditioning sump pump had clogged and overflowed.

Great, Diane thought. Just great. The last thing she wanted to do was spend the night cleaning up this mess. But she did not want a moldy, wet carpet smell in her newly renovated basement. So she grabbed the wet vacuum and a handful of towels and got to work.

For all her insecurities, Diane was not a crier. And despite all she had been through in the past week, she was not about to cry now. The wiring was bad, and Matt would fix it. There were hornets, but she'd hired an exterminator. The basement was flooded, and she'd fix that, too. She stayed up until two in the morning cleaning up the mess on her hands and knees. She scrubbed and scrubbed, determined not to let her fatigue, her desperation, her loneliness overcome her.

She was strong, she told herself. She would get through this.

Matt, bless his heart, who had stayed there with her until after midnight, was back later that day and graciously helped Diane dump the water from the wet vacuum outside. As they stepped out into the backyard, Matt reached out and touched the door frame. Little bits of wood flaked off.

"How long have you had termites?" he said.

A joke. Ha ha. I get it, Diane thought. But she was operating on just a few hours' sleep and frankly was not in the mood to be teased.

"I'm not kidding. Look," Matt said, brushing away dandrufflike flakes from the doorframe. "And here, too," he said, bending down to show her the chewed-up baseboard. "You've got termites."

He could see Diane's face drop. She was blinking away tears. And for a moment he felt as if he were sticking the knife in even further and regretted telling her.

"You can treat this," he assured her. "Happens all the time."

Diane was dumbfounded. She was not superstitious, but she couldn't help but feel as if fate was testing her. It wasn't just the problems at home. Diane was the manager of the local public library branch, a job she normally loved. But during this trying summer, a long-simmering dispute between two of her employees had begun to escalate. One accused the other of slamming a file cabinet drawer on her hand and even got a restraining order. The other employee retaliated by filing a lawsuit for malicious prosecution and defamation. It was a nightmare fit for Jerry Springer, and after all the problems at home, it was the last thing Diane wanted to deal with.

Then one Sunday morning before church during all this madness, she went outside to find that her car had been egged. One had hit the bumper, and three more were splattered across the driver's side. All had dried into a sticky yellow mess. Her daughter, Sara, burst out laughing.

"What's so funny?" Diane asked.

"Just this."

"What do you mean?"

"Just this. Our luck. I mean, come on."

Sara couldn't stop laughing.

But Diane was not about to have a sense of humor about any of this. If everything else—the flooding, hornets, and so on —was just bad luck, this was intentional. She felt violated. And increasingly angry at Ray for leaving her with this mess. At first, she just blamed the army, but now she started to blame him, too. He had told her countless times that there was nothing he could do; the army had forced him to go. But why was he still in the army? Why hadn't he retired already?

Sara kept laughing. But Diane couldn't. To laugh about it would be to allow emotion to rise, to let go, and she couldn't do that. She felt she was getting close to a breakdown, and she had to stay strong. She wasn't about to get emotional, even if it meant letting herself laugh. Laughter, she knew, would only give way to tears.

So when Ray called, she did her best to keep a stiff upper lip. She didn't tell him that his newly refinished basement was once again a construction zone. She didn't tell him about the flood or the hornets or the eggs. But there were so many problems piling on top of one another, she had to vent about at least one, otherwise she'd go insane. So she told him about the termites.

"But it would be fine," she assured him. "Everything's okay. Don't worry about me."

It took Matt six weeks to get the wiring in the basement fixed. But holes dotted the walls. Furniture was strewn about. There were paint cans and tarps everywhere. But by now it was October and Ray was soon coming home for his two weeks of R and R. Everything had to be back to normal before he saw it.

She knew the military counseled army wives not to change their appearance while their husbands were at war. Best to keep everything comfortable and familiar for them. That also meant no painting the house a different color. No rearranging the furniture. But Diane kept getting stood up by the contractor who was supposed to come to patch and paint the drywall, and Ray would be home soon.

Finally after the guy failed to show up for the second time, Diane pleaded with a friend to come help. He came over a couple of days later and patched the holes right away. The night before Ray was to arrive, Diane stayed up painting, hoping it would dry in time and that Ray wouldn't notice the new-paint smell. His plane wasn't supposed to land until four the next afternoon; that should be enough time, she thought.

The next morning the phone woke her. It was Ray. He had caught an earlier flight and was now in Atlanta. Could she pick him up in a couple of hours? He sounded giddy—and he was. After eight months in Iraq, he couldn't wait to finally get home.

Diane was freaking out. "You're not supposed to get home until four," she said frantically.

Ray was crestfallen. "Aren't you excited to see me?" he said.

"Yes, but if I'm going to get there on time, I'm going to have to hurry," she said.

She hung up and bolted downstairs to the basement like a teenager cleaning up after throwing a party while her parents were out of town. She hid the paint cans and tarps in the storage room, put the furniture back the way it was, re-hung the pictures. Then she rushed to the shower.

At the time Ray left for Iraq, she had worried that the man who came home would be very different from the one she'd married. But now, staring at herself in the mirror, Diane knew she was the one who had changed. She had become stronger, more independent—changes she welcomed. She had been tested by what felt like a conspiracy of dark, nefarious forces, by indiscriminate misfortune and human incompetence, and she had emerged intact, if not victorious.

But she also feared she was less sweet and quick to lose a temper that had rarely ever needed reining in. She had used the F-word. A certain layer of innocence, guarded nearly all her life, had been lost.

As she applied her makeup, she hoped it would mask the new Diane born of the exhaustion and stress of the past few months. It was important to show that, in appearance at least, nothing had changed.

7

Kate

Jody's Got Your Cadillac

Eight men missing: seven marines and a navy petty officer, all most likely dead. Killed not by insurgents but by Iraq itself when their seven-ton truck was washed away in a flash desert flood. The MIA were from big cities and small—Nashville and L.A.; Victoria, Texas; and Warwick, Rhode Island—and now their bodies were lost somewhere in the desert. Word of the flood reached Al Asad, and members of the 2-224th revved up their helicopters. That night they pulled two dead bodies from a wadi, a desert gully that instantly turns into a riverbed with the deluge. But there were still six more out there.

Kate volunteered for the search mission, not as a medic—these guys would probably need body bags more than emergency first aid—but as another set of eyes. The 2-224th had a full-fledged physician who in civilian life was a surgeon, and it also had a physician's assistant and a paramedic who had twelve years of experience in the back of an ambulance in civilian life. They were the ones who went out on missions when the battalion was inserting troops into dangerous situations. Kate spent most of her time manning the aid station at the base, organizing records, dealing with bumps and bruises, the occasional cold and diarrhea caused by the brown water they showered with. She'd been trained to deal with trauma, but that didn't mean she was going to see any. Certainly not today, anyway, as she scanned the desert looking for the men. Today her job was to spot a shred of uniform, a rifle barrel glinting in the sun, anything. For two full days the Black Hawks swept the desert floor skimming dangerously low and slow, but they found nothing.

Mid-morning on day three of the search, Kate, hoping for any sign even if it were a mirage, began to wonder if the desert had simply swallowed the men whole. Out of the corner of her eye she saw one of the pilots jump. Captain Mark Baush was not one to rattle easily. A former infantryman who had completed army ranger school and risen to officer through the enlisted ranks, he was on his second overseas deployment (the first was to Bosnia in 2001), and he had promised the soldiers under his command that he would bring every one of them home alive. Kate had such faith in that promise she was confident everything would be fine. But now Mark was twisting around in his seat so that he could catch her eye. He shot her a look that was at once so intense and sympathetic, Kate knew instantly what it meant: You're on.

She wasn't wearing a radio headset, so she couldn't communicate directly with anyone on the helicopter. So she reached for the notebook in the pocket of her flak jacket and scribbled a message to the crew chief next to her.

"What's going on?"

"Change of plans. Casevac mission. IED exploded," he wrote back. Casevac meant casualty evacuation, which meant she'd be needing that medical kit after all.

"How many casualties?" she asked.

"We don't know," the crew chief wrote. Then he added, "You've got your aid pack, right?"

A navy doctor who had volunteered to help search for the marines was sitting next to Kate, and she showed him the notebook. He asked to look in her aid bag to see what she had, and it was then that she realized he hadn't even brought his. What kind of doctor goes outside the wire without his aid bag? she wondered.

Soon Kate could see that the marines had set off to mark their position; tufts of purple smoke drifted skyward like cotton candy. "Every possible medical scenario went through my head, and I was scared shitless I was going to fuck up," she wrote in her diary later.

As soon as they landed, Kate yelled at one of the door gunners to remove the backseats from the helicopters so they could make room for the patients. Then she jumped out the side door and started running toward two marines carrying another marine in a stretcher made from a sleeping cot. Perhaps if her heart weren't beating so hard, she would have remembered rule number one in her training: "You're a soldier first. You can't help anyone if you're injured as well." But instead of pausing to make sure the area was secure, she went running toward the wounded marines.

As a medic, Kate had extensive training. Before the army she knew virtually nothing about human anatomy, but now she could tell the difference between the bright, spurting blood of a severed artery and the dark ooze of a venous bleed. She could treat sucking chest wounds, stabilize broken bones, perform CPR, tie a mean tourniquet, spot internal bleeding, patch a gunshot wound, and even make a stretcher out of tree limbs and a blanket. Fort Lewis, where she'd received much of her training, had all kinds of dummies to practice on, fake severed limbs and gallons upon gallons of fake blood to make the experience all the more realistic. Kate was pleased to discover that she never got squeamish—she was always too focused on what she was doing to let the blood bother her.

And she was able to stay calm, even while the patient was wailing in pain, even if he was acting.

But in nearly four years of active duty, the most severe injuries she'd treated in reality were when soldiers got banged up playing pickup basketball on base. Dislocated shoulders, broken fingers, twisted ankles, bruised knees. As part of her training she rode along with the base paramedics, which she looked forward to because she entertained thoughts of becoming one after the army. But most of the calls were for overreacting hypochondriacs, drunks, and the occasional drug addict who was hurting for a fix. Outside of the emotionally disturbed kid threatening to kill his parents, "it seemed really boring," she said. So she crossed that career path off the list.

She was happiest during a mandatory hospital rotation and got to spend a whole week in the emergency room. She worked with real patients, assisting the nurses and doctors. She saw a man go into cardiac arrest and die, despite doctors' zapping him with defibrillators. She saw doctors save another patient who had been drinking on his boat, fell off, and gotten chopped up by the rotor blades. A woman came into the ER complaining that she hadn't had a bowel movement in two weeks. Kate just happened to be the only woman working that night, so she performed the enema.

But she did not have a lot of experience with actual trauma cases. In the weeks before shipping out to Iraq, Kate and the other medics of the 2-224th went to a special training camp in Texas designed to give them a taste of what practicing emergency medicine in combat was really like. Instructors fired blank rounds over their heads and blasted gunfire and artillery sounds and Arabic prayers out of a stereo. They treated patients in the dark with strobe lights going off and fog machines emitting a dense haze that would make their eyes water. Meanwhile, the fake patients were combative, and instructors screamed at the medics, "FASTER. FASTER," trying to fluster them.

It was unlike anything Kate had ever experienced, and she couldn't help but feel confident that she was ready for Iraq. But a few of the soldiers heading out on their second and third deployments warned those who had not yet seen combat that there was a big difference between treating a soldier acting injured and hearing a soldier screaming in actual pain. Real blood doesn't wash out so easily, they said.

Running through the dust being kicked up by the helicopter, Kate could see the marines coming toward her. One had a patch over his face where he'd been hit by shrapnel but otherwise seemed to be okay. He could walk. The one in the stretcher was in much worse shape. His right leg had been blown off above the knee; his left was a mangled mess. It looked like the only thing keeping his foot attached was his boot. Blood was everywhere.

"What happened to him?" Kate yelled over the roar of the helicopter to the marines carrying him.

"IED hit his humvee and fucked up his legs," one said.

They got them on the helicopter as quickly as possible, and Kate went to work. A corpsman traveling with the marines had already put a tourniquet on his right leg but didn't have time for his left leg, so she put one on that leg and started an IV. The navy doctor, who had much more experience, seemed content to stay out of the way while Kate worked. Meanwhile, the marine's face had gone white with the blood loss, and he was slipping in and out of consciousness. He must have lost two pints of blood at least, Kate thought. And now she was worried she might lose him.

She held his hand and yelled at him to squeeze hers back.

"What's your name?" she asked.

He mumbled in response.

"How old are you?"

"Nineteen," he said, grimacing through the pain.

He had dirty-blond hair and blue eyes and whiskers on his chin, which made Kate think he must have been out in the field for days. He had an all-American-kid look that would have made him popular in his hometown but was now a mess of blood and tendons and bone. Flecks of blood spotted his face. He had cuts on his arms, neck, face—virtually every place that wasn't protected by his helmet or body armor. Behind those blue eyes was a look of utter fear and shock that made him seem even more young and innocent. But as the morphine he had been given in the field wore off, his fear was replaced by an excruciating pain.

"Morphine. I need morphine. Please," he was saying. "Please. The pain."

But she didn't have morphine. She didn't keep it in her aid bag. Only the unit's two full-fledged medical doctors were authorized to carry the drug in their kits. Plus, she thought she was going to be searching for dead bodies, not treating marines with their legs blown off. She had nothing to ease his pain. And neither did the navy doctor, who probably kept some in his aid bag at all times. Kate was sick that she didn't have any morphine for the marine. And she was angry that the navy doctor hadn't brought his own aid bag. You should take that with you everywhere you go, she wanted to lecture him.

"It hurts," the young marine was saying. "Please."

He was begging her. Desperate for something to make it stop.

"I'm thirsty," he said. "Water. I need water."

But giving water to a trauma patient can be dangerous. So once again, Kate had to say no.

The corpsman who had been traveling with the injured marines was freaking out. These were his buddies, after all, and the sight of his friends' blood, which was now all over the deck of the Black Hawk, was too much. "Is he going to make it?" he yelled over the whir of the helicopter. "Can you save him?"

Kate needed him to get out of the way and stay calm, and so she gave him a task: "Write down all your friend's injuries and what treatments we've given them," she directed. That way the doctors on the ground will have a complete picture of what happened.

Soon they arrived at a nearby base. The marine with the patch over his eye now had a face swollen to the size of a cantaloupe. But he could walk off the helicopter. The other one was passed out cold as they loaded him into the ambulance. Kate watched as he was whisked away to the hospital, hoping she had done enough to save him.

By the time the Black Hawk got back to Al Asad, it was evening. The sun was beginning to set over the dunes in the distance, and Kate wanted nothing more than to head back to her bunk and collapse after a shower. But she had one more task to complete before the day was over. She grabbed a brush and some bleach and joined the men scrubbing the blood in the helicopter until it shone like new, as if nothing had happened.

When she slept in the weeks that followed, she slept uneventfully. No nightmares. No waking up with the sweats. Just a dark, empty sleep, suspended just below the surface, that came only after hours of replaying the events of that day in her mind, over and over. It was as if she were trapped. Here was Captain Baush's "You're on" look. Here she was running toward the injured. Here was the burnt and torn flesh where his legs should be. Here was the *thwap* of the helicopters. Here was blood. Blood seeping through bandages. Blood on her uniform. Blood on her hands.

"Sometimes when I close my eyes I can see [his] legs," she wrote in her diary about three weeks later. "I can feel him squeezing my hand and begging for water. I can see the morphine wear off and him grimace in pain. . . . I remember the blood on my uniform and the blood in the Black Hawk. . . . I remember Capt. Baush jump in his seat and look back at me. I remember not knowing what was happening. The shock of it all is wearing off and I'm getting a little emotional."

But she didn't show it. Around the other soldiers she was the same old happy-go-lucky Kate, who was always up for a smoke break. She was a medic, after all. Treating the wounded was her job. She couldn't let it affect her. She told herself that the insomnia would pass, as would the troubling tick she developed: Her left hand started shaking uncontrollably. At first she thought it was nothing. A muscle spasm, or maybe she had banged her elbow. It started out as an infrequent inconvenience, but soon it was happening all the time, as if she were a Parkinson's patient, especially when she was stressed, or at night when she replayed that day in her mind again and again. Like her emotions, she found ways to hide her tremor—stuffing her hands in her pocket, crossing her arms—but was worried that someone would soon see.

No matter how hard she tried to cover it up, those who knew her best could tell by her vacant, sleep-deprived eyes that something was wrong. After a few weeks, her boss at the aid station finally confronted her with a simple "How are you doing?" It was no mere "What's up?" It was meant as a sincere question, and her tone made it clear that it was an attempt to get Kate to open up, if only a little.

The pressure had been building for weeks, and given the small opening the rote question provided, Kate's pent-up emotions came tumbling out. She started to sob, then shake, and no matter how many times her boss told her everything was okay, Kate could not stop.

She felt awful that she hadn't had any morphine for the wounded marine. Angry that the navy doctor hadn't either. Guilty that marines prowled the streets and sometimes got blown to bits while she lived in relative comfort. Sick at the blood and exposed bone and the gore, which she knew would stay with her for a long, long time. Exhausted, please-just-let-me-sleep exhausted. But mostly she felt completely overwhelmed. She had collided, head-on and unexpectedly, with the war, and it had shaken her.

Captain Baush and her fellow soldiers repeatedly tried to reassure her by saying she had saved the marine's life, and she had. The unit was putting her up for an award. But that only made her cringe. Yes, she had reacted as she'd been trained, quickly and with authority, barking orders to soldiers who outranked her. She'd applied a good, tight tourniquet and set up the IV and then looked into the man's eyes and told him to look into hers and told him to hold on. What else could she have done?

She'd had a man's life in her hands—a boy's, really—and he would never be the same. In the moment, of course, she didn't think of his future. But now, sleepless night after sleepless night, she could think of nothing else. Even though Kate heard that he was recovering nicely at Walter Reed Army Medical Center, she couldn't help thinking about what his life would be like now. Did he have a girlfriend? Would she stay with him? Was he angry, or bitter? Did he remember her holding his hand? Did he remember begging her for morphine?

In that moment on the helicopter, the trajectory of his life—whether he'd make it home to his parents, whether he'd walk, marry, have children, grow old—had depended on her. That was what overwhelmed her. That was what made her hand shake.

What she needed was her husband, the sweet man whose voice, even from across the ocean, could restore calm, no matter what. Everything's going to be all right, he'd say. And she knew it would be. The war would end, and she'd go home and they'd have their life together. This is what would get her through Iraq, which is why she had subjected herself to that embarrassing wedding ceremony in the empty chapel with the framed hologram of Jesus mocking her. No matter how awful the war was, she knew her husband was keeping their apartment, with its tapestries and candles, located in the cool part of town, warm and ready for her return.

Her husband was a great letter writer. He would sit out on their front porch and paint vivid pictures of what life was like at home—the people passing by, the neighbors, the crazy college kids. In autumn he'd provide poetic details about how the leaves were turning orange and red and gold, and in spring he'd meticulously document where the flowers were blooming, and when. He'd send her corny letters from her dog, Lola, signed with paw prints he'd draw. He sent care packages full of mix CDs, water guns to beat the heat, all sorts of junk food—including Pringles, blessed, blessed Pringles—he figured she couldn't get in the desert, and books he had just finished that she just had to read. All of it made her ache for home. And best of all, if, after a long shift, she needed to call home, she could. Even if in Richmond it was the middle of the night, he'd answer with a sleepy "Hey, Katibug" and she knew that everything was going to be all right.

Until, it wasn't.

As May turned to June, the letters, e-mails, and packages that once arrived in droves stopped coming. Every time she called, she either got voice mail or an excuse about how he had left his phone in the car and couldn't talk now.

By July, she was starting to get concerned, and nervous thoughts about her marriage were clouding her mind as much as the injured marine. Other soldiers in the battalion were going through the exact same thing. It seemed almost everyone was having marital problems, and a few were getting divorces. But Kate was sure that if she and her husband could just talk, everything would be okay. They loved each other. They were going to be together forever. Marriage is hard enough as it is, Kate told herself. Throw a war into the mix, and things get complicated. But it would be over soon, and they'd just pick up where they'd left off.

While on a few days' pass in Qatar, Kate called from a military phone bank, and finally he answered. He'd been avoiding her, she was sure of that now. So she called him at work where he couldn't avoid her. He was abrupt, saying, "I can't talk now. Call me after work."

"Well, I've been trying to call you for days but you haven't been answering," she said. "Are you going to this time?"

He said he would. But his voice was so cold it gave her shivers.

"We're going to be okay, aren't we?" she asked.

"No. I don't think we are," he said. Then he hung up.

By the time he got off work it was 4 a.m. in Qatar, but Kate hadn't been able to sleep anyway. She trudged back to the phone bank in the predawn darkness.

"I want a divorce," he said.

He hadn't told her he'd been cheating—she found that out later. But even if he had told her, she probably would have reacted the same way: with utter denial.

"No," she said. She would not grant him a divorce. Their only problem was that there was a war going on, and soon it would be over, and she'd be home. Everything would be all right.

The phone bank was packed with soldiers calling back to the States, and many of them were now staring at Kate as she sobbed into the phone. "We'll go to counseling," she pleaded. "This is going to work."

Even though he told her it was too late and he didn't love her anymore, she went straight to the Internet café on base and ordered him $150 worth of flowers. Then she called Captain Baush and her first sergeant at Al Asad, and they told her to get home as quickly as possible. She was so upset and lost that she didn't even think of it as weird that they were now referring to Al Asad as "home."

Like the soldiers in earlier wars, service members in Iraq, including those with the 2-224th, often talked about Jody, the guy who was sleeping with your girlfriend while you were away. In Vietnam they marched to the cadences written for Jody:

> Ain't no use in going back
> Jody's got your Cadillac
> Ain't no use in feeling blue
> Jody's got your sister too

And while Kate had heard many stories of marital disintegration throughout the battalion, she didn't think it would ever happen to her. Waiting to get back to Al Asad, she felt the news slowly start to sink in and, without thinking, she wrote an e-mail from Qatar to her friends and family back home, telling them that her husband was leaving her.

"I have no home to go to," she wrote. "I have no future. I have nothing. My life is over. . . . Now there is nothing. I have no car, no dogs, no apartment, no college education, no dream of one day having children, no happiness, nothing."

Both her mother and twin sister received the e-mail while at work. Both were so upset after reading it that colleagues told them to go home.

. . .

Kate had no idea that shrinks were allowed to give their opinion about their patients so forcefully. She thought they mostly sat and listened at a detached distance, nodding their heads, occasionally asking vacuous, open-ended questions such as "Why do you think that is?" But this psychiatrist, in his navy uniform, was nothing like that at all. He started off their first session by bluntly telling her, "I want to forewarn you that it's going to be difficult for me to have any objectivity because this is my third deployment. And on my first my wife cheated on me, and we got divorced."

Kate liked him right away.

Like his demeanor, the setting was not what she expected for a therapist. Then again, this was Iraq, where she was surprised to have even found a psychiatrist in the first place. Instead of a comfortable armchair and a room painted in soothing pastels and decorated with neutral art—all the trappings she associated with therapy—she sat in a metal folding chair and talked about her problems in a stark beige room with concrete floors. Outside, the building was protected with concertina wire and sandbags.

At first she was worried. Not about the therapy. She knew she was having issues and desperately needed someone, preferably a professional, to talk to. She was concerned that other soldiers would find out and think her weak, or damaged, unable to do her job, sort of like if Tony Soprano's Mafia buddies discovered he was seeing a shrink. Not that everyone felt that way. It was her supervisor who had learned that there was a psychiatrist on base and urged Kate to see him. Captain Baush, whom Kate leaned on for advice, also exhorted her to get help. He could relate. Shortly before he was to deploy for Iraq, his relationship with his fiancée had collapsed.

The more Kate thought about it, the more she realized just how many soldiers in the battalion were having marital trouble. And the longer they were away, the more problems popped up. There was the soldier who complained that his wife was sleeping around and spending his money. Another talked about how her husband suspected she was cheating on him (though she wasn't) and was sending her increasingly angry and abusive e-mails. And there was the soldier whose wife simply left while he was in Iraq. I've got the name of a great divorce attorney, he told Kate.

In a way it made Kate feel better to know she was in such plentiful company. And it felt good to open up to her psychiatrist, especially because he wore the uniform and had at least some sense of what she'd been through. He never pushed, which she liked as well.

At the end of their first ninety-minute session, he said he thought he could help her and asked if she wanted to continue. She was surprised at how much she did. So twice a week, Kate quietly made her way to his office and talked through her two issues: the guilt she felt over not having morphine for the injured marine and her divorce.

What worried her about the divorce was that she had married a guy who was obviously an awful choice for her. If she could make such a bad decision in choosing a mate for life, she wondered, what else was she getting wrong? She felt as if she couldn't trust herself to make any more decisions, which left her feeling somewhat paralyzed. "It made me question every decision I had ever made in my life," she said later.

"That's perfectly understandable," her psychiatrist said. "Though it may not seem like it now, you will date again. And you will marry again. The key will be to make a better choice. So let's make a list of what characteristics you'll look for next time."

Kate started slowly. "Financially stable, educated," she said while he wrote them down on a dry erase board. Soon Kate was rolling, talking so fast that the therapist could barely keep up: "Wants to have children. Keeps ties with friends. Is close with his family. Comes from a stable environment. Honest."

The whole exercise seemed kind of corny and simplistic. But it worked. Here was a practical guide to love and life in black and white, a way forward, that made her feel, for the first time in a long time, that she was taking control of her life. As the weeks wore on, the psychiatrist also went well beyond simply letting her vent about that day with the injured marine. He comforted her by saying that if she hadn't been there to treat him, he would have been a lot worse off, and possibly even dead. He reassured her that she'd helped the wounded marine. She hadn't planted the IED.

In the end, it felt good hear that, on the whole, she was a healthy, normal person who had been through two awful, traumatic events, back to back. Still, he wanted her to seek help once she got home. You never know what might trigger the nightmares, he told her. And going home could be more stressful than you think.

So she promised she'd find a VA counselor when she got home.

"No one will know who you are, or what you've been through. You'll be standing there in the grocery store, without your uniform, surrounded by civilians, just trying to get on with life, and suddenly you'll get furious at the people around you. You'll be mad at how they're living their lives comfortably, uninterrupted by the war. 'Don't they know what's going on? Don't they care?' you'll think. To them, it will be as if there is no war.

"This is what happened to me when I was home on leave," the Reverend John Weatherly, the 2-224th's chaplain, explained to small groups of his soldiers in the weeks before they were to go home. He had grown furious at the people around him, and you will too, he cautioned. The transition to home is not going to be as easy as you think. You'll feel naked without your rifle. You'll feel "a sense of entitlement," he told them, "that [you] deserve to be treated well." And when you're ignored by civilians—and you will be ignored—you'll get angry. It's as if your wife were dying in the hospital, and you come from visiting her and can't understand why people outside are smiling. "You want to feel like when you're grieving the world should be, too," he said.

Some of the soldiers were incredulous and laughed under their breath. I'm not going to be grieving when I get home, they thought. I'm going to be partying. And later they derided it as the Don't-Beat-Your-Wife briefing.

But Kate could picture exactly what the chaplain was saying, and she was getting mad just thinking about it. It already felt as if no one at home cared about the war. It seemed as if it was barely on the news programs the soldiers watched on base. Earlier, in her blog, she had asked: "Do people back home even know we are still over here? That is something we are beginning to worry about. . . . Is there a war still going on or what? When one of our neighboring units lost a Black Hawk last week and two soldiers died, did the news ever give it more than 30 seconds of their time? I can tell you for a fact they did not. . . . So many of us are scared this is turning into another fucking Vietnam. The soldiers will come home forgotten or even worse, hated. And when it is a slow news day and Bill O'Reilly is discussing some fucking fluff piece we all look at each other and shake our heads. Because we know the news doesn't care about us anymore.

"Thank goodness for friends and family, otherwise no one would remember.

"And I can always say 'At least I am not in Afghanistan.' Those poor bastards were as forgotten almost as quickly as they were sent over there. Wtf.

"I hate so much right now."

When she went home on leave, she got a taste of what the chaplain was talking about. To her friends she was something of a novelty, their only real connection to the war. She was paraded around parties and bars like a zoo animal on display. Come see the soldier home from Iraq! It angered her so much that now she knew that what the chaplain was saying about watching her anger was important.

The chaplain went on to discuss reuniting with spouses and family, a notion that made Kate wince. "Remember," he said, "their lives didn't just come to a standstill while you were gone." You got that right, Kate thought.

Where once going home was all she wished for, now it was a prospect that filled her with dread. Her husband was gone. She had no place to live. No job. And no certainty, after more than a year away, that she'd be able to function outside Iraq. At the beginning of the deployment she had planned on returning to college soon after getting home. But now there was no way she could stomach being a twenty-five-year-old sophomore in a class full of nineteen-year-old know-nothings whose biggest worry was what party to attend Friday night.

Kate had come to feel "institutionalized" as she wrote friends back home. The feeling was widespread among her fellow soldiers. One "actually told me that if she had the opportunity, she would stay another year," Kate wrote. "She doesn't want to go home."

What was foreign was now familiar, and vice versa. Kate knew how the soldier felt: "Going back to a home and a life that was not what I left is absolutely scaring the bejesus out of me," she wrote.

So she had a request for her friends and family about her return: "I would like my visit to be somewhat quiet," she wrote in an e-mail home. "One night, yes, I will answer any and all questions you might have of me. But let's try to make this a visit of reconnection and talk about the future, the little things, and laughter. After all the questions have been asked I really don't want to spend too much time dwelling on the nasty aspects of this deployment. I am more interested in sharing with you the bonds I have made with the wonderful people I have met over here."

It turned out the good chaplain needed to heed his own advice. Two weeks after getting home, he was driving his wife and two children to dinner (even though his wife had thought him still too jittery from the deployment to drive). He came to a stop sign in his neighborhood that he had long considered superfluous and had rarely obeyed. On this night, however, a county police officer was parked at the intersection, obviously looking to nab someone. The officer was in plain view, and the chaplain saw him, even made eye contact, and then proceeded to roll the stop sign anyway.

When the officer pulled him over, the chaplain explained indignantly that he was a National Guard soldier just back from Iraq, where for safety reasons you often blew through stop signs.

The officer was not impressed. "I've been back for eight months myself," he said. "You have to remember: You're not in Iraq. You're in the United States. And here we stop at stop signs."

The ticket cost $85.

8

Miranda

Graduation Day

Miranda could still remember the security code to the front door of the sorority house—1897, the year Kappa Delta was founded. Amazing how such a seemingly insignificant bit of data could remain embedded in her memory when over the past eight months so much had changed. She had worried about coming back for graduation, uncertain it was the right thing to do even as she walked back onto the campus for the first time since September. Recalling the code, though, gave her hope that, for a moment anyway, it would be possible to fit back in.

Come Sunday, graduation day, she'd be virtually indistinguishable from all the other students in their caps and gowns. She'd spend the week until then with friends, partying, catching up. She'd attend the senior dance and wear makeup—real makeup, not just the Chapstick that passed for lip gloss in Iraq—for the first time in what seemed like forever. Best of all she'd wear an elegant, purple dress made of satin, which after such an ascetic existence, after all the grit and sand and unrelenting flak-jacket sweat that gave even the most careful girl rashes, was a luxury in itself: satin against skin. She couldn't wait. As they said, Iraq was like hitting yourself on the head with a hammer—the longer you do it, the better it feels when you stop. And she was ready for a break. She hadn't realized it while in country surrounded by the tan desert. But despite her experience at the airport, once she got home to Virginia, saw the dogwoods and magnolias, the flowering pear trees, she couldn't help but think, It's good to be home.

The war had robbed her of virtually her entire senior year, but she was not going to allow it to take away the culmination of her fitful college career, interrupted first by army basic training, then by war. She had worked too hard for this degree—had been forced to complete her studies over an unreliable Internet connection from the Middle East and study after long hours in the supply office and tiring Black Hawk missions. Now she was going to celebrate alongside her classmates, even if she now felt so much older than everyone else.

Proud she had not forgotten the code, she punched in the secret numbers. She was eager to burst into the sorority house and yell out a big, "Hello, I'm back!" But the door wouldn't budge. She tapped out 1-8-9-7 again, more deliberately this time. Still, the lock remained stubbornly set against her. Then it hit her: While she'd been gone, someone had changed the code. So she had no other choice but to ring the doorbell as if she were just any other visitor and wait for someone to let her in.

She brought back souvenirs for her friends—stuffed camels, T-shirts, patches, baseball hats, trinkets, and other kitsch she had picked up in the Middle East. She handed them out at the sorority house like a "crazy aunt who came back from a trip," her close friend Portia Ross remembered. "It was almost like she was studying abroad. You never would have thought she came back from combat."

Miranda certainly didn't seem any different. Handing out the gag gifts, she was the same sarcastic, quick-witted jokester her friends remembered. Which was exactly the image Miranda wanted to project. She didn't want to be seen as a soldier coming home from war. And she was prepared for the questions about Iraq that inevitably came, answering them with the same don't-worry-about-me tone that had laced so many of her e-mails home. As word spread that Miranda was back, the girls crowded in around her, some sitting on the floor, wanting to know what it had been like. She told them about how as the unit's social chair she had gone to great lengths to obtain enough hamburgers for the battalion barbecue. She told them about how soldiers had access only to non-alcoholic "near beer," as if that were the most severe hardship of the war. She complained about her short hair and gushed about how excited she was now to curl her hair and wear makeup. And she adeptly changed the topic to the upcoming graduation, the parties, and the latest campus gossip.

She did not mention that in less than two weeks, while everyone else was at the beach, or home beginning their postgraduate careers, she would be back in Iraq, with eight months left to go in her tour.

Miranda's old roommate Ashley Slaff sensed that Miranda was painting a rosy picture so that no one would worry about her. It was, Ashley thought, a noble act of selflessness, and typical of Miranda, who, before she left for Iraq, hid notes she had written to Ashley all over their room. There was one in a purse Miranda had once borrowed that thanked Ashley for letting her borrow it. Then there was the one Ashley had found months after Miranda had gone that was stashed under her keyboard that gave her goose bumps. "I always wanted to thank you for being a great friend," it read.

She knew Miranda had signed up to be a door gunner, and that there had to be more to the war that she wasn't telling the rest of the girls.

She sensed there was another level below the facade Miranda was working so hard to construct. But she didn't want to be yet another person pestering Miranda for details and get the same clichéd response. If Miranda wanted to tell her about the war, she would. If not, well, Ashley wasn't going to push. Maybe she'd hear about it when it was all over and Miranda was home for good.

The night of the senior dance was perfect: clear May skies, a temperature that had that afternoon risen to the mid-seventies and was by evening mild and pleasant. The soon-to-be graduates were mingling under the big white tent spread out on the Sunken Garden, dancing away. The soft lights and the warm Virginia spring evening made Iraq seem very far away indeed. Miranda, wearing her satin dress, was as happy as she had been all week, floating away on the dance floor with friends. It felt good to just live as her former self, if just for a night, dancing carefree to the DJ.

Exhausted from dancing, Miranda took a break when she spotted Lance Zaal. He was tall and athletic and very cute. But that's not why she stopped to talk to him. Lance was a former sergeant in the Marines Corps who had also had a college career postponed by Iraq.

"I hear you're back from Iraq," he said.

He had gotten back himself just a few months before, and as it turned out they had been to some of the same places, including overlapping at Al Asad for a few weeks, though neither of them knew it at the time. Miranda could tell that as they spoke of the war, Lance was being whisked back there, away from the dance lights and music. Soon he was telling her about the first time his platoon was pinned down under fire. He called in to his command for support, he told Miranda.

"My lieutenant, the idiot, asked how I knew we were being fired at," Lance continued. "And I said because there are fucking bullets whizzing by my head!"

Miranda burst out laughing. Here they were, a soldier and marine, sharing war stories. It seemed completely normal except for their surroundings. This was a conversation better suited for the Elks Lodge or the American Legion hall, not the middle of the senior dance.

Like Miranda, Lance felt isolated on campus. "No one understood what I had just been through," he said later. And it felt good to talk to a fellow vet.

"So, you seen any action?" Lance asked her.

She nodded. A little bit. She hardly knew Lance. They ran in different social circles and took different classes. But she realized that if there was one person on campus she could talk to, it was Lance. He had been there. He knew. She was careful not to exaggerate her experience, which was nothing compared with what a marine like Lance had faced. But she told him about the guys digging the IEDs. How she had them in her sights. How they were so close, she could see one's face. How she could see it still. How she would have pulled the trigger.

"Well now you know you can do it," Lance told her.

Yes, she could. That was something probably no one else on the dance floor could say.

No matter how hard she tried to make everything seem normal, Miranda knew it wasn't. She knew the questions would come, and that friends would get overly emotional, and she'd have to hold back tears, to be strong. But even her friend Portia noticed, "People were looking at her as though they were trying to memorize her face in case they never saw her again."

On campus, Miranda had become something of a local celebrity: William and Mary's very own Iraq warrior. Shortly before graduation, the Associated Press wrote a story about Miranda's coming home to graduate. Even the college's Web site prominently featured a story about Miranda for a few days during graduation week. But she still very much felt like an outsider. She had been gone just eight months, but it felt like a lifetime. She had missed virtually all of senior year, the dances, a Caribbean cruise over spring break.

It hurt to see the girls who were merely "Potential New Members" when she deployed now fully ensconced in the sorority. Watching the campus's new dynamic was a little like witnessing the growth of a child: You don't really appreciate how much he's growing unless you see him only once every few months.

There had always been a difference between Miranda and her classmates because she served in the National Guard and they did not. It's why she didn't want to be seen on campus in uniform. But when she took the uniform off, she could, for the most part, shed her military persona and become a normal college student. But now at graduation, she felt even more removed from her classmates. Uniform or not, she was not like them.

Jody, as Miranda discovered, was not just the person at home sleeping with your wife or husband. Jody took many forms. Jody was all of the things that happened while you were away. For some soldiers in the battalion, it was their kids' growing up while they were gone. Missed first words, first steps. For Ray, Jody was the mounting problems his wife was facing at home. Even Diane, who had never put on a uniform in her life, got Jodied.

Jody wasn't so much a person as a concept—a verb and a noun, seeing as how the act of getting "Jodied" was what mattered more than who, or what, did it.

"So I have been back in Williamsburg for a couple of days, doing my damnedest to pretend like I am a normal graduating senior," Miranda wrote in an e-mail to friends. "I am, of course, not. I find myself in the curious position of being the only person saying hello on a campus full of people saying good-bye. I can't lie, it's been really good. I have had the chance to see so many people and to not care about a lot of things that I normally have to care about. But it's also been harrowing. I suppose that there are certain moments in a person's life where they are forced to see exactly how far they have come in life. I can see now the impression that WM made on me. But now, after being away and otherwise usefully engaged, I can see that I do not cleanly fit into that mold anymore."

. . .

Graduation was at noon on Sunday. William and Mary had been sending its students out into the world since the Colonial days, and in his speech the college president noted that in 1762 Thomas Jefferson had left the grounds a William and Mary graduate. The former Supreme Court Justice Sandra Day O'Connor, who weeks before had been appointed the college's chancellor, was on stage for the ceremony. As was Archbishop Desmond Tutu, who in his Commencement address extolled the virtue and energy of the young, how for generations they have risen up against injustice, from fighting the war in Vietnam to apartheid. "God says you young people, you're just fabulous," he said. "You are in the forefront of the campaign to make poverty history. You are part of the exhilarating movements for peace. You are amongst those who demonstrated against the war in Iraq. Give peace a chance. Give peace a chance."

Even though there weren't enough seats for all of them, Miranda and her friends crammed themselves into a single row. To fit, they had to share seats and sit on one anothers' laps. They were huddled together so tightly it was uncomfortable. But no one would leave the pack. It reminded Miranda of the way soldiers are often thrown together.

The college president carried on about the overachievers who were graduating with perfect 4.0s, the prodigy who co-wrote a paper with his economics professor, the neuroscience major who worked in an orphanage in the Philippines and volunteered at the local hospital.

"And I'd also like to take this moment to acknowledge one special member of the armed forces, who is receiving her bachelor's degree today," he continued. "Sergeant Miranda Summers flew in from her active-duty assignment in Iraq so that she could attend this Commencement." Miranda froze at the sound of her name. No one had warned her that she'd be singled out. Oh no, please don't, she thought. Her friends needled her, thrilled that one of their own was being recognized. And as soon as the president said the word "Iraq," the audience started to applaud, forcing the president to pause.

"Her National Guard unit was activated and sent to Iraq, and while she might have taken an alternative to leaving with her unit, she didn't. She remained, determined to graduate today, and Sergeant Summers is not to be denied. A few weeks ago, while still in Iraq, she received our Ewell Award and she wrote, 'I now know what it feels like to try to study, to learn, and to thrive when there is literally a war going on outside your very walls. I know that it was not just my classes, but all my activities at William and Mary that are enabling me to survive here. I am grateful to the college for everything it has taught me in and out of the classroom.'

"And we are immensely grateful to you, Sergeant."

Again, applause broke out.

"Stand up," her friends urged. "Stand up!"

Miranda could feel her face turning red as she stood and looked out over her fellow classmates. Hundreds of faces looking back at her. Bright faces. Young faces. Adults, but not yet adults. Faces that reminded her of the soldiers of the same age who were right now in Iraq. How similar they were.

And how very different.

At the beginning of the deployment, Miranda had thought that the war would help her decide what she wanted to do in life, as if combat would confer a previously absent level of clarity. But when she returned to Iraq, all she was clear on was that she was glad to be back. It didn't matter that she was soon transferred from Al Asad to the 2-224th's detachment at Al Taqaddum, even though TQ, as it was called, was much closer to Baghdad, much smaller than Al Asad, and more dangerous. Iraq was her normal, her home, and, at least for now, where she wanted to be.

Before the war, there had never been any question that when the deployment was over she'd go to graduate school. The only decision to make was whether she'd go for law or for a field such as American Studies that would help her land a job in a museum. But the more time she spent in Iraq, the less she could imagine life in an isolated academic bubble. Though she would not have dared tell her father, she began seriously exploring a postwar career in the services. She could get a full-time job with the Guard. Or, now that she was a college grad, she could apply to Officer Candidate School. Or maybe she should think about going to flight school. Heck, if she was going to stay in the military, why not sign up with the marines? And so she started talking by e-mail with some recruiters back home before realizing that maybe that was a little too hardcore for her.

"I love the army. It's an abusive relationship, but I keep coming back," she wrote her friends at home. " . . . I knew that although I keep thinking of the army as something I am doing to prepare myself for something bigger, maybe this really is my life. Although I tell myself that I want to go to graduate school and work in a museum, I have consistently wanted nothing more for myself than to be in the army. Really, I have been wanting this since I was about nine, and training for it since I was twelve. I cannot say that I see myself as a warrior or even a leader, but I know that I am a soldier. Even if the army could do better than me, I don't think that I could do better than the army."

Miranda was self-aware enough to realize that part of this drastic change of plans was the result of her current situation. She was a creature of context. If the 2-224th had not been called for Iraq and she had finished the rest of her college career on campus, the thought of going active duty or joining the marines would probably never have entered her mind. Part of her knew that she was, in a sense, hypnotized by the war and wasn't thinking clearly about her future. But part of her also realized that when she was home for good, she might very well be ready to take a break from the military.

So she also sent out applications to the State Department and the National Archives. And as much as she resisted the idea of graduate school—what would she have in common with all those young kids right out of college?—she thought it best to keep her options open. In a single weekend, she wrote her essay and shipped out her application to the most prestigious school she could think of that offered a master's in American Civilization/Public Humanities: Brown University, the New England Ivy that was perhaps the most liberal campus in the entire country. Even if she was accepted— and Miranda figured that was a long shot—graduate school in her mind was still very much the backup plan.

For the first time in her life, she had no idea what was next on the horizon. But she told herself to be patient. She would have to get home before she could fully take stock of just how much the war had changed her, and who she had become.

9

Craig

Welcome to Game Time, Lieutenant Lewis

The curious whistle in the distance was getting closer fast. But to Lieutenant Craig Lewis it didn't seem anything other than an innocuous distraction, and he didn't even look up from the Black Hawk's transmission filter he had been inspecting as part of the pre-flight routine. Out of the corner of his eye, he noticed that his instructor pilot was diving to the ground. But Craig didn't associate this odd behavior with the hissing, high-pitched whistle and just stood there wondering why his instructor would suddenly hit the deck.

"GET DOWN!" his instructor screamed.

The mortar hit a few hundred yards away with a titanic boom that shook the ground and kicked up a huge dust plume. Shrapnel and debris came bouncing past Craig on the tarmac.

Brushing himself off as he returned to his feet, Chief Warrant Officer-3 Shane Leipertz was incredulous. Any rookie in a war zone was suspect, but what kind of soldier doesn't know to hit the deck when there's incoming?

Craig was a replacement, a twenty-seven-year-old FNG ("Fucking New Guy") who had just joined the 2-224th fresh out of flight school six months into the deployment. It was Shane's job to get him ready to fly in combat conditions, an awesome responsibility that he didn't take lightly. But you never knew how such a green pilot was going to make the transition to Iraq, and judging from Craig's reaction—or nonreaction—to the mortar, it seemed as if Shane had his work cut out for him. He just hoped that this young lieutenant had at least half a brain and the good sense to do as he was told.

"Lesson number one: When you hear that whistling sound, you get down," Shane groused at him.

What a welcome, Craig thought. He had been in Iraq less than a week and already mortar fire had nearly taken him out. And now his instructor thought he was an incompetent buffoon before he was even able to take his first training flight.

Craig was one to follow orders. And he certainly was not the kind to question the wisdom of his commanders. But part of him thought it was crazy that he be allowed to fly a Black Hawk in Iraq. His flight school training at Fort Rucker, Alabama, had been intense and comprehensive, and he had passed all the tests. But everything was moving so fast. A little over a year before, he had never even set foot in a helicopter, and now he was going to be asked to fly one under fire into places like Fallujah and Baghdad. It seemed reckless at best. At worst, suicidal.

In flight school the conditions were almost always ideal; in Iraq, with its sandstorms, blinding desert winds, and 120-degree temperatures, not to mention the terrorists with guns and rockets, they were anything but. Craig had never even flown with door gunners on board, and he shuddered at the thought of having to give the order to fire. When the bullets started flying, he had no idea how he'd react. And his response to the mortar didn't do much to boost his confidence.

But what scared Craig the most was letting down his fellow soldiers, which wasn't so much a fear of disappointing them as it was of getting someone killed. One look at him, and everyone would know he was new to Iraq. It was obvious from his brand-new uniform, so crisp and clean he might as well have been walking around base with a sign around his neck that read "Replacement."

The mortar had carved a nice little crater off the edge of the flight line, but fortunately no one had been injured. Still, Craig wondered if the training flight would be postponed. The explosion had been awfully close. But this was Iraq, after all, and he figured he'd better just get used to bombs going off every once in a while. Shane, who seemed every bit as tough as the instructors at Fort Rucker, continued with the preflight routine poker-faced, as if nothing had happened. If this were a live mission, a near-miss mortar attack wouldn't get in their way. And Shane certainly wasn't going to let it interrupt his training session.

Shane hadn't ordered up the mortar attack, but with no one injured he was almost glad it had hit so close. Now he'd see what his young charge was made of. This could be a great, if unplanned, training exercise, he thought. He wanted Craig rattled. Pilots had to get used to flying scared, with bullets whizzing by, an engine out, fuel leaking, smoke billowing from the engine, an incapacitated co-pilot unable to help. One or all of those scenarios were a distinct possibility in Iraq, and his job was to make sure Craig could handle every single one of them—in addition to the unforeseen. The battalion had not lost a single pilot, but it had lost a Black Hawk, which crashed during a night landing in the middle of the desert.

Flight instructors have all sorts of Jedi mind tricks they use on young pilots that are designed to overwhelm them and expose their weaknesses so that when the crisis comes for real, they're prepared. "Task saturation," it was called in the world of aviation: Flood the poor bastards with so much information that they make mistakes. Then teach them how not to repeat those errors.

Shane was particularly inventive when it came to taxing his students and was known in the middle of training to assume an alter ego he called "Bubba." Bubba was a bumbling idiot of a co-pilot who spoke with a slow southern drawl and did everything he could to make flying as difficult as possible. Bubba would enter the wrong coordinates into the GPS, then suddenly forget how to operate the radio and start flicking switches on the control panel. He'd take the controls and force the helicopter into a nosedive, making his co-pilot-in-training retake the controls and right the aircraft. Anything could go wrong in the air—especially in Iraq—and Bubba was Shane's way of getting his pilots prepared. But Bubba was not going to make an appearance on Craig's first flight. There'd be time for that later.

Though he wouldn't show it, Shane liked Craig almost immediately once they were in the air. He sensed Craig was a dedicated soldier, one who didn't get too flustered and who, above all, listened. It's not easy flying in a desert environment for the first time. If Craig learned nothing else, he now knew what an incoming mortar sounded like, and Shane could guarantee that he'd be quick to hit the deck the next time they got hit.

Later, in the chow hall, some of the other pilots asked how the new guy did. "He's looking pretty good," Shane said. But one day didn't prove anything, and Shane retained a healthy dose of skepticism. Craig was not ready to fly any real missions yet.

"Flying with a guy as green as the Lt is a real test of everything I am about," Shane wrote in his journal. "I do not have the words available to me to describe the experience. They say the best way to learn is to jump in the deep end and swim, I just hope I can keep this guy from feeling like he is drowning. . . .

"Welcome to game time, Lt. Lewis."

The recruiters like to brag that any job you can find in the civilian world, the army has too. Only the army calls them "military occupational specialties," not jobs, and Uncle Sam pays you while you get schooled. Good with your hands? We have metal workers and machinists, the recruiters say. Interested in medicine? We got everything from to emergency medics to mental-health counselors, they say. You want to write? Our Public Affairs Office writes more damn truth in a day than the *New York Times* prints in a week. Good at math? We'll have you breaking codes and saving lives in no time. Think you're tough? Try the Army Rangers. You want to kill? Well, let's just say that ain't a problem. Firefighters, carpenters, chaplains, tank drivers, ship captains, dentists, spies, lawyers, morticians, translators—the army's got you covered.

But when Craig first considered that catch-all career center known as the U.S. Army, he decided to go for the glamour-boy slot, one of the more exclusive clubs the army had to offer. He had decided early on that he wasn't going to be an on-the-ground grunt, humping it into some God-forsaken hellhole, sleeping in trenches. He was going to fly.

Unlike the nonplussed air force recruiter, who told Craig his application would be added to the heap already piling up on his desk, the recruiter for the National Guard was enthusiastic and more than willing to spend all the time Craig needed explaining the ins and outs of the army. When Craig asked about flight school, the recruiter told him, "We've got an aviation unit right here in Virginia that flies Black Hawks." He couldn't guarantee that the unit would accept Craig and send him to flight school—such decisions were not made lightly and were subject to all sorts of physical and intellectual requirements and then the capricious whims of who knows how many members of the chain of command. Craig thanked him for his candor, but just knowing flight school was a possibility was all he needed to hear.

He'd grown up on a two-hundred-acre beef cattle farm in Kents Store, Virginia, a rural outpost halfway between Richmond and Charlottesville, where there was a post office, a volunteer fire department, a general store, and not much else except acres upon acres of farmland. He was the all-American kid, a star high school baseball and football player who hunted deer with his father, a short, spry man with twinkling blue eyes who decorated his auto-repair shop with the antlers and busts of game they bagged.

For teenagers in Kents Store, the military had long been a popular option after high school. Within a mile radius of his home, Craig could point to several neighbors who had served—the retired colonel across the street, the air force pilot around the corner, the army grunt two farms over.

So when Craig joined the Guard during his senior year of college in 2002, his mother, a hearings officer with the Virginia Department of Corrections, was pleased that he had taken the initiative. But his father was skeptical. Even though Craig played fullback for the Bridgewater College football team and could throw up 425 pounds on the bench press, he wasn't sure Craig was cut out for the military. That feeling faded somewhat after Craig finished first in basic training out of about two hundred other recruits. And it dissolved completely when he saw Craig for the first time in uniform, at which point he took the "Uncle Sam Wants You" poster that had been hanging in Craig's childhood room and hung it proudly in his auto shop. Unlike some parents who protested that their sons and daughters were only in the Guard and should not have to be fighting abroad, Craig's were under no illusions. They fully expected him to get the call, and so did he.

Craig, still caught up in the post-9/11 patriotic fervor, was eager to serve, even if that meant combat. But he also looked at his relationship with the military as symbiotic: He'd give the army six years of service, and the army would teach him a skill he wouldn't learn otherwise, which would then help his civilian career. Soldiering was never going to be a full-time commitment, which is why he had chosen the National Guard and not the active-duty army. He figured that if the U.S. government trusted him to fly a $6-million aircraft, then future employers would definitely regard him as hiring material.

After college and basic training and then Officer Candidate School, Craig got a job teaching and coaching baseball at his alma mater, Fluvanna High School. Everything was working out just as it was supposed to. One weekend a month, he'd put on his uniform and be a soldier with the 2-224th waiting his turn to go to flight school in Fort Rucker. The rest of the time he was one of Fluvanna High's more popular teachers. So he was relieved when his commander told him that everything was going to work out just as Craig had hoped: He'd go to Fort Rucker, but not until after the school year had ended. That meant he'd miss an entire year of school while the army taught him to fly, and he'd return to teaching the following September. Which is what he reported in the fall to his boss, the principal, who was supportive.

Then during his National Guard drill weekend in January 2005, his commander told him he would have to go to flight school earlier than planned. Instead of June, he'd be going March 31. No more baseball season. No more finishing out the school year. The country was at war, and the army had called. Craig tried to explain this to his principal, who wasn't thrilled with the fact that he'd now have to find a replacement for the last few weeks of the school year. Still, it was only January. There was plenty of time to find someone else.

On a Saturday afternoon two weeks later, the army called: Your date for flight school is being moved up. We need you at Fort Rucker on February 1.

As an officer, Craig outranked the sergeant calling him with the news, and he treated the call as a request rather than an order. I've already got my flight school date, he said: March 31. It was the date he had given his principal, and he was going to stick to it. February 1 was a week away. There was no way he could leave then, he told the sergeant. He hung up without giving the conversation much thought.

The next day the sergeant called back. Again he said Craig needed to move up his flight school date. And again Craig demurred, saying he'd stay with the March 31 date. It wasn't until a few minutes later when the battalion commander called that Craig realized how serious this was.

"What's the problem?" the commander said. Lieutenant Colonel Robert E. McMillin II was as affable as army leaders come. As a commander, he liked to laugh, dip tobacco, and play touch football with his soldiers. But he hadn't risen through the ranks by making friends with those in his charge. And his direct tone made it clear he was not in the mood to be dealing with the protests of a brand-new soldier.

An opening at flight school had come up and he needed Craig to fill it, he said. Some sit on waiting lists for months, if not years, to get in. And here Craig was getting the opportunity a mere two months after receiving his commission. What Craig didn't know was that the 2-224th was getting ready to deploy to Iraq, and it needed all the pilots it could get—which meant he was being fast-tracked to flight school. Uncle Sam needed him in the air.

Craig repeated his protest, keeping his soft Virginia drawl as polite as possible. "Sir" and "Ma'am" were integral parts of his vocabulary long before he joined the army, and he rarely lost his temper. It was as if he forgot that anger was an option in his emotional repertoire, and it certainly was not going to emerge while he was speaking with his commander. But he could feel an unsettling brew of agitation, anxiety, and helplessness rising.

"My date for flight school was already moved up once," he pleaded, "and my principal wasn't thrilled about that. I can't go back to him and say I'm leaving in a week. It would jeopardize my career. If only I could leave for flight school in the spring, as I originally planned. I can't give my principal such short notice. It's just not right."

When Craig was finished, his commander spoke softly and said he sympathized. But didn't budge.

"I hear what you're saying," he said. "But I need you. We all have to make sacrifices. You're going."

He didn't say, "That's an order." He didn't need to. And that was that.

Craig's mind raced. How was he supposed to pick up and leave for an entire year? Who was going to take his place in the group house he was sharing with three roommates? What would he do with all his stuff? How would he break this to his students, to their parents? But what he dreaded most was telling his principal.

If he had to be in Alabama in a week, he could work only through Wednesday, which meant he'd be giving just three days' notice. He would need the rest of the week to pack and get ready to move to Fort Rucker for a year.

He knew this was what the National Guard is all about. Being a citizen one day, a soldier the next. But Craig was beginning to wonder how he was going to balance the two roles. Wasn't the Guard supposed to help his civilian career, not hurt it?

Three days' notice was just ridiculous, he thought. This was not going to go over well.

Monday morning, Craig spotted the principal in the hallway before first period, took a deep breath, and steeled himself for what he knew was going to be an unpleasant conversation.

"I've got some bad news," Craig said, getting right to the point. "They moved up my flight school date to February 1. My last day is going to be Wednesday."

The principal was more incredulous than mad.

"This Wednesday?" he asked. "As in two days from now?"

Craig nodded, trying to get out the word "yes," but speech was failing him.

"You've got to be kidding," the principal said.

He had wanted to be supportive. He hadn't complained when Craig told him he'd be missing the last few weeks of the school year. Though not ideal, he could always find a substitute, and Craig had prepared him for the fact that he could be called up at any time. But three days was crazy. Wasn't there anything Craig could do to get out of it?

Craig tried to explain that he'd tried. He'd even brought it up with his commander. But he had to go, he said. There was nothing he could do.

· · ·

The army chooses its pilots carefully, and to make sure he was fit for flying, doctors poked and prodded Craig like a lab rat. They measured his arm span to make sure he could reach the controls. They tested his eyesight and depth perception. They stuck his face into a gogglelike device that created a map of his eyes. They dilated his pupils and shined lights into his skull until he felt as if he were in a sci-fi movie. They gave him an EKG to make sure his heart was healthy, drew his blood, tested his urine, checked his reflexes, asked him about how much he drank, and threatened him with a $100,000 fine and jail time if they discovered he was lying.

Flight school is so intense that some of those who make it through say it's like trying to take a sip from a firehose. From the beginning, Craig felt as if he were drowning. Unlike some of his classmates, Craig was not a natural pilot. Before getting to flight school he'd flown in an airplane only twice—once to basic training in Oklahoma, the other to Las Vegas for a bachelor party.

"I was totally overwhelmed," he said. But he was also determined. What he lacked in natural talent or instinct he compensated for with hard work. Every morning, his alarm would go off at three thirty, and he'd study his flight manuals before class at five thirty. At seven, he'd go out with his instructor to fly. Lunch was at noon, then class again until four, then a workout, then study some more after dinner. He fell asleep at his desk with his books open more times than he could count.

The instructor pilots at Fort Rucker were of two types—Santas or Satans, depending on how they treated, or mistreated, their students. At first it seemed to Craig that he'd lucked out. In class or on the flight line, his instructor pilot was polite and gentle, the kind of guy who empathized with what the students had to endure. But in the air he became an entirely different person, screaming as loud as any drill instructor. His stentorian, saliva-laced derision could rival the high-decibel whirl of the helicopter's blades. "What the fuck are you doing? Are you an idiot? How many times have we gone over this?" he'd yell, often all in one invective-filled rant. He was more Jekyll and Hyde than Santa or Satan, Craig thought.

In class, Craig's round-the-clock studying paid off, and he earned a 96 average. But when it was time to fly, he froze, and the abuse inevitably would begin. The instructor would get them in the air, let Craig take over the controls, and within a few seconds the helicopter would start jerking wildly all over the place like a bucking bronco. Once it started spinning out of control, there was no way Craig could get it to straighten out again. Inevitably, the chopper would tilt to a perilous angle, the instructor would grab the controls—"I got it," he'd huff—and right the chopper with what seemed the slightest effort. "Look at how easy this is," he'd say.

But it seemed impossible. There were three sets of controls that had to be used in harmony. Mess one up, and the others would go completely out of whack and the instructor would be yelling. Flying, then, was a little like juggling, but with both arms and both feet. But what surprised Craig was how delicate you had to be with the controls. Anything more than a feather-light touch could send the aircraft reeling. Some instructors even told their students that to nudge the helicopter forward you had to only think about moving the control.

For Craig, the hardest part wasn't getting the chopper to move, it was getting it to hover, a skill every pilot had to master to pass their first test, known as a check ride. No matter how hard he tried and no matter how loud his instructor yelled, he couldn't get that mass of metal to sit still in the air.

How am I going to do this for real, he thought, with people shooting at me?

Craig's first check ride was coming up, and he knew there was no way he'd be able to pass. Demoralized, he went to the flight commander and begged for more time to practice before the test. The army wasn't about to postpone a check ride for anyone, but the flight commander decided he'd administer it himself to see how bad Craig really was. Within a few minutes, they were spinning wildly out of control, and the instructor failed Craig on the spot. "You're letting the aircraft fly you," he admonished.

Craig thought for sure he was going to get booted from the school. Every other member of the class but one had passed their check ride. But as the commander reviewed Craig's file and saw his stellar classroom grades, he decided to give Craig some extra time—with a warning: "You have no business here if you can't control this aircraft." The army had already invested a lot in Craig and the other students and wanted them to succeed. But that didn't mean that they wouldn't boot someone who wasn't getting it.

As Craig took to the air again, he slowly began to get the feel of the helicopter. There was no sudden epiphany. Flying a helicopter came with gradual improvement, getting a little better, a little more confident each time, until eventually all four limbs were working as one, and the instructor was for once blissfully quiet.

After Craig's second check ride, this one administered by yet another instructor pilot, Craig's teacher, Mr. Jekyll and Hyde, rushed over and asked how it went.

"Well, I didn't crash," Craig said.

"I'm sure you did fine," his instructor said. And sure enough he did. He passed the next test, too—the solo ride, a short loop around the airfield by himself. But because of his early troubles, he was the last in the class to complete it. And he knew what that meant: He'd be hazed.

A few days later, Craig was greeted by the instructors with a flight suit a couple of sizes too small that had been spray painted orange and black. They made him wear swimming goggles and a pair of purple water wings that kids wear in the pool. Then they presented him with a bike that had been outfitted to look just like a helicopter—rotor blades, a rear tail, even landing skids—that he had to ride around the base's courtyard while the rest of the class pelted him with water balloons and soaked him with the hose from a fire truck.

Normally, he would have been horrified to be the class dunce. But as he made his rounds on the bike, trying not to get knocked over from the spray, he couldn't help but feel a huge sense of relief. He was going to make it. Dripping wet, laughing, arms raised in triumph, balloons exploding off his chest and arms and face, he put one foot in front of the other while his fellow students cheered him on.

It was early spring of 2006 when Craig returned home to Fluvanna. His favorite time of year. The green valley of central Virginia was coming back to life. Baseball season was about to begin. He had graduated from flight school near the middle of his class. He had earned his wings, but now he was ready to get back to teaching.

While he was in flight school, the 2-224th had shipped out to Iraq. Craig had been assigned to a different unit, so he figured he was safe from deployment. He got an apartment, and he left the principal at Fluvanna High a phone message to let him know he was home. Much as Craig would have liked to coach the baseball team through the rest of the spring, Craig didn't expect the school to give him his job back with just a few weeks left in the school year—even though by law it was required to. Days passed. But Craig didn't hear back from the principal.

In a way it was a blessing. At his Guard drill weekend in May, he was told he was going to be meeting up with the 2-224th in Iraq. It was bad enough that he was fresh out of flight school and had yet to fly a mission that was not under the supervision of an instructor. But he'd never even flown with door gunners before or in a desert environment where the blinding clouds of sand kicked up by the helicopter's blades can wreak havoc for even the most experienced pilots. To prepare for Iraq, the battalion had spent two months in the Arizona desert to get a sense of what it would be like over there. But Craig had missed out on that. And now he'd be the Fucking New Guy. Please, he prayed, don't let me mess up. "I didn't want to be the guy who didn't know their job," he said later.

Shortly before he shipped out for Iraq, he stopped by Fluvanna High one last time to say good-bye to his former colleagues and students. The principal's secretary said he wasn't available when Craig swung by his office, so Craig left another message.

He never heard back.

Craig had been in Iraq a week and he still considered it crazy that the army was going to have him fly combat missions. His evolution from citizen to soldier, from high school teacher to war-time pilot, had been so quick, so jarring that part of him couldn't believe it had really happened. How could he be ready for this when he hadn't even known to duck when under a mortar attack. But Shane, who had been charged with getting Craig ready in Iraq, continued to run him through the gauntlet, keeping a poker face throughout the training. Privately he was pleased with the way Craig handled the stress. There was an unflappable persistence in him that Shane admired. Even when Craig made mistakes, which he often did, he seemed determined to learn from them. And wasn't shy about giving it another go, even if he did fail again.

"I am pushing him hard, and he seems to be responding well," Shane noted in his journal. "I let him fly quite a bit, and he did well. The temperature was 50 C [120 degrees Fahrenheit]. The aircraft was struggling and so were we."

With each training flight, Craig slowly grew more confident. But when he saw on the flight schedule that his first real mission would be to Ramadi and Fallujah, he again thought his commanders were out of their minds. Did they have to start him out with two of Iraq's most dangerous places?

"There's a guy getting out of a truck. Looks like he's got an AK. He's shooting at us."

The crew chief's voice was steady and unexcited, without any hint of alarm. For a split second, the content of what he had said didn't even register with Craig. Then it hit him—*someone is shooting at us.* Keep the aircraft level, Craig thought. Don't panic.

Don't do anything rash and make the situation worse. For his first flight he was assigned a new senior pilot, someone he had never flown with before. And the other pilot was just sitting there silently, as if everything was okay. If he was playing it cool, Craig thought he should, too.

"What was that?" the senior pilot said. Three or four seconds had passed, but to Craig it had felt like forever.

"We're taking fire," the crew chief said again, almost nonchalantly. How can he be so calm? Craig thought.

But by then, they had already passed well out of range. "No point in returning fire now," the senior pilot said. He alerted ground troops to the insurgent's location and carried on as if nothing had happened.

Only then did Craig realize he was so focused on his most basic task—keeping the helicopter in formation—that it didn't even occur to him to give the order to fire. Not that he was authorized to; as the junior pilot, it wasn't his call. Still, the fact that it hadn't even occurred to him was troubling. He now had an answer to the question of how he would react under fire: He'd freeze.

But Craig couldn't dwell on that now. He had to stick a landing on a site near Ramadi that from a distance appeared to be no bigger than a postage stamp.

Craig followed the lead chopper in, keeping a safe distance, and slowly lowered the helicopter to the ground. Because it was a particularly steep landing and dust was swirling, he asked one of the crew chiefs to make sure the landing area was clear. When he said it was, Craig set the Black Hawk down softly. But when he looked out the window, he realized that instead of landing square on the pad, the helicopter was straddling the sandbags that formed the perimeter—the front tire on one side, the rear tires on the other.

"What the hell?" Craig said to his crew chief. "I thought you said I was good."

"I did," the crew chief fired back. "But you missed it."

One of the pilots from the lead helicopter whipped out a digital camera and snapped a photo, laughing. Craig could feel his embarrassment turn to frustration. He'd muffed his first landing, though part of him thought the crew chief had set him up. He was the FNG after all, and everyone likes to screw with the rookie pilot.

Within a couple of days the photo of Craig's Black Hawk half on the landing pad was posted in the flight operations center for all the other pilots to see.

After about a month of flying daytime missions, Shane thought Craig was ready to begin training to fly at night. The desert darkness could make Black Hawks disappear, which made it harder for insurgents to pick them out. But it also meant pilots had to fly with night vision goggles, which distorted depth perception and turned the landscape into a hazy, green blur. There were a lot of pilots who, during the day, flew flawlessly but at night seemed as if they had to learn how to fly all over again.

"He is smart, tough, and a good soldier," Shane wrote of Craig in his journal. "We will start goggle training tomorrow night and we will see just what he is made of."

Before the flight, Shane pulled one of the crew chiefs aside and told him that when he started to talk about football, flick the switch on the back of Craig's helmet that would turn off his night vision goggles and render him blind.

For a couple of hours, Shane put Craig through a series of normal flying drills just so Craig could get comfortable with the goggles. Then near the end of the session, just as Craig thought he had passed every challenge and was starting to relax, Shane told him to hold a hover at ten feet off the ground. Then he asked how the Redskins would do next season, and Craig's world turned black. It was as if he were suddenly locked in a pitch-dark basement closet. He had been trained for this moment and knew the drill. When your night vision goggles lose power, you are supposed to stay steady on the controls and report as calmly as possible that you have "goggle failure."

But Craig was so flustered he mangled the announcement. "I'm a failure," he said, panicking.

"What do you mean, you're a failure?" Shane teased him. He wasn't going to take over the controls or let the crew chief turn the power back on until Craig said it correctly. Meanwhile, Craig was doing his best to keep the Black Hawk from crashing into the ground, and just repeated the gaffe again and again—"I'm a failure. I'm a failure"—unable to form the correct sentence. Shane and the crew burst out laughing. Shane finally nodded to the crew chief, and just like that Craig had sight again.

For the next few days, any time one of the other pilots saw him they'd mimic him with a falsetto "I'm a failure. I'm a failure." The ribbing bugged him at first, but deep down Craig knew the truth: It's when they don't make fun of you that you have to worry. Sometimes the best you could hope for was teasing. And by the twisted rationale of army logic, "I'm a failure" was perhaps the best compliment Craig could have received. What it really meant was that Craig was anything but.

The truth was that while words may have escaped him during the test, his flying skills had not. He held that helicopter at hover the whole time he was blind.

Even though he was a replacement, Craig was eventually welcomed into the soldierly fraternity with open arms. His flying was progressing quickly. His commanders were giving him high marks. And because there was such a huge need for pilots, Craig was spending a lot of time in the air, seeing much of the country. Just a few months into his deployment and he had flown all over Iraq, performing every kind of mission the 2-224th had: inserting marines into combat situations, transporting service members and VIPs from one end of Iraq to the other, performing search-and-rescue missions.

Shane continued to give him more and more responsibility than Craig thought he could reasonably handle. But he seemed to rise to the occasion every time, unsure of how he pulled each mission off. Shane felt a fatherly pride. In a few months Craig had morphed from the kid in the clean uniform who didn't know when to duck from a mortar into one of the unit's rising stars.

Craig was so focused on his missions he had little time to reflect on what life was going to be like after he returned home from Iraq. He still very much wanted the military to complement his work in the private sector, not vice versa; his civilian career remained the top priority. But in the back of his mind, he feared that his military commitment, which had forced him to abruptly pick and up and leave his teaching job with just three days' notice, had inflicted irreparable damage. And even though the law mandated that Fluvanna High School hold a slot for him, he feared that his job would not be waiting for him when he returned. There was nothing he could do about it in Iraq, except hope—and worry. But there were more pressing concerns, especially near the end of the tour when helicopters started falling out of the sky.

The soldiers gathered in a squat chapel surrounded by tall, concrete blast walls that made it virtually indistinguishable from every other building at Al Asad. They took their seats quietly in the wooden pews to the soft sounds of a piano prelude, some red-eyed, some crying softly, wiping away tears on the sleeves of their uniforms. Chaplain Weatherly began to deliver the homily he had prepared for all year long but prayed he'd never have to deliver.

"After a year in Iraq," he said in a soothing, delicate cadence, "you've been bonded by your time together, by work, by war, by shared sacrifice. And now," he said, "you are bonded by death." The day before, Colonel Paul M. Kelly and Staff Sergeant Darryl D. Booker had been among the twelve soldiers killed when the helicopter they were traveling in was shot down near Baghdad. They had both served for years with the 2-224th before moving on to another unit, and they had both visited the 2-224th at Al Asad at Christmas.

"You know what it is to stand in harm's way," Weatherly said. "You know that deep fear. You know what it is to call another brother and sister who shared these days together."

Lieutenant Colonel Robert E. McMillin II, the battalion commander, took the lectern and made it clear that the even though Kelly and Booker were assigned to another unit, the 2-224th had suffered its first casualties of the war. Kelly and Booker were "as much a part of our unit family as anyone in this room," he said. "I can't help but imagine they are viewing this ceremony, watching over us, and praying for our safe return."

The soldiers sang "Amazing Grace" and then the chapel was full of the long, sad notes of Taps. And then there was quiet. Two soldiers stood at attention on either side of the altar, standing guard next to the symbols of the fallen soldiers—two pairs of empty boots, two helmets, and two erect rifles with dog tags dangling from them. Finally, in ones and twos the soldiers made their way down the center aisle to pay their respects. Some got down on their knees. Some saluted. Some reached out and gently touched the dog tags. Some bowed their heads. Some whispered prayers.

Craig crossed himself. He hadn't known Kelly or Booker, but their deaths shook him—just as they had nearly everyone. In a little more than three weeks, the 2-224th was going home. The dream was finally becoming exultant fact. But the news of Kelly and Booker snapped the soldiers back to the reality of war's danger—and it was just the first of a series of high-profile crashes that sent ripples of fear and shock through the battalion.

Three days later, a small helicopter operated by Blackwater USA, the private security firm, was shot out of the sky, killing 5. Two days after that a Black Hawk went down. In all at least 8 choppers were shot down in three weeks, killing a total of 18. "Planning Seen behind Attacks on U.S. Copters," was the headline on the front page of the *New York Times*.

It was January 2007. The battalion was about to finally return home, and Craig tried to stay positive. But he became utterly convinced that something terrible was going to happen. It was a bad feeling he couldn't shake, and pilots, like ball players, get superstitious. After a relatively safe tour, they were so close to going home. It seemed like the perfect time for disaster to strike.

Kate wasn't able to sleep at night knowing her fellow soldiers were still running missions up to the very end, which meant her friends were landing in hot spots like Fallujah and Baghdad and Ramadi on a regular basis. Up until now, she had seen more horror, more blood and gore, than anyone should ever see. But the injured had all been strangers. She didn't know what she'd do if she had to treat one of her friends. She wasn't religious at all, but she suddenly found herself praying every night for them to return safely.

"God, bring them home with me," she wrote her friends at home in an e-mail. "Bring them all back safe with me. God bless them. Just get us through these last few days."

Then she asked her friends, "Even if you don't really believe, could you say a little prayer for us? I am so scared right now."

So was Diane, who had seen the coverage of the crash of Kelly and Booker's helicopter on CNN. For the next few weeks she remained glued to the television, which seemed to be reporting nothing but helicopter crashes, wondering if she'd hear mention of Ray's name or the 2-224th. Every time the phone rang, Diane jumped, wondering if this was the call she had been dreading. And like Kate, she spent a lot of time praying: Please just bring them home safely.

10

The National Guard

The Nation's Best Defense Bargain

If privately the soldiers of the 2-224th were worried that something would happen on the eve of their going home, no one mentioned it. Talking about it was bad luck. Outwardly with one another they were giddy to be so near the end. Their time in Iraq was, in military parlance, "short"—and as they joked, so were they. They were so short they had to climb up Mount Toilet Bowl to take a piss. So short, they could parachute off a dime. So short, they had to rappel out of bed in the morning. Shane Leipertz, always quick with dark humor, joked that they weren't preparing to go home as much as they were getting ready for their next Iraq tour. "This is predeployment 2010," he'd say.

But they were careful to keep the joy and jokes confined to their ranks. There were still many other units on base that were nowhere near being able to go home, and that included their fellow citizen-soldiers at Al Asad, the Iowa National Guard's First Battalion, 133rd Infantry Regiment.

The Iowa Guardsmen's original orders called for them to go home in March, just a few weeks after the 2-224th. But then word leaked out to the families, who called their soldiers in Iraq with the news: You're being extended as part of the "surge," the Bush administration's attempt to tamp down violence by adding five more brigades to the fight.

That meant four more months in Iraq, and another stifling summer. Four more months of a duty—providing security for convoys along supply routes in deadly Anbar province—so dangerous that the soldiers likened it to Russian roulette. The soldiers groused and grumbled. But Kate and some of the other 2-224th soldiers were amazed at how well they handled the news. "If it had been us, I would have flipped out," she said later.

The commander of the Iowa battalion was grateful he didn't have a mutiny on his hands. Given the stress his soldiers had been under for the past year, given that every time they entered their headquarters they were greeted by the photographs of the eleven soldiers from throughout the brigade, including two from their battalion, who had been killed, and given the fact that his soldiers had had their home date pushed back another four months, Lieutenant Colonel Benjamin J. Corell was proud at how well they sucked it up and went about their business.

"You won't find anyone ready to throw in the towel and walk away from what they're doing," he said. "They're proud of their sacrifice."

But that sacrifice was being acutely felt, he acknowledged, in Iraq and at home, and it could have long-term consequences for the Guard. "There's a balance there that somehow we have to keep," he said. "Because we're crossing the line of what they're willing to sacrifice. And that's a concern. I'm not saying the sky is falling. But families have a big say in whether our soldiers continue their membership in the Guard."

It was an echo of what other military leaders had been warning as the wars in Iraq and Afghanistan continued to grind on. The Guard, which reports to state governors in times of domestic crisis and the president during federal emergencies, had been called up in numbers not seen since World War II and had constituted more than half of the army's combat force in Iraq at one point. As early as June 2004, Brigadier General John W. Libby, the adjutant general of Maine's National Guard, said, "The current pace [of deployment] isn't sustainable." That same month, Major General John E. Blair, the head of New Hampshire's citizen-soldiers, said: "As far as New Hampshire goes, we're tapped." Politicians soon chimed in. The U.S. senator Chuck Hagel of Nebraska said the war is "essentially ruining our National Guard."

The truth was, the Guard had been running in the red even before 9/11. The ending of the draft and the fulfillment of General Creighton Abrams's vow after Vietnam—"They'll never take us to war without the reserves again"—meant the reserves were, in fact, part of the Total Force. Though some key infantry brigades were left behind, the Pentagon simply had to call up its citizen-soldiers for the Persian Gulf War. In all, more than 60,000 National Guard soldiers were mobilized in 1991—a stark contrast to Vietnam, when only about 20,000 were called up. In other words, three times more Guardsmen were called for a war that lasted one hundred hours than for a war that lasted eight years.

Despite its participation in the Gulf War, which was hardly noticed by the general public, the Guard continued to be viewed as a force of last resort to be called out if the Soviet Union invaded Western Europe, ignited a nuclear conflict, and started World War III.

In 1991, after the Cold War, the massive military the United States had kept up—4.1 million total Department of Defense personnel, including civilians—in anticipation of the Soviet confrontation was no longer necessary. The United States, still wary of large professional standing armies in peacetime, drew down the force. By 1999, the force dropped to just over 2 million. The size of the active army under Presidents George H. W. Bush and

Bill Clinton was reduced from 770,000 in 1989 to 482,000 in 2000. The Army National Guard was also cut to 353,000. By 2000, by a narrow margin, the Army Guard and Army Reserve actually outnumbered active-duty soldiers, 564,000 to 482,000. The reserves, made up of the Guard and the Army Reserve, would once again become an integral part of the military force.

Instead of fighting World War III, the military throughout the 1990s was involved in smaller peacekeeping operations from the horn of Africa, to the Balkans, to Central America that, except for Somalia, where eighteen American soldiers were killed, would attract little public attention. And with an active force that was a fraction of its former self, the Pentagon had no choice but to increasingly rely on the Guard and Reserve. The National Guard had two components, the Army Guard and the Air Guard, which fell under the air force. Both reported to state governors and the president. The Army Reserve, by contrast, was strictly a federal force meant to augment the army in emergencies.

Throughout the 1990s, the reserves were sent to Haiti, Bosnia, Kosovo, and the Sinai. In 1997, President Clinton's secretary of defense William S. Cohen ordered the service branches to remove "all structural barriers" between the regulars and reserves. By the late 1990s, Guard and Reserve soldiers spent thirteen million days on active duty a year, up from less than one million in the late 1980s. A Pentagon study said the demand for Guard and Reserve units "is likely to remain high over the next 15 to 20 years."

The reintegration of the Guard and Reserve into the nation's military involvement overseas was a dramatic policy change that received little public notice despite its profound consequences. But now, the country "simply could not undertake a sustained opera-tion anywhere in the world without the Guard and Reserves," as Secretary Cohen said at the time. In 2000, the Guard hit a historic first when the 49th Armored Division of the Texas Army National Guard was deployed to Bosnia for a nine-month tour. Not only was it the first time since the Korean War that a Guard division had been sent to lead an overseas mission, but, more significant, it was the first time in the long history of the country's citizen-soldiers that a Guard unit of this size commanded regular army units in peacetime. If there had been any lingering doubt about the Guard's necessity or ability, the 49th erased it. Given the Guard's recent history, the leadership of the 49th was well aware of the significance of their role. "This wasn't just any mission for us," the division's chief of staff, Colonel Garry D. Patterson, said. "We felt like we had to make a mark on the wall for the ones that are going to follow us."

The line between the active army and the reserves was beginning to blur. The active-duty commander of the Sinai peacekeeping mission, who had been initially skeptical about being sent reserve soldiers, ended up changing his mind and paid them the highest compliment: "Here in the Sinai we're all soldiers. You can't tell who's active, who's Guard and who's reserve."

The role of the Guard had fundamentally changed. In less than a decade they went from being a relatively untrusted and untested gaggle of backups that would be called up only for World War III to a mainstay in the country's fighting force, serving alongside their active-duty counterparts. And that was before 9/11, and before the country was fighting two wars simultaneously.

Just after the attacks of 9/11, the 2-224th was sent to Bosnia for an eight-month tour. And as the battalion's soldiers watched their citizen-soldier counterparts pour into Afghanistan, provide security for airports, and then ship off to Iraq, they knew it would be only a matter of time before they were called up again.

The 2007 surge in Iraq was designed to secure the country. But on the home front another surge was already under way. It was a battle to win the hearts and minds of not Iraqis, but Americans, a massive attempt to convince the country's young men and women to join the frontline troops that desperately needed reinforcements. Thousands of additional recruiters surged into the streets of America, fanning out to high school cafeterias, shopping malls, playgrounds—anywhere the young and potentially willing could be found. At stake was the future of the all-volunteer force, which was in the most serious trouble it had been since the draft ended in 1973. The future of the army—and the war—was in the hands of recruiters, who were under increasing pressure to fill the thinning ranks.

They got some help from the Bush administration. A little-noticed provision in the "No Child Left Behind" act required public high schools to provide recruiters with students' names and telephone numbers. But even with that treasure trove of data, the recruiters' task was as difficult as it had ever been. Soldiers were being sent to Iraq for two and three tours, some spending more time abroad than at home. The repeated deployments had serious consequences, especially in the Army National Guard, where enlisting almost certainly guaranteed an expenses-paid trip to the front lines at least once.

Predictably, recruiting plummeted, and the ranks of citizen-soldiers were hardest hit. The Army National Guard missed its annual quotas every year between 2003 and 2007. The nadir came in 2005, when it hit just 80 percent of its goal—the worst recruiting year since 1991. It fell short by 13,000 recruits, the equivalent of several brigades. The increased reliance on the Guard left many units without a full roster of soldiers eligible to deploy. So military officials were forced to transfer man power from other units, often from across the country, to fill holes that had been left by soldiers who had reached their limits of two cumulative years on active duty. That, wrote Anthony Punaro, the chairman of a congressional commission appointed to assess the state of the Guard and Reserve, "destroys the unit cohesion that is at the heart of an effective fighting force, and commanders know that any reduction in unit cohesion can result in a greater risk of casualties. 'Pickup' teams belong on sandlots, not battlefields."

To keep thousands of soldiers in the ranks, the Guard had to continually revert to a little-known power known as "Stop Loss." Pentagon guidelines prevented reservists from being mobilized for more than twenty-four months, and so three and a half years into the Iraq War only 90,000 of the 522,000 Guard and Reserve soldiers were available to be mobilized. An army chart depicted the data as a depleted barrel. "We're out of Schlitz," it said.

After the active army missed its recruiting mark by 7,000 recruits in 2005, it radically changed its standards. It raised the maximum age for recruits from thirty-five to forty-two. The army also started accepting more soldiers that otherwise would have never qualified for service because of past criminal activity, drug or alcohol abuse, or low standards of physical health. By 2007, a study found that only about 70 percent of active-duty recruits had a high school diploma, well below the army's goal of at least 90 percent. The number of waivers the army granted for felony convictions more than doubled between 2006 and 2007, from 249 to 511 out of 80,000 total recruits. Many cases involved robbery, burglary, and drug offenses. A handful were for sexual assaults, involuntary manslaughter, and making terroristic threats.

Meanwhile, the army adjusted its advertising campaign to target not just prospective soldiers but also their Vietnam-era parents who were seen as the main obstacles to military service. "If your son or daughter wants to talk about the army, listen," the narrator of the army's television commercial intoned. "You made them strong. We'll make them army strong."

Aware that the wars had transformed the reserves from "army lite" back-benchers to a key component of the fighting force, the National Guard also launched a new ad campaign. Instead of merely hyping college benefits, its television commercials played up patriotic themes. "When your country calls, you go. Proudly," a Guard soldier said with soaring music in the background.

"It's more than money for college," another soldier said. "It's built my character and given me a sense of accomplishment."

The ad depicted Guardsmen less as college students than as soldiers in Iraq and Afghanistan, and also at home fighting fires and rescuing people from raging floodwaters. Then near the end of the ad, an arrow-straight line of Guardsmen, chins up in their dress uniforms, unleashed gleaming swords with white-gloved hands in perfect unison. It provided a fitting end that was unremarkable except for this: The image of uniformed men drawing their swords was taken right from the Marine Corps. By equating themselves, if tacitly, with the marines, the meanest, toughest, most exclusive branch of the service, the Guard was acknowledging that its soldiers more closely resembled a frontline fighting force than their former rear-echelon selves.

Appealing to patriotism alone, however, was not enough; the post-9/11 fervor that for a short while had made recruiters' jobs easy was gone. They now operated in what Army Secretary Pete Geren called in early 2008 "a recruiting environment that has to be as tough as we've ever faced." And so the army returned to another good old American motivator: cash. Uncle Sam could no longer rely on his famous World War II exhortation—"I want you for the U.S. Army." Now he had to show recruits the money as well. And so like the active army, the Guard in 2004 began dangling unprecedented wads of cash before recruits. Signing bonuses doubled from $10,000 to $20,000, reenlistment bonuses tripled from $5,000 to $15,000 (tax-free if the soldier re-upped while serving in a combat zone), and the Guard awarded $2,000 to any soldier who convinced someone else to join.

This was a crisis that eventually got the attention of Congress, which appointed the Punaro Commission to study just how badly stretched the Guard and Reserve were. The commission's conclusion in 2007: Nearly 90 percent of Army National Guard units were rated "not ready" for combat because of shortfalls of man power and equipment. They were indeed out of Schlitz.

At the center of the storm brewing around the Guard was its bald, blunt, and barrel-chested chief, Lieutenant General H Steven Blum. He had taken a somewhat unconventional route to the top, starting not at West Point but as an enlisted man who juggled a civilian job of teaching history at a junior high school in his native Baltimore with his military obligations. Shortly after Blum joined the Guard in 1968, riots broke out after Martin Luther King Jr.'s assassination. Blum's first active mission was to help quiet the violence spreading through Baltimore, and he later said he heard more gunfire during that time in his hometown than he did in any of his other missions. In the fall of 2001, while deployed to Bosnia, he became the first Guard general since World War II to command the 29th Infantry Division in an overseas mission.

His reputation as a straight-shooting, no-nonsense, street-smart officer impressed the author Stephen Ambrose, who visited Blum and his troops while they were deployed to Bosnia. "At 55, he has had made 1,500 air drops," Ambrose wrote of Blum in his 2002 book *To America: Personal Reflections of an Historian.* "He has had open-heart surgery. He talks so well and thinks so swiftly and knows so much that he reminds me of Eisenhower in 1945, when Ike was fifty-five years old."

It was Blum's Ike-like tenacity that endeared him to Congress as well. At Capitol Hill hearings, his answers to Congress members' questions were direct, infused with intelligence—and wit—and almost always unscripted. "It bothers me that the army and the air force and the Marine Corps and the navy are at war, and the nation's watching *American Idol* and *Dancing with the Stars,*" he once blurted out in a Senate hearing.

Some members of Congress had even proposed promoting the head of the Guard to a four-star general, a position not available to Guard officers, and making him a member of the Joint Chiefs of Staff. If the Guard was going to be used as much as the other branches of the service, the politicians reasoned, its chief might as well have a seat at the table when decisions are made.

But Blum thought that promoting him would have little, if any, effect on the Guard's mounting problems, and he demurred when asked about it. What the reserves needed, he told Congress, were the money and the resources to wage war, not bureaucratic shuffling. At a Senate subcommittee hearing in April 2007, he reminded the senators that the Guard cost taxpayers a tenth of what it takes to maintain the active army. The Guard was "the nation's best defense bargain," he said. But it was in trouble.

"The National Guard today, I'm sad to say, is not a fully ready force," he said in his opening statement. It suffered from an acute lack of equipment that could delay response to natural disasters. "Lost time translates into lost lives," he said. "And those lost lives are American lives."

"To get up to strength, the Guard would need $40 billion," he said.

Forty billion? Senator Barbara Mikulski of Maryland, who grew up not far from Blum's Baltimore neighborhood, wanted to make sure she'd heard the general correctly.

"You used a staggering number: $40 billion," she said. "That's what you said. Am I correct?"

"Yes—" Blum said.

"And of that $40 billion, though, what are we talking about?" Mikulski interrupted. "Are we talking about Jeeps? Are we talking about airplanes? Are we talking about guns? Are we talking about bullets? When we say, 'Oh, we don't have enough equipment,' what are we talking about?"

"In gross—" Blum started, but again was interrupted.

"I don't want dollars. I want examples."

"Yes, Ma'am."

Providing examples was not going to be a problem. Blum knew where the equipment shortfalls were; they were everywhere, from beans to bullets, as the saying went. If the senator wanted an inventory, that's what she would get.

"Trucks, radios, medical sets, helicopters," Blum began. "Night vision devices, individual weapons for soldiers—you name it, we are short of it—this is meat-and-potatoes basic items. Aviation, command and control, engineers, engineering equipment—I'm talking about dozers, graders, loaders, backhoes, dump trucks, logistics—I'm talking about all classes of supply that we are short."

"Now—" Mikulski piped up. But it was Blum's turn to interrupt. He wasn't finished yet.

"Maintenance, repair parts we're short; medical—medical sets that—"

Mikulski regained the floor, but Blum had made his point.

"Is the shortfall, then, due the fact that you had to leave it in Iraq?" Mikulski asked. "Or is the shortfall due to the fact that the equipment is wearing out faster than it can be replaced? Or is it that it was never budgeted? And essentially we are hollowing out the National Guard."

"All three, Senator. You're exactly correct."

To illustrate the extent of the problem, Blum arrived at the hearing accompanied by two Guardsmen, whom he introduced to the committee as examples of fine citizen-soldiers—and of the severe troubles the Guard was facing. The first was a twenty-three-year-old Oregon Air National Guard staff sergeant who had already been deployed to Iraq three times. But at home, the equipment he used as a combat air controller had not been updated since 1953, Blum said.

Blum then introduced his other guest, a forty-year-old platoon sergeant from the Kansas Army National Guard's 2nd Battalion, 137th Infantry Regiment, who had just returned from Iraq. "He doesn't have a problem of *old* equipment," Blum said in typically straightforward fashion. "He has a problem of *no* equipment. His unit, when it came back in November, came back to two Humvees that were left because they were not good enough to go to war, not suitable to go to war. And that's the equipment that he has in his unit today.

"So if Governor Sebelius from Kansas would need the 2nd Battalion, 137th to respond to a tornado, or a winter storm or any other emergency, the capability of that unit is minimized, not because of the great people in it, but because of the lack of equipment that's in that unit right now."

Governor Kathleen Sebelius was, in fact, worried. So much so that she appeared on Capitol Hill to lobby for the ailing Guard units in her state and across the country. She told reporters that the Pentagon's response was that it would take six years for Kansas to get back two-thirds of its vehicles and equipment.

"That's a very inadequate response," she said at the time. "We don't have the equipment to keep our citizens secure."

The commander-in-chief of the Kansas National Guard even wrote a letter to the Pentagon, urging it to replenish the Guard's depleted equipment: "We must be able to maintain a high level of readiness because no one will know when disaster will strike."

And then it did.

At nearly 10 P.M. on Friday, May 4, 2007, less than one month after Blum's warning in the Senate hearing, the sky over the farming community of Greensburg, Kansas, lowered and contorted itself into a powerful tornado nearly two miles wide with winds that whipped around at more than two hundred miles per hour. The Category 5 tornado, the largest to hit the United States since 1999, flattened the town of 1,500, crushing city hall, the hospital, the grade school, and the fire department. All that was left standing of the high school was the front door. Eleven people were killed.

As Sebelius toured the rubble in the wake of the tornado, she complained in strong language that the response had been hampered by the strain the wars had put on the state's National Guard.

"I don't think there is any question that if you are missing trucks, Humvees and helicopters that the response is going to be slower," she told reporters a few days after the tornado. "The real victims here will be the residents of Greensburg because the recovery will be at a slower pace."

She wasn't the only governor complaining. As the summer of 2005 approached, a seven-year drought had left the Montana wilderness a tinderbox. February, when usually a thick blanket of snowfall covers the state, was one of the driest in Montana history. "It's dry, it's double dry, it's triple dry," Governor Brian Schweitzer told the *Boston Globe*. Two years earlier, wildfires had charred 736,800 acres. Schweitzer was worried. Not only were conditions perfect for another widespread wildfire season, but about half of the state's National Guard soldiers were in Iraq or Afghanistan along with ten of their twelve Black Hawk helicopters, which were crucial for dropping water in the remote hills.

So Schweitzer, a horse-riding, flannel shirt–wearing rancher and farmer, took an extraordinary step. Calling the Guard's repeated federal deployments a "staggering commitment," he asked Blum to return his troops and helicopters.

"Why don't you send Montana's Guardsmen home for July and August?" he said, explaining his request in an interview on CNN. "We have forty-nine other states. They can rotate at different times. We'll take up the slack—for example, at Christmas."

Schweitzer's request was denied, but he was promised that should the fires rage, Guard units from across the country would descend on Montana to help. That didn't placate him.

"The fires that we have in Montana are in wild lands," he said. "These are big mountains, and this is where we don't have roads. You fight them with helicopters. You fight them with people that are trained to fly in mountains. . . . You can't send me somebody from Indiana."

As the Guard continued to play a prominent role in Iraq and Afghanistan, the tension between the states and the federal government over control of the Guard reached a crescendo. States felt as if the feds had usurped their power and left them vulnerable. All fifty governors—Democrats and Republicans alike—urged President George W. Bush in a 2006 letter to supply their beleaguered Guard units "with the resources they need to carry out their homeland security and domestic disaster duties, while also continuing to fine-tune their wartime mission competencies."

The struggle over control of the Guard went right to its identity: Was it a stateside force used in the case of natural disaster? Or a frontline fighting force needed to fight overseas alongside the active military? Or both? And then there was this: How did the United States, the world's lone superpower, which spends as much on defense as nearly the rest of the world combined, come to rely so heavily in Iraq on part-time citizen-soldiers?

To much of the public, the Guard was a bunch of loosely trained "weekend warriors" who hung out at the armory one weekend a month and was only occasionally called upon. The Guard was where you went during Vietnam to *avoid* combat, not to face two or three overseas tours.

But the truth was that the Guard was one of the most venerable, if overlooked, American institutions whose formation in 1636 predates the country by more than a century. The existence of the Guard, which is directly descended from the Colonial militias, was preserved in the Constitution by the Founding Fathers, who viewed it as a central component of a democracy. The grand story of these citizen-soldiers included fending off the Red Coats at Lexington and Concord, fighting as part of Teddy Roosevelt's "Rough Riders," and storming the beaches of Normandy. (The 2-224th traces its history all the way back to the "Richmond Howitzers" of the Civil War.) To highlight its early-American roots, the Guard's symbol is the musket-bearing Minuteman. Twenty U.S. presidents, including Washington, Jefferson, Madison, Lincoln, Grant, Truman, and George W. Bush, served in the Guard.

But in the years after the 9/11 attacks, after it had been called to serve again and again, the Guard, the country's oldest military institution, was beginning to buckle under the weight of both its domestic and foreign responsibilities. The damage would take a long time to repair.

PART THREE

HOME

11

The 2-224th

Don't Take the War Home with You

You can bring shrapnel home as a souvenir as long as it's smaller than eight inches long. Cigars are allowed—but no more than one hundred, and no Cubans. Middle Eastern hookahs are okay, but they must be clean. Iraq War trophies—foreign helmets, uniforms, flags, training manuals—all of them are permissible, but only if an officer signs off on them.

What's not allowed, the Military Customs officer told the soldiers who were about to board a plane home: brass knuckles, disposable lighters, scissors four inches or longer, aerosol cans. With a straight face he added that body parts are also prohibited.

"This ain't no fucking Vietnam movie," he said. "So if you have a necklace full of ears, it's got to go."

You can, in fact must, carry your rifle on board ("Lay them at your feet, pointed toward the middle of the aircraft"). But no bullets.

"Then what's the point of carrying my weapon?" a soldier quietly groused.

Porn is also a definite no-no. And booze is banned: "I know everyone is going to be drunk soon, but not today," the Customs official said.

In other words, the official seemed to be saying, Don't take the war home with you.

It was, of course, an impossible request. But hours later as the battalion's three hundred fifty soldiers stepped into the cocoon of the plane—a commercial 747 that was a far cry from the put-in-your-earplugs military transports they had grown used to in Iraq—it seemed as if they had already left the war behind. Reclining in their seats, they humored the flight attendants and chose between the chicken and the pasta, luxuriating in being waited on.

"All I want is a beer and a ball game," a soldier in row 21 declared. "And I'm good." Another, sitting farther up, had been looking forward to something even simpler: her garage door opener. Nothing says home more than the welcoming yawn of the door's retraction.

Going home. They knew the drill. They'd turn in their gear and fill out paperwork, and then, just like that, they'd be civilians again. No more guns. No more bullets. No more war. Thanks for your service, now go home.

For some the transition would appear easy. One lieutenant, a tall, boyish-looking Black Hawk pilot, would take mere weeks off before he went back to work as a patrol officer in Lynchburg, Virginia, citing speeders, breaking up the occasional domestic dispute. When he was first called up for Iraq, he knew "the deployment was going to determine whether [he] was going to be with" his girlfriend. The absence only made them stronger, and a month after his return he would celebrate her birthday with a cake. "Will You Marry Me?" it would read in carefully laid cursive—a proposal in pink icing.

Sitting near the middle of the cabin, surrounded by people she now considered among her best friends in the world, Kate was not looking forward to the prospect of home without her husband. One row back, Miranda had no idea what was in store for her next—a career in the military, a job, graduate school? Near the back of the plane, Ray couldn't wait to get home to see Diane, but he worried about what the long separation had done to her—and to them. Craig knew that at some point he would have to visit his old high school to see about getting his job back.

The soldiers followed their progress on a digital map that showed them speeding out of the Middle East, across Europe, and, after a brief layover in Germany, over the dark Atlantic, then to Newfoundland, until finally the pilot said, "We're now over American soil." The soldiers erupted into a celebratory cheer. Soon the plane began its descent, and the soldiers craned their necks to get glimpses of the twinkling constellation of city lights piercing the darkness outside their windows.

"You ready to sign those reenlistment papers?" an officer teased a lower-ranking specialist, who just rolled his eyes in response.

In a disorienting swirl of snow, a million flakes dancing in the plane's lights, the plane touched down at McGuire Air Force Base near Fort Dix in New Jersey an hour before dawn one day in February 2007. It took some of the soldiers a moment to realize that was not sand outside their window.

"It looks freezing out," Kate gulped. And it was. A wet, biting cold they hadn't felt in months. As they got off the plane, they braced themselves against the harsh wind and snow, shivering as they took their first steps home.

12

Miranda

Learning to Talk about War

Miranda awoke bleary eyed in the predawn darkness, unsure of where she was. The red digital clock read 5:00 A.M. Harry Potter was riding a broomstick in a poster on the wall. She was in a bottom bunk and could hear her fifteen-year-old sister sleeping soundly above her.

Oh yeah, she thought. I'm home.

She had been back for a few days now, but she was still going through the same disorienting routine, waking up lost until some clue—her stepmother's heavy wool blankets, the snow outside, the sound of her sister sleeping—let her know she was no longer in Iraq. But realizing where she was didn't necessarily remedy her profound sense of displacement. All of a sudden there was no more eating the same old, same old in a chow hall. No formation. No uniform. No rifle over her shoulder. No countless hours in the supply room. No checking the flight schedule to see when she might be headed outside the wire, her fingers lingering over the trigger of the M240. No more being a soldier.

Instead she woke to days so normal they were bizarre. It wasn't just the new things that she had missed out on, the TV shows she didn't recognize, the movies she hadn't seen. She was prepared for that. Missing out on stuff was just inevitable. What shook her was how the stuff that should have felt so familiar now, suddenly, was not. How odd it was to open a fridge and bask in the glow of that little light while rummaging for a snack. When was the last time she had done that? There was a childlike discovery to almost everything. Snow. The way it crunched underfoot. The Christmas card–like way it hung on the boughs of evergreen bushes. Wall-to-wall carpet against bare feet. The smell of fabric softener. Her parents' golden retrievers. The wonders of WiFi. Diet Mountain Dew. Blow dryers. Grocery stores. Cooking oatmeal butterscotch cookies from scratch. Slipping a key into the ignition, grasping the wheel, and stepping on the gas with nowhere in particular to go.

Iraq was an abstraction no one talked about, because no one knew how to. At times, it was as if Miranda had come home from a European vacation. Her stepmother, Vanessa Summers, asked her husband how they should act around Miranda, how they should talk to her. He had no idea. "Let's not press," he said. "If she wants to talk about Iraq, she will."

Miranda didn't seem shell-shocked, or depressed, or irreparably altered by war. It was clear that she wasn't like Vanessa's grandfather, who had been so haunted by World War I that even decades later crying children were kept away from him. Miranda came home a bit more reserved, and definitely more mature. Even though her husband urged her not to push, Vanessa desperately wanted to know what the war had been like. She wanted to know what Miranda had seen, what she'd experienced. She wanted to ask what she did, how she spent her days. This was her stepdaughter, after all, whom she loved. But now Vanessa didn't know how to talk to her. There was a chasm between them, and Vanessa didn't know how to cross it, or even if she should try. It didn't feel right to simply ignore the fact that Miranda was coming home from war. But at the same time, she felt she should tread delicately.

"If you completely don't say anything, then that's bad," Vanessa later said. "But if you say, 'Thanks for your service,' that sounds too distant. If you say, 'How was it? Tell us about it,' that's too quick. I was glad to see her, thrilled she was coming home safely. But nervous. I'm usually very communicative, but in this case I was not quite sure what to say other than, 'Welcome home. We're glad you're safe.' And those were the things that we said. It's not like they're coming back from college or a week at the beach where you can say, 'How was it? What did you do?'

"What do they want us to say?"

The army ought to teach soldiers' families how to act and talk, she thought. Because no matter how many times Vanessa and Miranda's father said, "Welcome home. We're glad you're safe," it never fully conveyed the profound sense of loss they had felt when Miranda had deployed, or the euphoria they felt now that she was home.

For her part, Miranda didn't want to talk about Iraq, and she wasn't yet ready for the questions that eventually did come. But when one week after getting home, while she was out to dinner with her family, her uncle asked her matter-of-factly what was the worst thing she'd seen, Miranda was unprepared. So she answered truthfully.

She had been flying as a door gunner when her helicopter was tasked for an "angel" mission—transporting a service member killed in action on the first leg of the long journey home. Usually, the body bags were zipped tight and it was easy for Miranda to forget there was anyone inside. But this soldier had been blown into barbed wire, which was still embedded, preventing the bag from zipping all the way. His head and torso were sticking out. Miranda saw his young, lifeless face.

Now staring at her parents' faces, Miranda knew she should not have mentioned the dead soldier. Not here sitting in a booth at the Red Robin restaurant, surrounded by regular people, going about their regular lives, eating burgers and milkshakes. Not amid the din of innocuous chatter and the clinking of silverware. Not between dessert and the check, at home, in a safe place where there was no war.

Miranda sensed that Iraq had, in some profound ways, affected her. How could it not have? But by talking about it, she would be unbottling the emotions that were inextricably linked to the war. And exposing them to the daylight of this new reality would demonstrate just how much she had changed, and how different she was. Instead she developed a rote speech that focused on how hot it was and excluded the faces of dead soldiers sticking out of body bags, or aiming her M240 left low, left low.

She still had no idea what to make of the experience and wasn't ready for it to emerge in this new, strange context. Not yet. Not if her emotional transformation was anything near the changes her body had been through. Since leaving Iraq she had shed ten pounds, easy. The weight just melted off. She wasn't eating any differently, or exercising more. It was the stress, her fellow soldiers told her. Or the lack thereof, now that she was out of Iraq.

None of her old clothes fit. They hung on her like rags on a scarecrow. She took her younger sister with her to the outlet mall to buy some new jeans, but no matter how many pairs she tried on, they didn't feel right. After a year of a broken-in uniform, civilian clothes felt uncomfortably stiff, as if they were made of wood. She could barely bend her knees. Perhaps more troubling was the makeup situation. She had been looking forward to a little eyeliner and lipstick, but now that she was home, all her colors were off and nothing looked right. The problem, she suspected, was not with her products, but with her. The desert had given her skin a weird orange-tan tint and bleached out her already light hair.

Then there was the odd sensation that for the first time in a long time she didn't have to get up, or be anywhere, or do anything. If she wanted to, she could sleep until noon and no one would say anything. She had earned this luxurious, indulgent freedom. So why in those first few days was she up every morning before dawn, before her parents, before her sister, before, it felt, the whole world? Lying in bed, looking at the clock, she'd think that 5 A.M. was 1 P.M. in Iraq. The sun would be warming up good over the distant dunes. Soldiers would be preparing to go out on missions. Strapping the body armor tight, setting their helmets, checking their weapons. Flipping the safeties to off. The Black Hawks ready, rotors whirling, engines humming. Lifting off into the desert. The vast, vast desert—so peaceful and, seen through a rifle sight, so dangerous.

Was all that happening at this very moment? Was there really a war going on? As she lay under a heavy wool blanket in a bottom bunk, with her sister softly snoring above her, in the half-sleep of the predawn quiet, it all could have passed for a dream.

At first, every day was like her birthday. What does Miranda want for breakfast? What movie does Miranda want to see? Where does Miranda want to go for dinner? It was a nice, pillow-soft landing. Even her parents' golden retrievers sensed that Miranda merited special treatment and followed her around the house like a pair of loyal bodyguards.

Eventually her dad and stepmother went back to work, her sister to school. The dogs no longer doted on her. Miranda was left home alone with hour after empty hour to fill. She caught up on the *Gilmore Girls* episodes she had missed. She surfed the Internet. Read *Vogue* and *Glamour* magazines. Went for long, long runs. And she lounged about for hours on end, amazed at how a day could pass without her accomplishing a single thing. Soon, though, it got old. Miranda was not the type to waste away the day. If only to keep her sanity, she was going to have to figure out what was next.

Ensconced in the military bubble in Iraq, she had been convinced that her future was with the army and had inquired about going active duty, or to Officer Candidate School. Graduate school was the backup plan. But now she wasn't so sure. Problem was, she didn't know what she wanted to do. She didn't want to get a job, or go back to school, or sit around the house any longer. She wanted to do something worthwhile. Something necessary. Iraq may have been tedious and awful at times, but even at its low points it had always felt significant. She was part of the United States War Machine, and it provided purpose and clarity, even if she played but a small role. In Iraq, she never woke up wondering what to do that day. If nothing else, war keeps you busy.

While in Iraq, the ever-resourceful Miranda had landed herself a summer internship with the National Park Service at Harpers Ferry, where she would dress up as a nineteenth-century matron and teach visiting schoolchildren about the abolitionist John Brown's raid. But that was months away. February turned to March, and still Miranda had no leads, or any sense of what to do in the meantime or after the internship was over. Thankfully, her parents never pestered her about her plans. Her future, like the war, was apparently a taboo subject. But Miranda would have to figure it out soon, and not just because she wanted to get out of her parents' house.

Waiting for her at home was a $13,000 mountain of college-loan debt. The GI Bill and the National Guard's tuition assistance program helped cover the cost of William and Mary. And she had scrimped through her undergrad years. When her friends asked to go to the movies, she said she had exams to study for because she couldn't afford a ticket. She ordered water at coffeehouses. And during her junior year, she was the only one of her friends who wasn't on the college's meal plan, which meant she often ate her pasta and pizza bagels alone in her room. After watching her father struggle financially throughout most of her childhood, she felt it important to get through college with as little debt as possible. Given the alarming cost of college tuition—even at state schools like William and Mary—$13,000 in debt was not as bad as it could have been. While in Iraq, she could defer payment. But now that she was home, the bills would soon start appearing. She'd have to figure out what to do next, and fast.

A couple of weeks after returning home, she was lounging on the couch in her sweats—the only clothes that felt normal—drinking a Diet Mountain Dew, clicking through her e-mail, when she came across one that read, "Congratulations." It was from the head of the Public Humanities Department at Brown University. She had been accepted.

If she wanted to, she could be not Miranda the directionless vet but Miranda the Ivy League–bound graduate student. Still, there was one major problem. The e-mail said nothing about the scholarship she had hoped for. Without the financial aid, there was simply no way she could afford Brown's $35,000-a-year tuition plus fees.

"Congratulations," her father said when she told him the news. "How are you going to pay for it?"

That was the question.

Easter weekend in Providence, Rhode Island, was raw—not like Virginia, which was already starting to show the first signs of spring. The rain came down cold and slanted, running in rivulets down the city's Colonial cobblestone streets, while the low clouds turned the horizon into a forbidding, gray smudge. Miranda, visiting Brown for the first time, took the inclement weather as a bad omen.

Touring the campus, she was looking for signs that Brown was the place for her. She missed academic life and was interested in returning to it. But the cost was staggering: two years of tuition, plus fees and living expenses equaled nearly $100,000. The only reason she was even considering attending was that the university had offered her a generous scholarship that cut tuition by 40 percent. Her GI Bill and military benefits would help as well. But how much, she would not know until she met with the new unit in Rhode Island she hoped to join.

Not only would transferring involve all kinds of bureaucratic army paperwork, but the National Guard unit the army wanted her to transfer to was an hour from campus. Rather than join that unit, she hoped to transfer to a Civil Affairs unit. Only there was a problem. The unit was in the Army Reserve, not the Army National Guard. While both the Army National Guard and the Army Reserve were part of the army, and while together they constituted what is commonly referred to as the "reserves," they were distinct species. Unlike the Guard, which reports to state governors in times of domestic crisis and the president when placed under federal control, the Army Reserve is exclusively a federal force that has no state responsibilities. By transferring to the Army Reserve, Miranda hoped she would be eligible for a lucrative signing bonus. But depending on how much she scrimped and how much the military chipped in, Brown would still increase her debt, perhaps by as much as an additional $20,000, she figured.

Strolling through Brown's venerable campus, she realized how much she wanted it to work out. Brown was one of the best schools she could have hoped for. It dripped with Ivy League class. The professors she met were smart and engaging, and they seemed genuinely interested in her. Her department was small enough that everyone knew everyone else, and it seemed like an academic fraternity of sorts. She pictured herself with books under her arm, crossing the Common en route to class on an autumn morning. How serene that would be—and how utterly different from what she had just been through. She could feel the citizen breaking out of her soldierly body armor. Accompanying her on the trip was her stepmother, Vanessa, who was thrilled with the place and urged Miranda to attend.

Still, Miranda worried. After her year in combat, she feared, as she said, that she had "gotten dumb," and she wondered if she would be able to keep up academically and fit it. Brown students were, for the most part, the polar opposite of the soldiers Miranda had served with. Indeed, the students at Brown and soldiers in Iraq

were so different it was hard to believe they were the same age, sep-
arated only by a choice. One group chose to go to college; the other
chose the military and, by extension in the post-9/11 world, war.
One was dedicating itself to intellectual enlightenment, the other
to serving the country. Noble goals both. But seeing all these carefree students frolicking on their well-manicured campus, Miranda
couldn't help but see the difference in stark terms. One group was
fighting and dying. The other she saw in the coffeehouses ringing
Brown's campus, seemed like young, frivolous children. It was perhaps an unfair judgment, but one she couldn't help but make.

To be sure, Brown would be a huge culture shock. The university was not only one of the most prestigious in the country, but
perhaps the most liberal. And even though the university bent over
backward to make it clear that it welcomed students from every
walk of life, the war didn't affect the overwhelming majority of
Brown students. There were no massive protests on campus. No
sense that the country was at war.

Although her visit lasted just a few days, she could sense the
disconnect between herself and the other students. While she was
getting ready to deploy to Iraq in the fall of 2005, the big controversy at Brown was that a producer for Fox's *The O'Reilly Factor*
brought a video camera into the university's annual "Sex, Power,
God" party and aired footage of drunken, naked students dancing
in a bacchanal the producer called "pure debauchery." More than
thirty students were treated for alcohol poisoning.

Not that Miranda had anything against blowing off steam on a
Saturday night. She had been to her share of frat parties at William
and Mary, and had, after all, streaked the sunken garden on her
last night on campus, though she later felt guilty about it. But the
more she learned about Brown, the more she realized it might be
a little "out there" for her. And despite all the talk at Brown about
inclusiveness and openness, she wondered how such a community
would react to a real live soldier and veteran in their midst. Everyone
said they supported the troops, even while criticizing the war.
That sentiment seemed to flourish at Brown. She knew she would

never be spat on and that no one would blame her for the war. In fact, she would probably be treated politely, maybe even with respect. But it was clear to her that at Brown she would be not just an outsider but a curiosity.

When she went to meet with the school's veteran affairs coordinator, the secretary in the admissions office stared at her blankly.

"The who?"

"Your veteran affairs coordinator," Miranda said.

When the secretary looked at her blankly again, Miranda added, "You're required by law to have one. I'm going to need help with my GI Bill."

The secretary thumbed through a campus directory but found nothing.

"Surely, I can't be the only vet on campus," Miranda blurted out.

After three days exploring Brown, she was still unsure if it was the place for her. She knew she would love the classes and the professors, but here her "otherness," as she called it, would be pronounced. A lot would depend on whether she'd be able to transfer into the new unit.

Civil Affairs would be for Miranda the dream job of her military career. They were the soldiers building schools, helping run elections, fostering fledgling governments, and bringing sewer lines, running water, and electricity to places without. They were part soldier, part diplomat, and they drew from a wide range of civilian fields whose expertise could be applied to many different situations: lawyers, teachers, police officers, economists, bankers.

To get the right mix of experience, Civil Affairs units can be picky about whom they accept. And soldiers wanting to join typically have to go through an interview process and have the rank of at least sergeant if enlisted, or captain if an officer. On her way to meet the battalion commander, Miranda felt confident. She had a college degree and combat experience, and she had studied both Russian and Arabic, though she was fluent in neither.

The commander was a genial gentleman who took to Miranda right away and said he thought she would be a great fit for the battalion. But joining the unit, he cautioned, meant she would have to go through intensive training school over the summer. And because Civil Affairs units were in such high demand, Miranda probably would be deploying again in the near future.

But those concerns were washed away by the allure of the job, the possibility of doing something significant in her military career while at the same time getting an Ivy League graduate degree. It was the ultimate marriage of her citizen and soldierly ambitions. Here in the commander's office, she had gotten the sign she had been looking for on Brown's campus. It was almost as if she would attend Brown just so that she could join this Civil Affairs unit. Her decision was solidified when later that day the recruiter told her she could be eligible for a bonus as high as $40,000 because she'd be considered by the Army Reserve a new recruit and because Civil Affairs was one of the most deployed specialties and in increasingly high demand in the world's hot spots. It was as if her future was being taken care of in one fell swoop.

As she drove back to Virginia, she knew what her next step was going to be. She was headed to the Ivy League, even if in the back of her mind the recruiter's promises sounded a little too good to be true.

13

Kate

Practicing Normalcy

They were home but not home. Fort Dix was technically on American soil and in the United States, a stone's throw from the New Jersey Turnpike. Freedom was just outside its tall gates. But to the soldiers of the 2-224th, unable to see their families just yet, it felt like a cruel stutter step on the long road home. They would be confined here for one more week, turning in weapons, seeing doctors, filling out paperwork before they would finally be released into the civilian world.

One of the more dreaded of their post-deployment chores was a mental-health screening that most of the soldiers considered a joke. Few spoke up in these sessions because they feared that if the counselors sensed they were the slightest bit unstable, they would be kept on base for further screening while the rest of the unit finally went home. But Kate had promised the navy psychiatrist in Iraq that she would seek help when she got home, and this was her chance.

She didn't realize, though, that she'd be expected to open up in a group counseling session. She would not have hesitated to talk one-on-one with a counselor, as she had done in Iraq. But when she showed up for the session there were about a dozen soldiers sitting in a circle, and while they were all from the 2-224th, these weren't people in front of whom she felt comfortable discussing her personal problems. No wonder soldiers were famous for strictly adhering to a code of silence, she thought. Who wants to spill their guts in front of a room full of soldiers?

Leading the group were a civilian counselor and an army chaplain, who thanked them for their service and explained that the transition they were about to go through was a difficult one. Then they asked the soldiers to list some of the things that worried them about coming home.

"Let's start with you," the chaplain said, indicating Kate.

She could feel the anticipatory stares of the other soldiers and her face turning red, but she summoned her courage. Over the past weeks, as her homecoming had drawn closer, the nightmares had returned. Her hand continued to shake whenever she felt the slightest bit of stress. She needed help. She was as scared about coming home as others were excited. Even if it meant embarrassing herself in front of her fellow soldiers, she would talk.

"There are two things bothering me," she began.

The first was her divorce. The second was treating the wounded marine. She talked about her sadness at losing her husband, and how she was terrified to go home and face the fact that he was no longer there. I have no future, she said. Everything that was familiar—married life, my home, my past life—has all been taken away from me. I have no idea what I'm going to do next.

She didn't even know where she'd be living. After her husband announced he was leaving her, Kate sent an e-mail to virtually everyone she knew in Richmond asking if anyone knew of any housing leads. A fellow National Guard medic whom Kate had gotten to know through various training exercises wrote that she had an extra bedroom in her house that she'd be happy to rent.

"I feel like I'm homeless," Kate told the group.

Then she talked about the marine, how he had writhed in pain, begging for morphine, but she'd had nothing to give him. For hours on end, especially at night, she'd obsess over that moment, unable to think of anything else, or to sleep.

"I can still remember his name," she said. "I still hear him screaming. For me he is the war."

After the session, the counselor and chaplain pulled her aside and said she needed to seek additional help. There was a therapist on base and they'd make an appointment for Kate to see her privately the next day. The chaplain, a sweet, tall man with a soft Sunday-sermon voice, was particularly comforting. He took her phone number and e-mail address and promised that when she got home, he'd follow up with her. Everything was going to be okay, he promised. She was home now, and they would take care of her.

The next day, the chaplain personally escorted Kate to the therapist's office, and before saying good-bye he repeated his vow that he'd be in touch. He was not going to let her fall through the cracks.

To the therapist, Kate repeated her story—the sleepless nights, the fear of being alone, the feeling that she was having to start over. There were times when an inexplicable rage would well up inside her, usually when she thought about the wounded marine and the mass casualties that came into the Al Asad hospital. "The deployment taught me how to hate," she said. She was afraid she was a ticking time bomb, waiting to go off.

"There is a name for your condition," the therapist said. "It's called PTSD."

Kate knew what the abbreviation stood for: post-traumatic stress disorder. Every soldier did. One in every seven soldiers who had served in Iraq was reportedly suffering from it. Except for the stifling group session, Kate was relieved to see that the army seemed so intent on getting her help. The army chaplain had taken a personal interest in her. And now having her PTSD officially diagnosed blunted some of the fear associated with it. Even though her fellow soldiers had warned her the Department of Veterans Affairs was a joke, Kate promised the therapist she would make an appointment when she got home. Still, she was worried about how she'd react in a few days when all of her fellow soldiers scattered back to their families, leaving her alone.

As a former active-duty soldier, she knew all about the camaraderie of soldiers. But the 2-224th had become her family. They had lived together, traveled together, eaten together for so long, she couldn't imagine what life was going to be like without them. Her good friends, Captain Mark Baush chief among them, had helped her through her divorce. Like everyone else, Kate was glad to be out of Iraq. But part of her didn't want the deployment to end if that meant leaving her friends.

Shortly after getting out of the counselor's office, she ran into Mark and some of her other friends in the unit and immediately broke down.

"I just found out I'm crazy," she said, holding back tears.

The soldiers cheered as the buses pulled past the Fort Dix gates. They cheered again as they crossed into Virginia and a phalanx of state troopers escorted them the rest of the way home, lights flashing. Like schoolkids on the precipice of summer vacation, the soldiers were ecstatic. As the buses drew close, the soldier sitting next to Kate pulled out his cell phone and told his wife, "We're almost home, baby. No more than an hour now. I can't wait to see you."

Everyone else's happiness only made Kate's loneliness more profound. When she first deployed, she had imagined what coming home would be like: She'd jump into her husband's arms, and they would cry, ready to start the rest of their lives together. Instead, newly divorced—she had signed the papers a couple of days earlier at Fort Dix—she had no one to meet her. She pulled out her phone and begged her best friend to come to the ceremony.

"This is so depressing," she said softly so the other soldiers wouldn't hear. "I don't have anyone there."

The families went wild when the buses pulled up as if they'd break through the barriers restraining them while the 2-224th filed into formation one last time. Kate saw her best friend and smiled.

The battalion commander reported to the state's adjutant general, "All personnel accounted for."

"Go home," he urged his soldiers. "Hug your families. Put your feet up. You deserve it."

When he dismissed them, the soldiers broke ranks in a mad rush. Family members descended on them with tearful hugs. Kate's friend ran over to her and enveloped her in a huge, warm hug. It felt great to see her, and Kate was so thankful she had come on such short notice.

Still, it was not the welcome home Kate had imagined.

The directions to Kate's new home were scribbled on a piece of paper, but she had only a vague idea of where she was going, and soon she was completely lost. The streets of Richmond, Virginia, were suddenly unfamiliar, and the further she pushed on, the more disoriented she became.

After the welcome home ceremony, Kate wasn't ready to face her new, strange life—and sleep in her new, strange house—just yet. So she walked through the emotional reunions and made her way to a nearby Mexican restaurant, where she celebrated her homecoming with friends over beers and margaritas. Then she crashed in a motel.

Now, as she tried to find her way to her new home the next morning, she was lost somewhere in a rough neighborhood, thinking this can't be it. She pulled over, consulted her directions, then scanned the street signs for clues. But she had no idea where she was. Finally, she called her new housemate, Steffanie, who told her the way.

A few minutes later Kate walked up the front steps of a pink house with a chain-link fence and a gazebo in the backyard.

Tentatively, she rang the doorbell the way a stranger might. This is so weird, she thought. I can't believe I live here.

Steffanie opened the door and gave her a huge hug. "Come in, come in," she said. They chatted and hugged again, and soon Steffanie said, as if she were a concierge, "Let me show you your room."

The boxes of Kate's past life were stacked in the corner. They had been packed by her ex, who was kind enough to list what was in each box, and Kate opened a couple of them slowly, unsure of what memories her belongings would evoke. "My purses!" she exclaimed at one point. "My shoes!" at another.

But she left most everything else untouched. She decided not to rush things. She was unfamiliar with the person who once belonged to the things in the boxes, and she wasn't ready to face that stranger just yet.

Before the divorce and the wounded marine and the sleepless nights and the unsettling fact that sometimes her hand started shaking uncontrollably, the plan after Iraq had been to resume her college career. She had dropped out after she was unable to complete a single semester of community college and joined the army to straighten herself out. After Iraq, she'd finally be ready, and mature enough, to take on college again. But now it was obvious there was no way she could handle sitting in class with a bunch of sorority sisters and frat boys with whom she had little in common. In the fall, she would be ready to resume college, but not now.

What she wanted was to do a whole lot of nothing. She would put some distance between the war and herself by turning life into one big party, living a life of beer-soaked frivolity while collecting $350 a week in unemployment insurance. Like her first night home, her second was spent drinking, as was the third. Though this time, surrounded by friends she had not seen in months, she took it to the extreme—beer after beer, kamikaze and Jägermeister shots—and ended up puking in the alley behind the pub.

She had spent more than a year under the direct supervision of the U.S. Army, an experienced that left her feeling "institutionalized," she said, like a prisoner. No laundry, no grocery shopping, no cooking, no cleaning the toilet, no rent checks, no filling up the car with gas or taking a drive. For more than a year, she knew where she had to be and when and whom to salute and when to say "Yes, Sir" and "No, Ma'am." She did her job. She treated the wounded. She followed orders. Now she was home and free to do as she pleased. And she was going to make the most of it.

"this past week i have made some decisions about my immediate future," she wrote in her online blog a few weeks after getting home.

"i don't want to work.

"i want to have fun.

"i want to travel.

"i want to chill out w/ friends and do a lot of drinking."

The pink house with the gazebo was where she lived, but it was not her home. It belonged to a friend, a lovely, caring friend who had given her a place to stay. And although it had a comfortable couch and a television and a coffee maker and a peaceful front porch, Kate felt most what it didn't have. Without her husband, the place, like the rest of her life, felt foreign. Without her husband, any place would.

She'd just gotten home, but now she needed to get away. A road trip. An escape. An exercise of her newfound freedom that would postpone the inevitable moment when she would have to confront this new, strange reality.

In Knoxville, where she grew up, she hugged her mother and partied with high school friends. In North Carolina, she partied at her first sergeant's house. In Savannah, Kate stayed out all night and ended up sleeping in the car. Kate woke in the front seat slumped over in the driver's seat with a raging hangover. She brushed her teeth in a Starbucks bathroom, then hit the road for home.

The party continued in Richmond, where day after idle day passed. A posting on her MySpace blog read:

> yesterday was completely wasted as far as being productive. instead i chose to spend time w/ my little [dog], lola, and my friend, jordan. she and i started drinking around 2 P.M. and that was pretty much the end of that day. lol.

About a month after getting home, she woke up crying. She had been dreaming. She was certain of that. But now the dream escaped her. She searched her memory for clues of what it had been about, as if the ritual of remembering would deliver her from this unexplained, frightful sadness. Maybe it was the marine begging for morphine. Maybe it was her ex saying, "I want a divorce." Maybe it was simply the fact of the hard, real present that her mind for some reason chose to acknowledge this early March morning: She was waking up on a lumpy, borrowed futon to a strange ceiling, all alone, with the boxes of her past life piled still unpacked in the corner. But whether it was something from the past that had been brewing in her subconscious, or her present reality, she was left with a sick, hollow feeling she could not escape. She pulled her knees and arms to her chest in a defensive, fetal crouch, but she was still shaking uncontrollably. This is what descending into madness must feel like, she thought.

In Iraq, dust storms would occasionally roll over the base. From a distance they were awesome and vast and terrible, blurring the line between the ground and sky, rendering the horizon nothing more than an obscure smudge. Like a tsunami, they were all-consuming and had the power to erase the distance between here and there, swallowing trucks and tanks and tents. Everything. Which was where Kate was now: lost at the epicenter, feeling around in a cloud of sand and dust for some way out.

In truth, she had been there for some time, torn between twin realities: war and home, home and war, unsure of where she belonged. A week before her own sobs woke her, she had e-mailed some of her fellow Guard soldiers an *Esquire* magazine article titled

"I Miss My War" that was written by a former Iraq war infantryman who was wistful for the harrowing thrill of combat and the sense of purpose it gave him: "War peels back the skin, and you live with a layer of nerve exposed, overdosing on your surroundings, when everything seems all wrong and just right, in a way that makes perfect sense."

In the e-mail, Kate added her own thoughts about the war: "i kinda miss it too."

Lying on her borrowed futon, she could not stop crying, which only compounded the problem. She was trapped and scared. Something was seriously wrong. Barely able to speak, she called her twin sister in Knoxville, who told her it was time to get help.

The VA hospital south of Richmond was a squat brick building with a circular driveway and an American flag out front. When Kate had finally called for an appointment at her sister's urging, the receptionist told her the first opening wasn't for another six weeks.

"Six weeks?" Kate had said. "You don't have anything until then?" She needed help now.

"Sorry," the receptionist had said. "That's the best we can do."

In a building full of World War II, Korea, and Vietnam vets, Kate was by far the youngest, drawing stares from older men who must have thought she was a nurse, not a patient. Although she had asked to see a mental-health specialist, she was told that first she had to see a general practitioner, who could then refer her to one. While she was there, she figured, she would finally have him look at her shoulder, which she had injured years before and had recently started aching again.

But the doctor didn't so much as look at her shoulder. And when she told him she had been diagnosed with PTSD by a therapist at Fort Dix, he nodded and typed away at his computer but said only that the referrals she needed would be sent to her in the mail in the coming weeks.

More waiting? Kate couldn't believe it. The morning she'd woken up crying was, she was convinced, her subconscious's way of telling her she was in trouble. The referrals would take another few weeks to arrive. And then it could take another month after that to schedule an appointment. Combined with the six weeks it took to get this appointment, months would pass before she ever got in to see anyone. So, she thought, this is why everybody says the VA sucks.

If she had been in one of those moods she increasingly found herself in, when she was liable to explode in a fit of rage, she might have grabbed the doctor by the white lapels of his lab coat and demanded to see a counselor immediately. Instead, she directed the anger inward, where it morphed from rage to a deep, immobilizing sadness. So when the doctor ended the brief session, mentioning that he was late for lunch, she quietly nodded her head and said nothing.

David Dahlstrand was new to Richmond, and outside of the people he worked with at the corporate offices of Circuit City, he didn't know a soul. Richmond was, by every definition, the model of a good old southern town. People were unfailingly polite and gracious. But David was having a hard time penetrating its seemingly closed-off social circles. He'd been here just a few weeks. It seemed as if everyone else in Richmond had been friends forever.

Where to meet people? He wasn't the kind to go up to strangers in bars. And he wasn't getting invited to many parties. The dating Web site eHarmony.com seemed a logical place to start. It cost a little more than some of the others and involved a lengthy questionnaire, which he thought would attract a higher caliber of person—someone who, like him, was serious about meeting people and having some fun. Plus, the Web site picked out matches for you based on your profile. If there was a romantic spark, great. If not, he would just be happy to have made a connection with another human being in this big, strange city.

But he was a little puzzled when one of his recommended matches was a female soldier who according to her profile had recently returned from Iraq. What could we have in common? he wondered.

Even though Kate's divorce had only recently been made official, it had been nearly a year since her ex told her over the phone that he wanted to end their marriage. She was ready to move on. She wasn't in the market for anything serious, but it would be nice, if a bit frightening, to date again, to flirt. Putting herself back on the dating scene was, she suspected, another way back. And she was also ready, after a prolonged absence, to start thinking about college again.

But because her marriage had not turned out as she'd expected, Kate figured she was no longer qualified to pick men suitable to date. She needed professional help. She'd let eharmony.com pick the men for her. But how to fill out her online profile? Would men be lining up to meet a recently divorced female soldier just back from Iraq? She didn't think so. But she also figured that if they weren't okay with the fact that she was in the military and a veteran, she wouldn't want anything to do with them, either. If her date turned out to be some bleeding-heart civilian who was going to trash the Iraq War while pretending to support the troops, she wouldn't last five minutes. Be up front, she decided. Don't hide who you are.

But when David and Kate met for drinks on a Monday night, she steered clear of talking about the army, an association that in the presence of this civilian suddenly made her feel dowdy and unfeminine. She didn't want to scare him away. David was tall and blond with blue eyes. He was a cute, white-collar professional. He wore a dress shirt that she thought had to have been dry cleaned, shoes that shone, a belt that matched, and slacks—not khakis, but real slacks that still held their nice, neat crease at the end of the day. He had gel in his hair. She was in jeans, a purple V-neck, and a leather coat. He ordered a rum and Coke, which made her Miller Lite seem so pedestrian by comparison.

Like Miranda, Kate had become adept at masking her army persona around civilians and deflecting questions about the war.

She was relieved that David seemed content to stay away from Iraq too, and she made sure he wouldn't bring it up by playing conversational defense: What do *you* do? Where are *you* from? His job at Circuit City's corporate offices sounded technical and, frankly, boring. But she kept the conversation steered toward him. Anything was better than opening herself up to questions about herself. What was she supposed to say? "I recently woke up crying so hard, I thought I was going mad"? That wasn't really first-date stuff.

The first Miller Lite went down quickly. So did the second. And the third. She was so nervous, they just sort of disappeared. Thankfully, he drank, too, one rum and Coke after another. This was the most fun he had had since he'd moved to Richmond. This girl seemed down to earth and real. He loved her infectious laugh and the fact that she was nearly always smiling, even if it was a nervous affectation. Above all, he was grateful to have met someone so fun. By the time he finished his first drink, he was completely at ease.

After the date Kate concluded that he was sweet, and it was nice to get out again. If nothing else, she'd proved to herself that she could. But he was too much of a starched-and-pressed preppy for her. Too much of a civilian. To be with him, she had to play the part of the well-adjusted vet, home from war, ready to get on with life, when in reality she was stuck in limbo, unsure of what was next. They were at very different stations in life. Where, she wondered, could this possibly lead?

But David was persistent. They had fun together, so he kept calling her and asking her out, and she couldn't find a reason to say no. What was the harm in a little fling, even if she knew it couldn't go anywhere? This was good practice at normalcy. When she was with him, she forgot about the war. She wasn't Kate the soldier or Kate the vet. She was just a young woman on a date with a cute guy who appeared to be smitten. He was a real gentleman, who always took care of the check and called when he was running late. On the night he had been caught up at work and was really late, he showed up with a vase of roses. He was fun and spontaneous and romantic. Dates were adventures that could take them anywhere.

Where would you like to go? he'd ask when he picked her up in his canary yellow sports car. When she shrugged, he punched the "find restaurant" function in the GPS and let it decide for them. They ate Brazilian and Chinese. One night they ended up at Texas Road House, another at the Waffle House. It didn't really matter where they went; they always had fun.

Over those first few weeks, they talked about everything: their childhoods, his work, her friends, their desire to have kids one day—everything, that is, except for Iraq. Kate just could never find the appropriate time to bring it up. And why should she? Everything was going great. She didn't want to ruin it by bringing the war into it. So she buried it away, as if it had never happened. It felt good to have something else to fixate on, something good like a cute boy who could turn a Tuesday night into a romping escapade.

Kate's friends kept asking her how it was going with the eharmony guy. But she was worried about how they'd get along. Her friends were beer-drinking, blue-collar construction workers, tile layers, grouters, soldiers. Like her, they wore jeans and drank Miller Lite and drove trucks. They'd take one look at the stiff in the slacks with the yellow sports car and laugh. Plus, they were prone, especially after a few, to start making a production of every part of Kate's life that she was working so hard to conceal. Buy this girl a drink! they'd say. Don't you know she's an Iraq War vet? That was the last thing she wanted to expose David to. She didn't want to talk about the war with anybody—especially her new civilian boyfriend—and thankfully he had the good manners not to press. With David, she was starting fresh, from a clean slate. She had buried the war. It was behind her now. She was moving on.

At least that's what she told herself.

By the end of April, spring had settled into Richmond, and Kate was feeling better than she had in a long time. It was a Saturday night, and David had taken her to a pizza joint. She was full and content and, above all, glad to be going back to his place for the night.

Two days earlier she had written a little poem on her blog:

> i like the boy.
> he grows on me everyday.
> he treats me like a princess.
> this is a very healthy thing that is
> developing between the two of us.
> he gives me goosebumps.
> i am falling.
> la la la

That was Thursday, a good day. Friday, though, was a bad day, another fearful reminder of how quickly she could swing from elation to sadness and back again, sometimes all within the span of just a few hours. In a blog entry titled "this is for my mental health . . ." she detailed what had happened that day with the marine, knowing that David, unaware of her blog's existence, wouldn't read it.

> To be honest, and I apologize in advance if I offend any of you for what I am about to say, but I really could not care less what you think about what I am about to tell you.
> This is a form of catharsis for me. A form of therapy. I have only really talked to a few people about this and there was a reason for that, because unless you were physically there, unless you saw what I saw and dealt with the mental anguish and aftermath with me, there is no true way to understand what happened.

By Saturday evening Kate was feeling good again. The warm air hung tight like an embrace. David opened the sunroof and turned up the radio. Kate let the warm wind whip up her hair, and as the music blasted, she settled into her bucket seat, comfortable and relaxed.

Then she heard a familiar sound that sent chills through her body. The *thwap, thwap, thwap* of two military helicopters flying in formation overhead. She hadn't heard that sound since Iraq, but it transported her back in an instant. She tried to push the thought from her mind, but the flashback of that day with the marine was so intense she could barely breathe. It was as if she were having an asthma attack, and so she started inhaling and exhaling deliberately. David thought she was getting carsick and turned down the stereo.

"Are you all right?" he asked.

She shook her head and tried to explain. But she was having such a hard time breathing that speech eluded her. "The helicopters," she gasped, unable to manage more.

He knew she had been a medic in Iraq, and he assumed she had seen some pretty awful stuff. But she hadn't said much about the war, and he wasn't going to push, not even now, as she labored to catch her breath. His job, he figured, was to be supportive and loving. If she wanted to talk, now or later, she would, he said. And he would be there for her.

"You're okay," he said. "You're safe here with me. I'm not going to let anything happen to you."

He was calm and quietly strong in a way that was reassuring. Kate was stunned by his pitch-perfect response. Slowly she regained her breath. No longer did she care if he was too much of a civilian for her, if he was too preppy, or if he wore pressed shirts. None of that mattered.

"It's okay to be afraid," David reassured her. "We all have things we're afraid of. Take me. I'm afraid of straws."

Kate had no idea what he was talking about.

"Drinking straws," David continued. "They totally freak me out. I'm always scared that when I go to take a sip I'm going to poke my eye out."

She couldn't tell if he was joking or serious. But this was such an absurd, unexpected thing to say that her panic loosened a bit into little ripples of laughter.

"What are you talking about?" she said.

"I'm serious," he said. "Here, look in my glove compartment."

Kate opened it up, and sure enough there was a stash of white plastic straws.

"See, that's my collection of 'safe straws,'" he said. "They're not nearly as sharp as the other kind. I keep them with me just in case because I eat a lot of drive-thru."

Kate was laughing now, hard.

"I'm telling you," he said. "Those clear straws are dangerous."

He was so weird—a good weird, a funny, distracting weird—that she forgot about the helicopters and Iraq and her own fear. Her hand stopped shaking. The crisis had been averted by his drinking straw phobia.

"here is this civilian, who never knew me before the deployment, and i was completely unloading on him," she wrote in her blog a couple days later. "i thought for sure that i had ruined everything, that i had totally freaked him out and that this would be the end of our short, but sweet, relationship. david surprised me, reassured me, told me that i was safe and that he would protect me, and then proceeded to distract me by telling me silly and funny stories until i calmed down and started laughing again.

"bless his heart. he really is an awesome guy."

First they said she was going. Then suddenly, she wasn't. Steffanie Pyle's name had been scratched from the list. Who was in charge of the list, how one got on or off it, she did not know. But if her name was no longer on it, that meant she wasn't going to have to deploy to Iraq. Which was a relief because she wouldn't have to leave Kate, her housemate, all by herself and she'd be able to continue her college studies. It also meant that Steffanie could go ahead and get her two weeks of annual National Guard training out of the way.

A couple of days later, her commander pulled Steffanie and about ten of her fellow soldiers aside. Steffanie saw he was holding a list and her heart sank. She knew there was always the possibility of going. That was just life in the Guard. But she'd been told not more than two weeks earlier that she was safe. The commander read down the names and Steffanie winced when he read hers aloud. Then she heard him say, "Kate Broome."

"That can't be right," she piped up. "Kate's my roommate, and she just got back from Iraq."

"Well, she's on the list," the commander responded. "Maybe if she just got back, it'll be her choice to go. But she's on the list."

By the time Steffanie was released to go home and pack, she was so upset about having to deploy she could barely talk. What was worse, she had to report in a week, which was not enough time to get everything in order before she was to take off for a year or more. Sobbing, she called her boyfriend with the news. Her cell phone battery was dying, so she told him to call Kate and tell her she was coming back to pack up her stuff. Don't tell her that her name was on the list, too, she said. But she was crying so hard, he didn't hear her.

At home, Kate's lackadaisical spring had lulled her into a state of complacency. It was now June. She'd been home four months but hadn't had a job, or registered for classes, or done much of anything, which was fine with her. Her high school friend Cecil was staying with her for a couple of weeks, crashing on the living room couch, which is where they were when Kate's cell phone rang. Cecil couldn't tell who was on the other line, but whoever it was, he or she was clearly upsetting Kate.

"I can't go back there," she said, hanging up. "I can't go back."

"Go back where?" Cecil said. "Slow down. Tell me what's wrong."

"That was Steffanie's boyfriend," Kate explained. "She's going to Iraq, and she saw my name on the list as well."

How could this happen? She had just gotten back, and had even been diagnosed with PTSD. She was stunned, and soon she was having a hard time breathing. Then her hand started shaking.

"I can't go back," she kept saying.

Cecil tried to reassure her. He gave her a hug, then started rubbing her shaking hand. He'd seen it once before, a few days earlier.

He had been making dinner, and looked over at Kate. Her face had gone white and her hand was jittering at her side like a leaf in the wind.

"What's wrong?" he said.

"I'm having a panic attack," she said. But after a cigarette she seemed fine, and didn't want to talk about it.

But now her hand would not stop shaking, and Cecil could not get her to calm down. Breathe, he said. Inhale. Good. Now exhale. One breath at a time. He was afraid she was going to pass out.

"This doesn't mean anything," he said. "Just because Steffanie saw your name on some list doesn't mean you're going anywhere. It's all a nasty rumor that hasn't been confirmed by anyone. What we need is hard information. Is there anyone you can call?"

Kate had the cell phone number of the training sergeant, but he didn't pick up. So she left a message.

"I can't go back," she said again. She was freaking out. The more she thought of having to go back, the more distressed she became. She was enveloped again by the sandstorm, crying uncontrollably.

She called David at work, and he had an immediate calming effect. "You're not going back," he said. He was so firm, so resolute, she believed him. "You're not going back," he said again. "I'm not going to lose you."

This was a problem, and they would find a solution, he said calmly. Probably, he reasoned, this was all a mistake. You just got back from Iraq. But if they do in fact intend to deploy you, we'll find a way out. We'll get you some pot, and make you fail the drug test. We'll go to Canada.

An hour or so later the training sergeant called her back.

"Sergeant Broome, how the heck are you?" he asked.

"I don't know," Kate said. "You tell me. I heard my name's on the list."

"Hold on, let me check," he said. "I have the paperwork right here."

Kate waited as he riffled through the papers.

"Yeah, you were on the list," he said. "But not anymore. You got scrubbed out."

Kate was furious. "I just got back," she said. "You guys shouldn't be able to touch me. How did my name even get on there?"

"Orders are orders. They needed medics, and so they listed all the medics in the state. We had other assets that had not deployed yet so we were able to scrub you. But if we didn't, you'd be going. Needs of the army."

That's it, Kate thought, I'm getting out. I'm an "asset" to them. That's all. Her enlistment would be complete in October 2008 and she would not re-up. She had been in the army for nearly eight years now, but no more. She'd have fifteen more weekend drills and one more two-week training, and then she would be done. That meant she would be forfeiting a $15,000 reenlistment bonus and would have to find a way to pay for her last year of college on her own. But she didn't care. No amount of money was going to keep her in the army now.

There had been a time when she pictured herself going the full twenty years for the retirement benefits. But now what she envisioned was a life with David, who agreed wholeheartedly with her decision to get out. When she was worried she might have to go back, he had been great, just like he was the night when the helicopters induced an Iraq flashback. And she couldn't help but reflect on the fact that he had said: We'll go to Canada.

We. As in together.

Smoking cessation. That's it. A smoking-cessation program and an appointment at a women's health clinic were the grand total of the referrals Kate received from the VA. Nothing about her shoulder. And nothing about seeing a psychiatrist.

Forget it, she thought. If this is how they treat their soldiers, I'm done with the VA.

By now it was July 2007. She'd been home nearly six months. The nightmares, the hand tremors, the panic attacks were still a disturbing, if less frequent, part of her life. She could get used to the fact that every once in a while things were just going to go south. "When I get down, there is no darker place in the world," she wrote on her blog. She'd just adapt by accepting the occasional meltdown. Meanwhile, she'd get on with life. She had recently visited the campus of Virginia Commonwealth University to register for classes. It had felt good to do something productive, even if was odd seeing all those young kids on campus.

What she couldn't tolerate, though, were the questions people asked about Iraq. Dumb questions, hurtful questions, questions that revealed just how different she was from even her closest friends. Normally, like Miranda and Ray and Craig and so many others home from the war, she usually just replied with rote answers that kept the truth at a safe distance. "It was hot," she'd say, which was both true and accessible. Reduce the war to meteorology, and maybe then there would be some common ground so that people could understand. But the heat was so stifling that even then there was a disconnect. This was an otherworldly heat. Planet Mercury heat. A heat so bad the breeze wasn't a relief, but rather like standing in front of a hair dryer. It was worse than the stickiest, humid August day in Richmond. Worse than being stuck in the backseat of a Volkswagen Bug with no AC and the windows rolled up sitting next to a Great Dane that's breathing in your face. It was a heat she couldn't describe and they wouldn't understand. And so even as Kate dismissively used the stock "It was hot" line, she thought, You have no idea.

If she didn't talk about weather, she would talk about the sand. How the sand wasn't sand, not the way Americans think about it anyway. The sand of Iraq wasn't gritty and granular like you found at the beach. It was soft and smooth, like talcum powder, and got into everything: your eyes, your clothes, your hair, even your bed. "In Iraq," she'd say, "you lived in sand."

But occasionally people would probe beyond the sand and heat. "What was war really like?" they wanted to know. "Did you shoot anybody? Did you see any dead bodies?" They asked as if it had been a movie, as if it hadn't been real. Because it hadn't been. Not to them, anyway. Civilians. That's when Kate would lose it.

"I saw dead people . . . there. Does that make you happy?!" she vented on her blog. "I saw dead people and I saw terrible injuries and I heard people screaming and crying quietly in pain.

"I guess this is what everyone wants to know, right? I mean, otherwise they would stop berating me with ignorant and painful questions. . . .

"How was it over there? Did you see bad things? Tell me something horrible that you saw. . . . What sticks in your mind the most? Was it hard being over there? Did anyone die on you? Did you see a lot of nasty wounds?"

For saving the marine, she'd been awarded the Bronze Star. But she never talked about the prestigious medal with friends. She never bragged, or showed off the citation that said her "efforts saved the Marine's life." In spite of what was printed on the piece of paper, she didn't believe she deserved the award and had taken it off her chest fewer than ten minutes after it was pinned. When she got home, she stuck it in a box and stashed it under Christmas decorations in the guest bedroom closet. Maybe one day she'd be able to look at the award and be proud. But not now. Now she only wanted to forget.

On the bad days, when David could tell she hadn't been able to sleep, or could see that distant look in her eyes, he would gently urge her to try the VA again. "They are specially equipped for what you went through," he'd say. "It's not like you have a broken bone that any doctor can fix. The VA specializes in this kind of treatment." Kate had received a letter in August, saying she needed to schedule her annual checkup, but she'd ignored it. They always put you on hold, she complained. It was such a pain just trying to make an appointment. But as weeks and months passed, and the nightmares continued, she began to wonder if she was ever going to get better. And so one day that autumn, nearly a year after getting home from Iraq, she finally called.

"I need to schedule a checkup with my primary care provider," she said.

The woman on the other end took her information, then asked Kate to hold. Surprised she had actually gotten a real person on the line, Kate began thinking that maybe it would work out this time. But five minutes on hold turned to ten. Cloying elevator music played. "Please remain on the line," a recording said. "We will tend to your call shortly."

Fifteen minutes passed.

"We won't keep you holding one second longer than is necessary."

Twenty minutes. Kate rolled her eyes. "This is why I was putting off making the call," she said.

"We look forward to serving you. . . . Please remain on the line."

After thirty minutes—she could tell because her phone recorded the length of the call—she hung up, disgusted. "I'm finished," she said. "I'll try again tomorrow."

And she did, this time waiting ten minutes before hanging up. She called back every day that week, waiting on the line for between five and fifteen minutes. In the end, she had spent a total of about a six hours on hold but never got through.

So when she later had to sit through a briefing with fellow medics about PTSD, and how the army and the VA were there to help, Kate began to stew. The more the first sergeant giving the presentation talked, the angrier she got. And when at the end, he asked if there were any questions or comments, she raised her hand.

"Everything you just said about the VA and how they are there to help the returning soldier, that's a bunch of bullshit," she blurted out.

The first sergeant's eyes got wide, and for a moment, Kate thought she was in real trouble for telling off a soldier who so out-ranked her. His eyes got wide, but he kept his cool.

"Now you see this is where a soldier has failed to take advantage of the services the military has to offer," he said, then asked Kate to see him later.

But Kate was still fuming after final formation and hopped in her car and went home. At the next drill weekend a month later, the first sergeant came looking for her.

"You ducked out before I could talk to you," he said. He knew she needed help, and he had dug up a phone number for where she could talk to someone.

Slightly ashamed, Kate took the number and thanked him. But when she looked at it she realized it was the same number that had kept her on hold for so long.

14

Mark

Keep Your Boots On

The soldiers filing in for the welcome home ceremony all looked alike. Same uniform. Same crew cut. Same shoulders-back posture. It was hard for Elaine Baush to figure out which was her son. But then she saw him. She caught his eye, smiled, and waved, her heart lifted. And when Mark smiled back with that twinkle-eyed smile inherited from his father, she felt like breaking through the barricade that sequestered the hundreds of families who had come to welcome their soldiers home. If she could just hug him, it would confirm that the sight of her boy standing in formation was no mirage. It would mean that for him—and for her—the war was finally over.

The invasion of Iraq was an atrocity, she believed, committed by an administration she could not stand, and it pained her that her son was a part of it. But like his father, Mark was set in his ways. There had been no talking him out of going to Iraq, just as there had been no talking him out of attending VMI. It had almost seemed as if he wanted to go, which she could not understand. But as she said good-bye to him back then, she couldn't help but feel proud of him—especially after everything he had been through.

Black Wednesday, he called it. The day he was called up for Iraq was also the day his fiancée left him. A double whammy that left him reeling. The wedding invitations had been printed, the reception hall booked. But Mark's fiancée didn't want to be a military wife, and so when he came home to tell her he was being sent to Iraq, she said she had some news for him, too. Perhaps he should have seen it coming. They were two different creatures. She was a planner who paid meticulous attention to detail and did not want anything to do with the military. He improvised life one day to the next, was so messy some of his friends called him Pigpen. And the news of his upcoming deployment only confirmed the fact that their relationship was fatally flawed. He took the blow hard, and when he called his mother that night he couldn't hide his despair.

He was worried, he told her, about flying Black Hawks in combat and leading soldiers so soon after getting his heart broken. He was a company commander, and he needed to be sharp—otherwise, he feared, someone could get hurt. He was going to promise every single one of the soldiers in his command, which included Kate and Miranda, that he would make sure they came back alive. But he couldn't afford to be distracted by his breakup. Distractions could be deadly.

"You'll do fine," Elaine had told him. And she was confident he would. Much as it pained her that her son was in the military and going to war, she knew he was an excellent soldier, and an even better leader who would protect those in his charge. The fact that he was concerned about how he would be able to look after his soldiers while broken-hearted was evidence of that.

Now he was home, standing proudly in formation in front of his company, his promise fulfilled. The battalion commander released them, and soon Elaine was hugging her thirty-seven-year-old son, tearing up. Even Mark's stoic father, Dick, had tears in his eyes, a sight Mark had seen only a couple of times before. He was home, safe and sound. Elaine would finally be able to relax, and Mark would move on with his life, find a new girlfriend, with any luck one who would stick around this time, settle down. She hugged him tighter still, not wanting to let go.

"I'm so glad you're home," she said.

"I am, too," he responded.

But there was something about him that was distant, she sensed, something he was holding back.

Getting up at O-Dark-Thirty had never been easier for the soldiers of the 2-224th. They were at Camp Virginia, Kuwait, a staging area for troops moving into and out of Iraq, and they carried themselves with the confident insouciance of those on the return leg. This was the day they were finally getting the heck out of the Middle East. And despite the early hour, they were exuberant as the buses pulled away from the camp to the airfield and headed toward the rising sun.

"Are we home yet?" a wisecracking soldier yelled less than a minute into the ride.

"We just got the order," Mark, sitting in the rear of the bus, snapped back. "We're being extended!"

The soldiers burst into laughter. Out of Iraq, about to head home, they could afford to laugh.

Like everyone else, Mark was eager to get home. A year in the desert, flying mission after mission, had left him drained. He'd had his hairy moments, seeing tracer fire light up the sky in front of his Black Hawk. With eighty soldiers under his command, he didn't feel he could take time off, and so he was one of the few in the battalion who did not go home for two weeks of leave.

While he was away his father had had another stroke, his third, and his health was failing. Mark's house, the fixer-upper he planned to renovate and flip, was in desperate need of attention. And he was ready to start scouring his Richmond neighborhood for other rundown properties he could fix up and sell. He might have chosen to be a soldier, but he still had ambitions to make that first million in the private sector.

But perhaps most of all, he was eager to spend some time with the woman he had been e-mailing from Iraq. She was an old friend from the neighborhood, on whom he had secretly had a crush even though she was married. But now she was getting divorced, and in her e-mails she let it be known she was looking forward to spending time with Mark when he got home.

Once the soldiers arrived at the airfield, the battalion commander asked Mark to take a walk. He had good news and bad. The good: Mark was going to be promoted to major. The bad: There was a strong possibility he was going to be transferred to another unit—an infantry brigade combat team that could be headed to Iraq in a few months. Nothing's certain yet, the commander said. And even if it does happen, no one will force you to redeploy so quickly. The choice was his.

Mark didn't hesitate. "If they go, I have to go, too," he said. "I can't accept the promotion and then pass on the deployment."

He didn't want to be the one person in the new unit who didn't go to Iraq. It made sense for him to go. He didn't have a wife or kids. Better me, he thought, than someone with a family. And if he sucked it up for another year, his military career would take off with another deployment under his belt. Ordinarily, it would have been a dream job. As the brigade aviation officer, he'd have access to a full arsenal—Black Hawks, Cobras, Apaches, fixed-wing gunships, even manless predator drones for reconnaissance—and get to help plan operations with the grunts on the ground.

Only why did the assignment have to come so soon?

All around him soldiers were celebrating going home, but suddenly Mark was quiet.

Kate thought he was crazy for even considering going back. So did his first sergeant, and so did many of the other soldiers Mark told, and so he stopped talking about it. He certainly was not going to worry his parents, not until it was official. He went through the welcome home ceremony doing his best to pretend that everything was fine, that he was just another soldier excited to be home and start the rest of his life.

The call came eight days after his return. Mark answered, groggy at nine in the morning.

"How would you feel about deploying again?" the battalion commander asked.

"I'll have to get back to you on that one, sir," Mark replied.

But he knew that going to Iraq was a foregone conclusion. And that meant he would have to tell his mother, which worried him more than another deployment. His going back to Iraq, he knew, would break her heart.

The road home was still covered with snow, and the air in late February held winter's chill. But the sun was out as Mark drove to his parents' cozy two-story brick house, which backed up to the woods. Mark wore a flannel shirt and jeans, the picture of a suburban civilian, except that since coming home he'd kept wearing his army combat boots. They just felt right, and so for whatever reason—laziness, inertia, the fact that he didn't have any civilian shoes—he kept wearing them. A few blocks from his parents' house, he pulled over to gather himself. His hands shook and he lit a cigarette to steady himself, thinking that the last time his heart had pounded this hard he was flying into Baghdad.

He arrived before his mother, who was thrilled for the midweek visit, a true luxury after his year in Iraq, and had set out steaks to defrost on the counter for the occasion. Soon she came in through the kitchen door, carrying groceries, and kissed her son. Since he had returned home three weeks earlier, she hadn't seen or heard from him much and was glad they would finally have some time to catch up.

She sat down at the kitchen table, settling herself in, eager to finally hear more about what Mark had planned now that he was back. Mark sat down with her, but he quickly popped back up as if the seat were burning hot. He paced back and forth, like a tiger at the zoo, rubbing his sweaty palms on his jeans.

"Mom," he said finally, unable to look up at her. "I'm going to blow your mind."

Her eyes narrowed and her mouth opened. She could read her son's moods better than anyone, and she saw the nervousness in his eyes, the irritability in his gait. Immediately she could tell exactly what was coming. Before Mark got out another word, she gasped, "You're not going back to Iraq."

It was a statement, not a question.

Mark continued quickly, as if tearing off a bandage, "I'm in love with a beautiful woman who has two kids, and I'm going back to Iraq."

Mark's plan was to soften the blow by coupling the news about Iraq with the fact that his e-mail flirtation with a woman in Richmond had blossomed into a romance over the past few weeks. But Iraq was all Elaine could focus on.

"You know what I told your father: 'If they send him back, they're going to arrest me for killing this president,'" she said, repeating her idle threat.

"Mom, I have a choice and I'm going back."

She was stunned, speechless. Tears welled in her eyes. Her lower lip quivered.

"Mark," she said softly. "Oh, Mark. Oh, Mark. Oh, Mark."

It was all she could manage. She let out a long, sad sigh and closed her eyes. Mark walked over and wrapped his arms around her.

"I'm sorry. I just don't think they should be sending the National Guard to Iraq at all," she said, her sadness momentarily edged out by anger. "And certainly not twice. The National Guard is supposed to defend the country."

It was inherently unfair, she thought. How could the army allow this? How could they be so desperate for soldiers that they would send her son back so shortly after his return home? This was ridiculous. He had done his time. Let someone else go.

"I'm not married," Mark said. "I don't have kids. Better me than someone with a family."

But the explanation did little to assuage her. You have me, she thought. No matter how much he tried to assure her that he'd be okay—he had survived Iraq once already and he'd come home from this deployment, too—she was devastated.

"Should we have a welcome home party, or maybe another going away party?" she said.

"Maybe combine them," Mark said, grateful for his mother's attempt to inject humor into the conversation. But the joke fell flat, and once again the reality hit Elaine and she started tearing up.

"Ah, I thought you had done your bit, and were home for good," she said softly.

"It sets me up," Mark said. "After this job I'll be an attractive commodity."

"To the Iraqis."

"Mom, they don't fuck with me."

Sure he was lying about the danger. Elaine knew it. And Mark knew that she knew it, which was what bothered him so much. Throughout his life, he'd had an almost preternatural ability to bury emotion and show no fear. But watching his mother wipe away the tears she couldn't blink back shook him in a way that getting shot at over Baghdad never had. Mark's eyes welled, and he hugged her in a strong, permanent way that under different circumstances would have meant, It's okay, Mom. I'm home. Home for good.

But no matter how tightly he held her this time, he was past the point of saying hello. Three weeks home and already he was saying good-bye.

"If you get killed this time," she said, "I'll never speak to you again."

Mark had six whole months before shipping out again in August. But was it enough time to shed the stress of one deployment and then prepare himself for another? Mark wasn't sure. He felt as if he had just run that marathon again, willing himself across the finish line, and was now being asked to run another one. He didn't know if his body, or mind, could take the whiplash he felt from having to begin a repeat performance so soon. He needed to relax, get back to normal life for a while. In the army, they called it "decompressing," and for once they got the terminology just right. For a year he had felt the strain of leading a company, the stress of flying, the weight of war pressing down on him until he had become hard down to the core, like a tightly wound baseball, or a diamond.

Mark tried to relax, and from a distance he might have even seemed successful. His capacity for fun was almost as great as his taste for adventure, and he dove back into his old social routine: Thursday night poker with the guys, Fridays and Saturdays at Poe's Pub, the neighborhood bar. Much as he loved the army, being a carefree civilian was fun, even more so after depriving himself for so long. He slept late, caught up with the neighbors, spent time with his new girlfriend and old friends. And in those moments he could feel the coil in his stomach loosening. He was neither back in Iraq, nor going there, but rather right smack dab in the Hawaiian shirt–wearing present, blissfully devoid of memory and foresight. If the ability to enjoy these moments came courtesy of denial, or the distraction of old friends and cases of beer, he didn't care. The only way to be ready for Tour Two was to let Tour One go.

But no matter how hard he tried to will himself into a blissful state of ignorance, the war was always there, both behind and in front of him, like two sentries bookending him in. While he could stay rooted in the present, he could not erase his memory, which was beginning to revisit Iraq subversively and in ways that suggested he was only beginning to realize how deeply it had affected him. Dreams of tracers lighting up the sky. The thrill and fear of flying into Baghdad under the cover of darkness. The young marine Kate had treated. Mark had been there. He'd been the one flying. It had been months since he'd thought about that kid. But now, like Kate, he couldn't stop thinking about him, wondering if he was okay.

If he couldn't keep his memory from revisiting Iraq, he could banish such thoughts, or try to, as soon as they entered his mind. He was only half joking when he told the chaplain who checked in on him from time to time that he was fine; he could drink away any of the ghosts he saw. He didn't have time to dwell on the past. Not when day after passing day was ushering him back to Iraq like a conveyor belt he couldn't get off. He was going. He had accepted his fate and its possible consequences. This was, after all, going to be an on-the-ground combat mission, and instead of processing the past he needed to gird himself for what could be an even more harrowing future. While he knew he had to use the time between deployments to recharge his batteries, he also feared that if he relaxed too much it would allow civilian softness to erode the warrior carapace he'd grown in Iraq and would need again. It was a delicate balancing act, which was why part of him just wished he could turn around and go now and get it over with. But Mark's new unit wasn't scheduled to deploy until August. Which didn't give him enough time to fix up his house or to find a new property to buy, renovate, and flip. It wasn't enough time to go out and get a real job, either. He was stuck waiting to go to war, which meant he was also waiting to come home. Because no matter how hard he tried to pretend he was home from Iraq now, he wasn't. Not entirely, anyway. He was stuck somewhere in between.

Richmond, set in its southern tradition, was not a city bent on reinvention and had in Mark's absence stayed true to itself. The old mansions off Monument Avenue were as regal as ever. The grand Confederate statehouse still stood tall, its pillars stalwart like Great Britain's Beefeaters, its front facade still facing south, giving the north its backside. The city's abiding backdrop was mimicked by the steadfastness of the small, forgotten details that had once made up his life and would, presumably, again. The same rack of baby backs and catfish at Poe's Pub. The same guys crowded around the poker table Thursday nights. The same rotted floorboards in his home, which was still in dire need of renovation. Everything was constant, and there was something reassuring about the reminders of how life used to be, offering hope that it would be possible, someday, to return.

Everything appeared the same, that is, except for his father. While Mark was away, Dick Baush had suffered two strokes. Not only was he constantly tethered to an oxygen tank that continuously force-fed oxygen up his nostrils, but he just looked old. Other soldiers missed the births of their children, their first words and first steps. What Mark missed was his father's slipping into old age. His father wasn't the picture of health when Mark had left, but now he was frail and weak, delicate almost, which was a word Mark never would have used to describe his taciturn, robust dad. Dick had always been a man of few words. But now when he spoke, the words were more labored than pensive. And so when Mark's mother called that spring, a couple of months after he returned home, and said, "Your Dad's in the hospital," he was not surprised.

His father's bout with pneumonia snapped Mark into the present. Here was something immediate and serious that demanded his attention. But not even repeated trips to the intensive care unit, where Dick Baush was hooked up to a series of monitors, could fully distract Mark from his upcoming deployment, though it did cast it in another, disturbing, light. With his father ill, should he really be leaving? His first Iraq tour forced him to miss his father's descent into illness, and now he was clearly in serious condition. But what worried Mark most was his mother, who was visibly shaken that her husband of forty years was now visiting the hospital with frightening regularity. Though she assured Mark everything was going to be fine, he wasn't convinced. Leaving her again seemed a cruel act of abandonment that was beginning to outweigh his commitment to serve. Mark would wait and see before making any decisions. He could still get out of going to Iraq. And if his father's condition didn't improve, he couldn't imagine how he was going to bring himself to leave again.

As for his new unit, he knew basically nothing outside of what he'd already been told: It was an infantry battalion combat team, deploying in August, that was going to see some real action. Since Mark's return from Tour One, he had taken a couple of months off from military life, and he assumed the new unit was allowing him some breathing room before they came calling with his new marching orders. But now it was spring, and Mark still had heard nothing. In the context of all that was happening at home, the silence started to concern him. So on the first Tuesday in May, he decided to check in, if for no other reason than to meet the guys he'd be going over with.

When he got to the unit's headquarters in Stanton, Virginia, he was impressed. The soldiers were moving with a real sense of urgency, getting ready as if they were on the verge of deploying in a matter of days instead of months. Which, as the battalion commander informed Mark, was exactly what they were doing.

"When are we going?" Mark asked, incredulous.

"Friday," the commander said.

"This Friday?" Mark gasped.

He couldn't believe it. No one had contacted him, an oversight for which the battalion commander hastily apologized. In the hustle and bustle to get ready on an expedited timeline, he explained, the unit had simply forgotten to contact its newest member. But there was also another bit of news. Instead of running badass, on-the-ground operations, the unit would be providing logistical support in Baghdad's heavily-fortified Green Zone. And instead of acting as the battalion's aviation officer, a position that would have given Mark the authority to call in all sorts of air support for the soldiers on the ground and maybe even the opportunity to see some action himself, he'd be supervising soldiers whose sole responsibility was to check people's IDs.

"Sir, if this is sitting at a desk for twelve hours, then I'm not your guy."

Mark couldn't believe the words were coming out of his mouth, and with such anger and authority. Part of him still thought such a statement was tantamount to the worst kind of perfidy. He had been ready to redeploy. He had girded himself for what he had accepted was an inevitability. He was ready for war and had again pledged his fidelity. But not for this. Not hanging out for a year performing the menial task of checking diplomats' identification cards. He couldn't stand a desk job in the civilian world. Why would he do one in the military? Not for a year. Not when his father was ailing. And certainly not if he had to pack up and be ready in three days.

His new commander was visibly disappointed, but also sympathetic. It was Mark's choice, had been all along. There was no changing his mind.

Driving home, Mark was a free man, a civilian, who was for the first time in months truly home, able to live the rest of his life, or at least the next few years, without the worry of war. He could commit to his new girlfriend, fix up his house, scout for new properties, finally make that million. Just like that, he had his life back. All of which was good—great, even. He should be feeling relief, the great burden being lifted, allowing at last the decompression.

Then why as he drove home didn't he feel the tightly wound knot in his stomach begin to relax, or feel relieved in the slightest, or any of the things he suspected he should have been feeling? Why instead did he feel as if he were falling through the earth?

15

Ray and Diane

Seeing Suffering

To everyone else at the Savannah airport it must have seemed a touching scene: the uniformed veteran stepping off the plane and being greeted by his wife and newborn son. The son had been born while the soldier was at war. The son the soldier had not, until this very moment, laid eyes on.

Ray Johnson held his baby boy for the first time, a five-month-old bundle in his arms. He would have liked to swoop up his young wife and given her a long, passionate kiss, like the sailor and the nurse in that Times Square photograph celebrating the end of World War II. But his wife was cold, distant. And Ray could tell immediately there would be no saving their marriage.

They had wed impulsively in the weeks before he left for Vietnam in January 1969. He was a young soldier, fresh out of flight school, convinced at twenty-one he probably wouldn't survive to see twenty-two. She was just nineteen, the petite and popular cheerleader, just out of high school. They met on a blind date, while Ray was in flight school, and married a few months later in a small ceremony and honeymooned in San Francisco amid the Haight-Ashbury hippies, who were burning their draft cards on the street and demanding an end to the war Ray was about to enter.

The Dear John letter arrived halfway through the tour. It was cold and sparse, and she urged him not to tell her parents that she was leaving him less than a year into their marriage because he might get killed and then they would never have to know. But Ray was in the middle of a war and needed something to help him survive. So he held on to the hope of his marriage like a talisman and convinced himself he could save it. He just needed to get home, that was all. Now Ray was back in Savannah, Georgia, holding his baby boy. He smiled at his young bride, but she averted her gaze. Jody, he suspected, had visited her while he was away.

"You can stay the night," she told him when they arrived at her apartment. "But tomorrow, you have to go." Ray kissed his baby boy good night and slept in the guest room, wishing he were back in Vietnam.

Unlike so many of his fellow vets, Ray was never spat on, never called a baby killer, never faced any profanity-laced derision for wearing the uniform. Savannah was home to a large military population, insulated from the protests and violence, and Ray hung with the crew-cut crowd that populated Hunter Army Airfield and talked about stopping the communists. His friends were soldiers and vets and pilots, people who knew what combat was like. People to whom Ray didn't have to explain himself. People who understood there was a certain safety to battle.

In other places, from the Lincoln Memorial to college campuses, and city after tumultuous city, the rest of the country was rallying against the war. MLK and RFK had been shot dead. The police were in the streets. Cities were burning. Nixon was president.

But Ray wanted no part of any of it. He was a young, and perhaps foolish, veteran home from a war he hadn't really left and was eager to return to despite the fact that he had barely survived the first time. Truth was, he was not ready to be a husband or a father. He was a soldier who thought the war could still be won. It had to. Too many people had died to give up now.

Newly divorced, he volunteered to go back, despite having a newborn. But his request was denied. With hundreds of hours of combat time under his belt, he had more combat experience than many flight instructors. And the army needed him to use his experience to train other young pilots to fly in Vietnam.

He would get there. Back to the safety of battle. Only it wouldn't be in Vietnam.

Diane arrived at the airport with a bouquet of red and white roses. At the ticket counter, she flashed her steely-eyed military ID and said with newfound aplomb that her husband was coming home from Iraq today and she wanted to greet him at the gate—not back behind the security checkpoint where everyone else had to wait. She was determined to be the first person Ray saw when he stepped off that plane.

Ray had told her that if she said she was a military spouse she'd be able to come through the security checkpoint. But Diane wasn't so sure she'd be allowed without a boarding pass, and so she girded herself for a fight. Before Iraq, she would have been too embarrassed even to ask. And if she were told that only ticketed passengers were allowed through the checkpoint, as she was sure she was about to hear now, she would have quietly nodded her head and retreated without so much as a meek "I understand."

But now she was different. Stronger and more assertive, yes. But with her transformation came a hardness she found disconcerting. She didn't want to come off as bossy or pushy. And above all she didn't want to be considered the dreaded B-word. The word so often used to describe a woman who always gets her way, a word she never would have uttered herself, not even under her breath. Since Ray had gone, Diane had changed for sure, but she hadn't changed that much, had she? She didn't think so, but she had learned this: Sometimes you had to stand up for yourself, maybe even assert yourself over others, and perhaps others would think you were mean, or pushy, or worse. But so be it. Sometimes a woman just had to look out for number one.

Toward the end of Ray's tour even the Mercedes he had bought her seemed to be trying to convey this message. The car was a beauty, sleek and gorgeous with 189 horsepower. But what Diane liked best about it was that it always made her feel safe. The car was as solid as a tank, with doors of steel that kept the outside world at bay and wide wheels that held the road. With Ray gone, the car's protection took on an even greater resonance. But then came word: The airbags were dangerous to smaller drivers like her and were being recalled, and in an instant her sense of security had been deflated. The irony was unmistakable: Not even Ray's protective present could keep her safe while he was away. Maybe nothing could. No matter how secure she felt, it was, she now knew, an illusion. The device designed to protect her instead could have done just the opposite.

Diane immediately made an appointment with the dealership to have the airbags replaced and took a day off from work to bring the car in. But when she arrived, she was told they were out of airbags.

"Come back tomorrow," the guy at the dealership said.

"No, you don't understand," she pressed. "I made a reservation to have the airbags replaced."

"What do you want me to tell you?" the guy asked. "We don't have any."

He was condescending, misogynistic. Shooing her away. A tactic he no doubt had used successfully before with others, which was perhaps why he thought he could get away with it now. Normally, he would have. In her past life, Diane would have retreated home and maybe even thanked him for his time. But not now.

"This isn't acceptable. I need to talk to someone else," she said politely but firmly, strong enough to show that she was not leaving until someone helped her.

The service manager eventually came out and told her the same thing, and with the same don't-bother-me-lady attitude: We don't have any airbags. You'll have to come back tomorrow. But Diane wasn't having any of it. "If you don't have any in stock," she said pointedly, "why do you take reservations from people to replace them?"

"Well," the manager said, "the girls who take the reservations don't know what we have in stock."

"The 'girls'?" Now Diane was mad.

"If I make another appointment, then am I guaranteed the airbags will be here?" she asked.

"Uh, well, no," he stammered.

"So maybe you can call around to other dealerships and find me my airbags."

If her logic didn't give her the upper hand, her tone, obstinate and tough, made it clear she was determined to bend the situation to her satisfaction. A moment ago he was treating her like one of his "girls," and now she was treating him like a little boy. He obeyed and made the calls. She even detected a touch of contrition when he reported back that no other dealer had airbags.

"Well, maybe I can leave my car here and take a free loaner until you get some in," she suggested.

The service manager had a better idea. "Would you like us to come to you when we get the part?"

"That would be just fine," Diane said, wondering why he hadn't suggested it two hours ago.

A couple of weeks later the mechanics showed up at her office and replaced the airbags in the parking lot. It didn't take more than ten minutes.

The ticket agent at the airport told Diane she could go right through security, no problem, which came as a relief. She wasn't in the mood for a fight and didn't want anything to spoil the moment. Ray would be home any minute.

She'd dressed carefully that morning: a red leather coat and a black turtleneck, her hair primped, her makeup just right. She wanted to look exactly like the woman she was when her husband had left. Ray, wearing his tan flight suit, walked off the plane, and Diane squealed. She buried herself in his arms, hoping her mascara wouldn't smudge. People were staring. But she didn't notice. Ray was home.

Outside the gate area, on the other side of the security checkpoint Diane was allowed to pass, Ray's colleagues from the Maryland State Police were waiting.

"It's good to be home, I'll tell you," Ray said, shaking hands with a trooper friend.

With Diane at his side, he was all smiles, a healthy, if graying, fifty-nine-year-old veteran of two wars.

A couple of days later the CNN crew came to interview him as a follow-up to the piece they had done before he went to Iraq. "After a year in Iraq, back home safe, what does this fifty-nine-year-old grandfather take away from Iraq?" the reporter intoned, as the camera turned to Ray sitting in his dining room.

"The best thing that I took away from Iraq," he began confidently as if the answer would just come to him. But he was clearly stumped, and for a split second he looked puzzled, as if he were searching his mind for an answer, any answer. But he could come up with nothing, and his face turned from puzzlement to sadness.

"I don't know if I can say that there's been anything good out of this tour," he continued. "I see a lot of suffering."

It wasn't clear whose suffering he was referring to. The Iraqis'? U.S. service members'? Perhaps all of the above. The answer, like the question, was open-ended.

Within an hour of their arriving home, the doorbell rang with the first of the deluge of well-wishers welcoming Ray back. Then the phone started ringing, and for the next few days it didn't seem to stop. Ray was, of course, flattered. The attention was wonderful, and the emotions were sincere. But coming so shortly after walking into his front door, it was all a little much. He felt a little like a prop. The lone war hero. And in between visits he confided to Diane, "I just want to get away with you."

She had hoped he'd feel this way because that's what she wanted, too. She was taken slightly aback by all the friends Ray had and humbled by the way they were welcoming him home, but she didn't want to have to share him yet. Anticipating his arrival, she had booked a little vacation for a week or so after his return.

"Pack your things," she told him. "We're getting out of here for a little while. Just you and me."

"Where?" he inquired.

She wouldn't say. As they drove south from Maryland, into Virginia, then down Interstate 95 into North Carolina, he badgered her, "Where are we going? Savannah? Miami?" But no matter how hard he pressed, she wouldn't relent. She stayed strong. Unusually strong. Since when is she this good at keeping secrets? he wondered.

She was bringing him back to the past. The year-plus absence had made her long not just for the time they had missed together but for something more. She wanted to go back to the beginning, to the place where they were married. And from that distant vantage point she wanted to look forward to the present, to where they were now, as husband and wife, and as individuals. Before they moved on with the rest of their lives, she needed to take measure of how far they'd come and maybe recapture a glimpse of their former selves, if only for a moment.

Diane, for one, knew that the thirty-three-year-old bride who'd married Ray that December day would barely recognize the fifty-year-old woman she had become. Perhaps that was normal. Who, looking at themselves from a distance of seventeen years, would believe their eyes? But at no point along the line had Diane changed more than in the past year. The sudden transformation, she now suspected, was so deep and profound it was tantamount to her own private metamorphosis, and it would be some time before she knew its full extent and what it meant for her—and her marriage.

The inn was just as they remembered it. They took a horse-drawn carriage to the mansion where they'd had their reception, and it, too, looked unchanged. They were married on a December night, not unlike the one they were now enjoying. After all the tumult in the past year, it reassured Diane to know that this place had remained just as she pictured it in her memory. It felt good to know that some things remained steadfast and unaltered, even if she didn't.

The night was freezing. Ray and Diane cuddled under a heavy blanket like newlyweds. Diane pulled the blanket up to her chin, feeling safe and protected for the first time since Ray had gone.

Ray was being obstinate. He didn't want a welcome home party. He didn't want anyone making a fuss on his account. But Diane quickly put him in his place. This isn't about you, she lectured. This is so that everyone else can welcome you home.

The tone was unfamiliar, but Ray understood immediately that it was impervious to argument.

There must have been almost two hundred people crammed into their house. Diane had ordered party trays of seafood and had made dips and appetizers, and she told people to show up as if it were an open house. Diane was stressed with all the guests in her house and making sure there was enough food and drink. And then suddenly she heard one of Ray's friends say something about how Ray had volunteered for Iraq. She stopped what she was doing and shot Ray a look. This was the second time she'd heard one of Ray's friends extol his virtue for volunteering. The first was a few weeks earlier when she took Ray to visit his old colleagues at the state police, and one of them said he had nothing to complain about. After all, he had volunteered for Iraq. Diane was incredulous and had confronted him, saying "You had a choice about going to Iraq?" Ray responded that the guy didn't know what he was talking about. He hadn't volunteered, he assured her. But now here was someone else saying the same thing. How could everyone know about this but me? Diane thought. It was humiliating. Had he lied to her about being forced by the army to go to Iraq? Could he have stayed home if he had wanted? She couldn't confront him now, not with a house full of guests. But she was going to get to the bottom of this.

After the party was over and everyone had gone, and she was finally given a moment to think, she wondered what the old Diane would have done. Broken down in tears. That much was definite. But would her former self have confronted Ray? Or raised her voice? Would she have told him how hard her year had been, or the vacuum his absence had created? Would she have brought up the hornets, the flooded basement, the bad wiring that turned the basement into a fire hazard? Or told him about how when she hit the bottom, she thought she was losing her mind?

But, really, what did it matter what the old Diane would have done? That person was gone now, and she had a decision to make. She was furious and part of her wanted to stay that way, make him grovel for forgiveness. This, she knew, was a tactic her old self never would have contemplated, let alone carried out. But there was a certain appeal to letting her anger fester, to unleashing the tension to start a fight that was perhaps long in coming. To what end, though? For how long would she allow this to drag on? Long enough to threaten their marriage? No probably not. But she did let him know just how difficult her year had been. And she let him know that if, at the height of her troubles, she had learned he had gone to Iraq by choice instead of under orders as he let her believe, it was entirely possible she would have left him.

But that was then. The truth was she loved him dearly. That was certain and unchanged, confirmed in absolute terms the moment she saw him stepping off the plane and reinforced countless times since then. She would stand by him and support him without condition, despite the fact that he had not been entirely truthful with her. Those were the bonds of their relationship, the covenant of her marriage, which she did not take lightly. She let him know that, too. But he was now on notice, if implicitly, that their relationship was different. She was different. And she wasn't going to take any more guff—not from the Mercedes dealer, not from her husband, not from anyone. Things had changed. If he couldn't live with that, well, then that was his problem.

In the months ahead, the new Diane would assert herself in all sorts of little ways that would often take Ray by surprise and make it clear that somewhere along the line the power in their relationship had shifted, and not in his favor. But if he protested, which was rare, because the shift was real and he knew not subject to negotiation, her answer came as quick and as encompassing as buckshot: "You created this monster," she'd say.

It was more accusation than apology, though it contained a little of both. The monster that Ray or, more specifically, Ray's absence had supposedly created wasn't really a monster at all, of course, just a stronger, more independent version of his wife, even though she continued to fear that people might, on occasion, get the wrong impression. In fact he kind of liked her newfound independence, even if it meant he was left to fend for himself with increasing frequency.

He'd run enough gauntlets to recognize that real growth comes from trial and experience, even from fear. There was a modicum of truth in the adage that whatever doesn't kill you, . . . well, probably not the best idea to repeat that to Diane now, not after what she'd been through.

He was learning already.

The blow of discovering Ray's secret was softened immensely by the fact that it was born of good intentions, though perhaps not toward her. Diane admired her husband's patriotism, even though she thought the country was way off course in Iraq. It was an opinion he shared, though sometimes she had to remind herself of that. The fact that Ray had gone off to fight a war he did not wholeheartedly believe in was, to her, an admirably selfless act that made her proud. She felt that admiration rising as he tried to explain why exactly he had volunteered, even though he kept insisting that he didn't "volunteer."

What he did, he said, was tell his commanders that should a unit somewhere, sometime need an extra body, even if that body was not quite as nimble as it once was, that fit his qualifications, he'd be willing to go. (That sounded to Diane like the precise definition of volunteering, but there was no point in arguing semantics now.) Because of his age and rank, he'd been able to get out of previous deployments. When his home National Guard unit in Maryland was deployed, for instance, Ray did not go with it, which made him feel guilty. Imagine training month in month out with a band of soldiers, and then when the call finally comes, you stay behind. Maybe that was the right thing to do for his marriage and civilian job, not to mention his personal safety. Lord knows, it would have been easier just to stay put. But just because it was easy didn't make it right. After a while it ate at him. He was a soldier. The country was at war. He had to go. That was the best he could explain it.

Fortunately for him, it was good enough for Diane.

It was not as if he'd been hiding an affair. He was going to war, which at his age must have been difficult, more so than she could imagine. He wasn't some green nineteen-year-old who knew nothing of war. Ray knew what he was getting into. He knew how awful war could be. And yet he went anyway, which meant he was either crazy or brave. Diane knew it was the latter. If that wasn't courage, she didn't know what was. Not that she had a clear sense from him about what either war was like. Her sense of his experience in Iraq was about as clear as her sense of what he'd been through in Vietnam, which was to say murky at best. When they talked on the phone while he was in Iraq, he steered clear of discussing the war. And now that he was home, he adhered to that policy rigorously. Whatever happened over there stayed neatly stored out of view, just like Vietnam, which of course led her to imagine something worse than the truth—in both cases. Though with Vietnam that would be near impossible; even she suspected that.

What little Ray did say of the war, he felt comfortable saying to anyone who would listen, including his interviewer at CNN, which was that, in his view, Iraq was another Vietnam. As one of the few who had served in both wars, he was well qualified to make the judgment. And it was a nice, tidy sound bite, perfect for TV news. But no matter how definitive or profound the statement was, it was also unclear. What precisely did he mean, Iraq was another Vietnam?

Maybe the answer lay at the end of the story, or the way it had ended for him. Maybe he meant American soldiers were once again coming home from a war that wasn't over and had no end in sight. Ray had now fought two wars but had never been in a victory parade, which was almost enough to make him wonder if those ticker tape–filled photographs from World War II were a fiction. In his lifetime, it seemed, the only people who'd had the honor of waltzing down Broadway under a cloud of confetti wore New York Yankee pinstripes, not army camouflage.

It wasn't the celebration of victory he longed for, though, as much as victory itself, and the closure it brought. The absolute finality. How nice it must have been for those World War II vets to come home knowing it was all over and done with. That the threat had been vanquished, peace had been secured, that they had won. And perhaps best of all: that they were returning to a country that had sacrificed greatly and could now share in the celebration. That was another thing. To have a parade you need people to cheer you on. Which wasn't a problem after World War II. Was it possible that the veterans of that war being dubbed the Greatest Generation had as much to do with the mood of the country they were coming home to as it did with their own valor? Because Ray had fought alongside some pretty damn heroic soldiers in Vietnam and then again in Iraq, and no one was calling them great.

Since Ray had come home, he and Diane had talked a lot about how she was the one who had changed during the deployment. But there was, Diane detected, something different about Ray, too, even if they didn't speak of it. He was, as he had promised before leaving, the same old Ray. But somewhere around the edges, there was an unmistakable hint of sadness. He had fought two wars, both deemed debacles by the majority of the American public, and, if truth be told, he didn't disagree. But he didn't spout off like those idiots on television, or the anti-war protesters. He didn't harp on it or complain, not once. Speaking ill of misguided leadership was to his old warrior ethos a form of treason. But deep down, Iraq bothered him. What were we doing there? What was the point?

As a good soldier, he could mask his emotions. Forty years in uniform had taught him that much. But his disappointment was there, lurking beneath the surface, if not on his face. Diane could sense it. And it was evident there on television during the CNN interview, if subtly.

"I see a lot of suffering," he had said.

Maybe he didn't mean it at the time, maybe he didn't even realize it, but the suffering, at least in part, was his.

16

Craig

The Two O'Clock Lull

"M r. Lewis," his students called him. "Mister Leewwwis," they would sometimes chirp in playful moments, teasing out his name like a piece of taffy. Craig couldn't remember the last time someone had addressed him that way. He'd been Lieutenant, or "L-T," or, to the enlisted soldiers, "Sir" for so long now it was hard to imagine being called anything else. He liked being called Sir. Had a nice ring to it. A single syllable, direct and precise, that conveyed respect, delineated authority, and evoked a perhaps antiquated etiquette that Craig found reassuring. He had grown up in a world of Sirs and Ma'ams, where the chain of command was clear and always respected. That often was not the case at Fluvanna, where sometimes he felt he was lucky to get "Mister." What a rowdy bunch they could be, difficult to keep focused on their assignments on the best of days. Flying into Baghdad could be horrifying, but nothing was quite as daunting as managing a classroom of twenty-five high school sophomores on a sunny spring day.

Craig was eager to get back to teaching, though nervous. Developing lesson plans for an entire fifty-minute special education class in virtually every subject—math, history, English—was no small task. It had taken him almost a full semester to get used to it. And now, after a two-year absence, he'd be starting from scratch. But of course that's not all that worried him. His boss, the school's principal, had not been pleased, to put it mildly, with the way Craig had left. The Guard had forced Craig to ship out to flight school much sooner than he had originally thought, and then deploy to Iraq. And after Craig gave his principal a mere three days' notice, he got the distinct feeling that he would have fired Craig if he could have. He couldn't, of course. Federal law prevented it. Reservists couldn't be fired simply because they were shipped off to war. That same law mandated that the school hold his position for him until he got back from Iraq. But while his job was guaranteed, that didn't mean he'd be welcome back.

Before he faced all that, though, he had to first finish up the deployment. At Fort Dix, where the 2-224th went through the final motions before being released for good, there was much to be done, especially for the young officers like Craig who had to sit through meeting after meeting required to move 350 soldiers, 30 Black Hawks, and all their equipment for the last leg home. Then, there was the issue of turnover. After the deployment, many soldiers would be getting out of the military; others would be promoted and transferred to different units. A new crop of recruits would come in.

"Some of y'all are going to get company commands," the battalion commander told the younger officers. But Craig wasn't paying attention. He was only a lieutenant (company commanders usually held the rank of captain) and had joined the unit only six months into the deployment. There was no way he'd be given a company command, so he tuned out the details of a meeting that clearly would not involve him.

It didn't even occur to him that he might be given command when later that day, one of the higher-ranking soldiers passed him in the hallway and gave him a big smile. "Congratulations!" he said.

"About what?" Craig said.

"Oh, you don't know?"

"No."

"Well then, never mind."

It wasn't until that evening that the battalion commander came over to him in the officers club, put his arm around him, and told him he'd be taking over Delta Company.

Craig was dumbfounded. Delta Company didn't just have more than seventy soldiers who would be under his direct command, it was the battalion's maintenance company, which meant it had a budget of millions of dollars that Craig suddenly was going to have to manage. It was a huge promotion that left him humbled and grateful and daunted all at the same time. The commander asked if he felt up to it, and Craig said he did. If he could manage flying Black Hawks in Iraq fresh out of flight school, he could handle this. With a tour of combat under his belt, and now a company command, he couldn't imagine his military career going any better. He just hoped things in the civilian world could keep pace.

Winter turned to spring, and by May Craig decided he'd put off going to see the principal long enough. He was nervous about it, of course. But he also wasn't ready to start work right away. He'd given such short notice that he was leaving and now he had waited almost three months to inquire about getting his job back. Not that he'd ask to start right away. It didn't seem fair to make the school find a position for him this late in the year. He'd start the following fall.

He'd been gone so long the secretary gave him a quizzical "Can I help you?" look when he walked into the front office. Then she recognized him. "You're back!"

"I am," he said. Then, referring to the principal, he asked, "Is he available?"

"Let me check."

Craig shuffled his feet nervously. The principal of Fluvanna High was a gruff, no-nonsense man who'd spent a long career as a public school administrator and teacher. On his desk sat a prop, an urn positioned so that the troublemakers who got sent to his office had a clear view of its thick, bold lettering: "Ashes of Problem Students."

Welcoming Craig into his office, the principal was warm but businesslike. And as Craig explained his circumstances—"I'm now home and would like to teach again"—he listened intently but with a professional detachment, his face devoid of emotion. Craig had been teaching special education but would prefer something in phys ed.

"I'd love to help you," the principal said. "But I don't have any openings." He was surprised to see Craig, who he hadn't heard from in so long and assumed had moved on. If Craig was serious about coming back, why hadn't he been better about staying in touch?

One of the physical education teachers might retire after this year, he offered, and that would create a slot. "I'll keep an eye out," he said. "But I can't promise anything. Plus, you've been gone more than a year, so the school isn't obligated to take you back."

For a split second, Craig's brow started to form a menacing crinkle, and he took a deep breath as if preparing to mount a protest. *I just spent a year getting shot at in Iraq, and you're not even going to hold my job for me?* But whatever confrontational spirit was rising within was quickly stifled, and Craig softened his gray eyes into a get-along smile. Best, he decided, to play it cool, to see if this can't be resolved amicably. His deployment had already caused enough problems.

"If anything does come open," he said, "please let me know."

The principal repeated the promise that he'd do what he could. As they shook hands, Craig told himself that it was only May; there was still plenty of time before the school year started again in August. Plus, he felt the law was on his side, should it come to that. He ran his hand along his crew cut, still at army standard, and thanked the principal for his time.

As he walked out into the hallway, one of his former students spotted him and came running down the hall.

"Mr. Leewwwis!" she said. "Mr. Leewwwis! You're back!"

Yes, he was back. For as long as he'd been gone, there was still so much familiar about this place. He remembered this end-of-school rhythm—final exams, Friday night baseball games, then prom and graduation, all of which he could see unfolding again in such reassuring repetition, as if nothing had changed.

His student disappeared to her next class, and Craig, now nothing more than a visitor, walked away in the afternoon sun, wondering what to do next.

The bright side was that he'd be able to look for something else now. Craig enjoyed teaching, but after flying Black Hawks in Iraq and now with his new company command, he felt ready for something a little more consequential. And if he couldn't find anything else, well, as a last resort he could make the school take him back. But it would work out. He was sure of it. He was an officer in that massive corporation known as the U.S. Army. He had combat experience, and a college degree. Plus, the government trusted him to fly $6 million helicopters.

With his experience overseeing dozens of soldiers and now, as a company commander, millions of dollars of equipment, he figured he'd make a great manager in the private sector. He updated his résumé, adding his promotion to company commander, and sent it out, first to large corporations—Sears, Lowe's, Wal-Mart—that always seemed to be hiring and sometimes talked up their efforts to recruit veterans, then to defense contractors, which is where he really wanted to work. It was only a matter of time before he'd be scooped up, he thought with the confidence of someone whose performance reviews in the Guard were always glowing.

"LT Lewis is one of the most talented leaders I ever had the pleasure to work with," read one. ". . . His potential for promotion and future service is unlimited."

"LT Lewis served with such exceptional skill and maturity he was selected above several more senior officers for company command," read another. ". . . He is intelligent, well studied, patient and demanding."

Once he landed a new job, he wouldn't have to worry about whether Fluvanna High would take him back or not. Thanks, he'd say when the school finally came to its senses and offered him his job back. But no thanks. Craig was so confident about his prospects that he went ahead and bought a house in the Charlottesville hills.

But then, nothing. Days passed, then weeks, and there were no callbacks inviting him in for an interview, not even a single pro forma e-mail saying, "Thanks for applying, we'll get back to you shortly." It was as if his résumé had disappeared into the maw of a big corporate black hole. It was summer, a slow time for business, he told himself. Plus, he had plenty of money saved up and would be fine for a while. He just needed to apply himself, use his con-nections, scatter a few more résumés out there. Perhaps most of all: Stay positive. Think about how he could take the extra time to relax and have a real summer. He'd been through a lot, and now he could use the time off.

The problem was, that was getting old quickly. He wasn't one to lie around, and after living the supercharged life of a combat heli-copter pilot he found it difficult, and demoralizing, to sit around watching TV all day. Don't take it personally, he told himself. But it was hard not to. This was rejection of the worst kind—where they don't even bother to tell you no. He'd rather someone look him in the face and say, You're not for us. But as day after day passed without so much as an acknowledgment, his calls and e-mails unreturned, it was as if he didn't exist or, worse, didn't mat-ter. That was what stung most of all. Especially after Iraq, where so many people had depended on him. He was part of an interlinking chain, each part crucial to the success of the whole, which made him feel useful. Vital even. And he was. People's lives depended on him, his ability to fly right, to perform under some of the most intense pressure a person could imagine. More pressure, he was sure, than he'd ever be under in the civilian world. Which was why he didn't understand why no one was calling him back. He was biased, of course, but if he were a millionaire starting a company, he'd want a whole lot of military guys just like him. And he vowed that if he ever did make it big, he'd cut veterans a break.

Stay positive, he told himself, even though doing so was becoming increasingly difficult. If it wasn't him, then maybe it was this town. Charlottesville was an oasis nestled in the verdant hills of central Virginia, home to Thomas Jefferson's Monticello and the University of Virginia. But Craig had to face facts: It wasn't the economic engine he had hoped it would be. He would have liked nothing better than to stay put in the area where he'd grown up, find a good job, meet a nice girl, and raise kids. But maybe that just was not possible. Maybe he had to start looking farther afield, to suburban D.C., to the tech corridor that had sprouted up in northern Virginia, fueled by the Pentagon's seemingly bottomless purse. And maybe he needed to broaden his search from his dream job in the defense industry to, well, everything else. So he tried medical sales, management positions for health-care companies, even the post office, which wasn't his first choice, but he figured the federal government would be amenable to hiring vets. He tried jobs whose titles he didn't fully understand: "media sales consultant" and "customer operations manager." He had accounts on monster.com and hotjobs.com. He tried nonprofits like a hireahero.org, dedicated to helping veterans like him.

More applications. More résumés. More networking. Still nothing.

It was humiliating, and it made him want to give up. But even if he could have slept late and lounged around all day in his pajamas, he made himself get up, shower, and get dressed. His roommate would go off to work, and Craig would go to his "job": scouring the Internet for employment. The days dragged on, repetitious and boring. Nine o'clock would crawl to ten. SportsCenter would rerun on ESPN, and he'd putter along on the Internet, checking his e-mail to see if anyone had responded, while waiting for lunchtime. Was eleven too early to eat? By mid-afternoon, he was stuck. The "two o'clock lull," he called it.

By three, sick with cabin fever, he often escaped to the gym, where he'd work out for hours, because like a prisoner he had nothing else to do. And who were these people who could come to the gym in the middle of the day? Were they, like him, unemployed? What an ugly, awful word—*unemployed*—a close cousin of *destitute*, or *homeless*, or *food stamps*. He never thought it would apply to him, even if it didn't really. He still had the salary he made in the Guard for drilling one weekend a month. And he was also paid for the required time he put in flying in order to stay current. But he *felt* unemployed. He felt its stinging rejection, as it drained his bank account. He felt it watching his roommate going off to work, day after day, while he sat on the couch until the game shows came on. He felt it with friends out at a bar, hoping the cute girl flirting with him wouldn't ask the dreaded question: "So, what do you do?"

This wasn't how it was supposed to be. He was a twenty-eight-year-old Black Hawk pilot in his prime. They made movies about guys like him. He had the flight suit, the aviator glasses, the big watch. He could land his helicopter in hostile desert country in the dead of a pitch-black night, and that made him a stud. Didn't it? He wasn't sure anymore. This whole job thing had shaken his confidence. And it wasn't just the job, or lack thereof, that rattled him. It was that it didn't seem as if Iraq was a big deal to people. Not that he wanted a parade or a party in his honor. In fact, that was the last thing he wanted. But he'd been in *Iraq*. He'd been shot at, flown in to all those places you heard about on the news—Ramadi, Baghdad, Haditha Dam—and here at home people outside his immediate family treated his absence as if it had been an extended business trip and wondered when he was going to get serious with his life and find a job, as if he weren't trying.

The posting for a youth counselor on the Internet job board was not ideal. A few months ago he would've probably not even applied because the salary was only $35,000—just about what he had made teaching. And it was nowhere near the direction in which he wanted to be heading, which was hooking up with a defense contractor and being able to marry his military skills with his civilian career. But it was a job, and he was a shoo-in. Not only had he worked as a special education teacher—great preparation—but he had worked as a youth counselor in college. Which was an even more depressing sign that he was moving backward.

But by now it was summer, and Craig was getting desperate. He'd chewed through $10,000 of his savings, which was supposed to be the beginning of his nest egg, not some sort of emergency fund. But he needed work, if only to get out of the house. So he sent in his résumé and got a call a few days later asking him to come in for an interview, which he aced. He was sure of it. They were impressed with his experience and, he felt, with his composure and comportment. He was good with troubled kids. The job was his. He could feel it. Any day they'd call with an offer.

Only they didn't. One day passed, then another, and when Craig checked the Internet job board again he saw that they were still seeking candidates for the position he'd thought was his. How could he not have landed that job? He replayed the interview in his mind again and again looking for where he went wrong and could come to only one conclusion. During the interview, they came across the part of his résumé that detailed his service in the National Guard and Iraq. Then came the question: "What's the likelihood of your being deployed again?"

Craig tried to make it clear that it wouldn't be for several years; he'd just gotten back. But when they pressed, he had to admit that he could be called at any moment for a domestic emergency. That's what the Guard was all about.

At the time, he didn't think the answer had hurt him. Wasn't it a good thing to be dedicated to your country? His training and leadership could only help. If he was qualified to lead men in combat, he certainly could handle a bunch of troubled teenagers. But thinking back on it, he realized that was the moment the tone of the interview had changed. And it wasn't long after that that they were thanking him for coming in and saying they'd be in touch. Perhaps it was naive of him, but he didn't want to believe his Guard membership could be the reason why no one was hiring him.

He was proud of his service, and it showed. On his résumé he featured it prominently, thinking it could only make him a more attractive candidate. Under "Relevant Work Experience," he highlighted the fact that he was a company commander who was "responsible for training and preparing over 60 soldiers for future combat operations." And he also played up his wartime experience, wherein he "planned and participated in over 50 combat missions while deployed during Operation Iraqi Freedom."

But maybe that had been a mistake. Maybe serving in the Guard was a hindrance, not an asset—at least at a time when reservists were being called for two and three overseas tours. When he mentioned his theory to fellow soldiers, a few said they had run into similar problems. It was known as the "military service penalty" in some vet circles, and Craig was starting to believe it really existed.

Federal law required that employers, and even small companies, hold jobs for deploying reservists. Swept up in the wave of patriotism after 9/11, many sent their citizen-soldiers off to war with pats on their backs, flags waving. Many employers even made up the difference in pay. But as the wars slogged on, and soldiers were called to active duty again and again, the word *reservist* suddenly had a stigma attached to it. Craig could understand why. He had seen firsthand how difficult it had been for Fluvanna High to find someone to replace him at the last minute. The way he'd been treated, though wrong, he felt, was clearly a result of his sudden departure.

But the law that ensured reservists' jobs, though well intentioned, had backfired. Employers were by now painfully aware that if they hired a reservist, they might very well be without that person for long stretches of time. Refusing to hire someone because of their membership in the reserves was illegal too, of course. But difficult to prove. This much, however, was easy to understand: Who would want to hire a reservist if that person was going to be gone one out of every four or five years?

17

Miranda

The Pedicured, Door-Gunning Ivy League Veteran

S tanding at the lectern under the image of a sun with pursed lips peering through the clouds, the dean gave a welcome that could not have been more inviting. The more than 400 graduate students, many straight out of the country's best colleges, were assembled in the auditorium. They were, the dean proudly told them, among the nation's best, and the university had chosen them very carefully. More than 7,000 had applied to Brown's graduate programs; 463 had been accepted, a rate of 6.6 percent.

Surveying the other students, Miranda sank in her seat. She had been admitted and had even been awarded one of the university's prestigious scholarships. Still, she didn't feel that she belonged on such hallowed academic ground. By now, Labor Day weekend of 2007, she'd been out of Iraq for six months. But still she felt more kinship with the soldiers and grunts than she did with the bookish students assembled around her.

In her enthusiastic welcome speech, the dean, a bespectacled, hippie-ish professor of anthropology, told the students, "The step you are taking is a courageous one." It doesn't matter if you're from another country, what religion you believe in, what race you are, whether you're gay, straight, or transgender, she continued. Everyone was welcome at Brown.

Veterans, Miranda thought. What about veterans? The only minority status you earn. Maybe she was being overly sensitive. Just give the place a chance, her parents had counseled. But as they had been during her visit to Brown the previous spring, her antennae were up. And even though she had decided to study here, she was still unsure that she had made the right decision. Of all the people seated in the auditorium, she had to be the only one who had fought in Iraq.

The first semester's tuition had already come due, and Miranda was in no position to pay it. The Guard had not released her from duty so that she could sign up with the Army Reserve Civil Affairs battalion and collect on her lucrative bonus. She had pestered and prodded, but the big army bureaucracy sat on her request to transfer from one branch of the army to another for so long that she missed out on the Civil Affairs training over the summer, which meant that if the Guard ever did process the paperwork, she would have to complete it next summer. Meantime, with her signing bonus on hold, she was forced to go deeper into debt than she had planned. Thankfully, she had landed a coveted spot in campus housing where rent was only $300 a month. Her car insurance would be $150 a month, then there was the $90 car payment, $50 for her phone and Internet, and a self-imposed limit of $200 a month for groceries and $100 for incidentals. If she scrimped, she could get by. But she was mad at the army for holding up her transfer, and it showed. In an unsuccessful attempt to speed up the process over the summer, she'd dashed off a heated letter that said if she wasn't soon released, "my being able to attend graduate school is in jeopardy." She continued, "I have done everything that the army has asked me to do. I have balanced the demands of work, school, and National Guard commitments. I graduated a year late and gave up my senior year of college to go to Iraq. I gave up opportunities to study abroad and possible internships so that I could train with my unit at drills and annual trainings. I have put my family through hell as they have tried to support me through college, deployment, and helping me get back on my feet after the deployment. I have never regretted this decision. I did it because I believe in the mission of the United States Army."

And now she wanted something in return. It's not as if she were asking to leave the Guard in order to get out of the military. She was asking to leave the Guard before her contract was up so that she could join the Army Reserve.

Making close friends at Brown was going to be even more difficult than Miranda had imagined. Perhaps she exacerbated the problem by a new unwillingness to hide her military persona as she had at William and Mary, where she hardly ever talked about the Guard and was very rarely seen wearing her uniform on campus. But for some reason she was much more willing to come out of the closet at Brown. Perhaps because she was older, more mature, more comfortable with herself. The war definitely had had that effect on her. But there was also a part of her that felt she had a duty to be a reminder of the war on a campus where there was scant evidence of its existence.

At the orientation where she met the other students in her graduate program, she included the National Guard and Iraq in her Hello-my-name-is-Miranda introductory bio along with her interest in women's history and collecting historical artifacts. Afterward, one of her fellow students came up to her and said she had never met anyone in the military and that Miranda certainly didn't seem like a soldier. If you've never met anyone in the military, then how do you know what one seems like? Miranda wanted to say—but caught herself. She was willing to discuss her service in a way she never had before, but that didn't mean she was ready for confrontation. Instead she told her fellow student that she probably had in fact met someone in the military before but just didn't know it.

"When we're out of uniform, we usually look like everyone else," she said.

Which led to a discussion about who serves in the army—rich or poor, rural or urban—and why, and Miranda found herself trying to debunk the myth that all soldiers come from the lower classes, though a great deal do. "It's more representative of society than you'd think," she explained.

Then, of course, came the inevitable: "Now that you're back, do you support the war?"

It was, Miranda suspected, a well-intentioned if not entirely sincere inquiry, loaded with self-interest. If Miranda said she supported the war, her answer would be discounted as biased and misguided. What else was a vet just back from Iraq supposed to say? That she'd wasted the last year and a half of her life fighting for a mistake? But if she said she did not support the war, then that would only confirm the notion that the war was an atrocity—a belief so obviously held by the woman asking her. That answer would allow the woman to say for who knows how long, "Well, I know this Iraq vet, and even she says the war was a mistake." Miranda was not about to justify anyone else's thoughts on the war, especially those of someone who had not been there. But she wasn't going to lie, either

The truth was that Miranda didn't believe in the war. Not for a second. Not before the war, or during, or after. Which is what she said. But it wasn't that simple. It didn't matter what she thought, which was perhaps hard for someone who had never even contemplated joining the military to understand. She was a soldier, in a democracy, who just happened to believe in her country and in the need for a military and in the notion that there are things in life worth fighting for. Soldiers aren't the ones who decide what those are; they're the ones who do the fighting, even if that means fighting for something they don't wholeheartedly believe in. Which, of course, kind of sucks. But patriotism is believing in your country, even if its government occasionally falters. Sometimes it's believing in your country despite its government. And really, isn't that the important thing? Isn't that worth fighting for? Even when you can conveniently forget about the war and the military and go about your merry way. But know this: Because this country has a healthy stable of volunteers, because there are people fighting for you and in your place, you can go off to fancy colleges and take interesting classes and have these theoretical conversations without any worry of being drafted.

Only in her daydreams and in her journal would Miranda offer such a bombastic "You can't handle the truth" response, which would in the fantasy leave people in awe of and grateful for her service. In reality, her answer was much more diplomatic, well within the confines of civilian politesse. It including the part about service to country and sacrifice but left out all the hoorah, steely-eyed, Jack Nicholson dramatics. But even her toned-down response seemed to go too far. The blank expression of her questioner told her that much.

Quick, Miranda chastised herself, change the subject.

So, she tried as normally as possible, "Where are you from?"

As someone who collapsed all sorts of stereotypes—How many lithe, blond, pink-toe-nailed Ivy League door gunners were there? How many young women listed both *Full Metal Jacket* and *Legally Blonde* among their favorite movies on their Facebook page?— Miranda was careful not to judge people, or institutions, too quickly. And she was not about to accept the caricature of Brown as a radical left-wing campus until she had spent some time there and found out for herself. She was heartened to find that there was, as she had suspected, a range of thought and ideals, as there should be on a college campus. There was, of course, a left-wing newspaper, but there was also a right-leaning student magazine that had espoused the idea of bringing ROTC back to campus. And though virtually none of her classmates had military experience, Miranda was relieved to learn that one of the professors in her department was a Vietnam vet.

Despite the school's disconnect from the wars the country was currently fighting, there was ample evidence of Brown's long-standing ties to combat. Soldiers Arch, a grand monument on the edge of campus, was dedicated to the Brown alumni who had died in World War I. "They gave their merry youth away for country and for God," the inscription read. Across campus on University Hall was a plaque for General Nathan Greene, who had fought in the Revolution. The same building bore another plaque, dated 1897, that noted Brown's commitment to that war: "For six years, all academic exercises in this university were suspended. Faculty, students and graduates, almost to a man, were engaged in the service of their country. May all who read this inscription be stimulated by their example to respond as loyally to their country's call."

It ended with "Dulce et decorum est pro patria mori." (It is sweet and fitting to die for one's country.)

Still, there was ample truth to Brown's stereotype as a liberal haven, and Miranda found herself colliding with it again and again. More pragmatist than conservative, her "otherness," as she called it, was pronounced against the backdrop of the lefty campus, and though she liked to think she was as progressive as the next person, Brown made her feel even more like "a 60 year old man in a 24 year old body," as she wrote in her journal. Particularly in class, where, as she wrote, "I've come to the realization in my first few weeks at Brown that maybe I don't entirely fit in. This is not your classic sense of not fitting, in that I don't seem to have trouble finding people to hang out with, and academically I don't seem to have a problem keeping up. It's actually kind of a new thing for me.

(1) I actually have opinions on what people are talking about, and (2) no one else seems to agree with them."

A few weeks into the school year, Miranda found herself dissenting during a discussion in one of her classes. The professor had asked what had seemed a straightforward question but it launched a heated controversy in the classroom: Should a museum doing an exhibit on wildlife accept donated animal skins from hunters? To Miranda, the answer was a simple yes. If museums accept donated works of art, why not accept a hide? But she was clearly in the minority.

"The debate in the classroom seemed to focus on how hunting was wrong, and accepting the donations encouraged it," she wrote in her journal afterward. "I was the one idiot who raised her hand suggested that hunting could be pretty badass, it's not illegal, and thousands of people love it and would love to go to a hunting museum and see things like taxidermied animals. . . . Generally, I said that it wasn't our job to put value judgments on killing animals, our job is to find the best way to present dead animals to the public so that they can grow and learn. And in a room full of vegans, I thought they were going to eat ME."

In another one of her classes on cemeteries and burial grounds, the professor was talking about the importance of wills as historical artifacts, and then asked if anyone in the class had a will. Miranda was the only one who raised her hand.

"And what prompted you to prepare a will?" the professor asked.

Miranda could have skirted the question—and in her previous life probably would have—but instead she answered directly. "I'm in the National Guard and was deployed to Iraq," she said. "The army requires everyone to have a will before shipping out."

She anticipated the sudden, awkward silence coming, as if everyone's breath had been simultaneously sucked from the room. She had been back long enough to know that this mix of confusion and incredulity was the predictable reaction. She knew her story would generate blinky-eyed expressions in others, just as it had when she had told her family about the dead soldier sticking out of the body bag. And she knew the best way to wipe the bewilderment from their faces was by making them laugh.

When she had gone to fill out her will, she told the class, the army lawyer had asked if she wanted to be buried or cremated. "Cremated," she had responded. "I don't want a big, expensive funeral. And I'd like the ashes put in an Etch A Sketch, where they could provide entertainment for others."

Any residual tension dissolved into laughter.

There had to be other vets on campus, or at least people who had served in the military in some capacity. At times, she felt as alone as she had at the airport coming home for graduation, halfway through her tour. All the soldiers she had been traveling with went their separate ways, leaving her the lone soldier in a sea of civilians. Miranda went to the registrar's office asking how many other students were using the GI Bill to pay tuition. "Oh, there are three or four of you," the secretary said. But near the end of her first semester, Miranda had met just one—a former soldier who had served his tour in Iraq, gotten out, and made it abundantly clear he did not want to talk about the war.

The 2-224th was still gathering one weekend a month for training that had become mini-reunions, despite the fact that just a few months after coming home there was so much turnover that about one-third of the faces were new. Miranda missed her old battalion, the people she had served with who had been like family to her for more than a year. After the war, she had been so preoccupied with getting home and figuring out what to do next, she hadn't given much thought to saying good-bye. It was weird to think that for a year and a half, she'd longed to get home and talk with someone, anyone, who was not in the military. But now she desperately wished she had just one friend who understood not only the military but also what she was going through now trying to get her intra-army transfer.

The Guard had finally agreed to let her transfer for the Army Reserve Civil Affairs unit. But the paperwork was screwed up and marred by bureaucratic glitches that left her hanging in limbo. Typical "hurry up and wait." A true SNAFU. Pure BOHICA. But who at Brown would know what BOHICA meant?

"This entire process has been frustrating," she wrote. "The worst part is that I don't seem to be able to talk to anyone about it. I think that I probably need someone in the army to talk to about it, but not my recruiter. I made the mistake of bringing this up with several classmates here. They were really trying to help out, but pretty clearly did not understand what I was trying to figure out. And it wasn't even that they didn't get the army and the convoluted forms, they really didn't seem to understand the army, why it exists, and why I'm in it. Everything they were saying was reverting back to not getting deployed. I tried to explain that getting deployed was kind of the point of being in the guard, at least to a certain extent. That I wasn't in the army because I just wanted college money, I was there because I felt like there were things in America worth fighting for. . . . It's been frightening and disheartening. It's not even so much about that they couldn't help me make this decision that was potentially important to me, it was that these very bright, educated people at some level had no clue what was going on. I want to be friends with them, I value their opinions, but we just cannot see eye to eye on this. I tell myself that the fact that I'm even talking about it could help. But I don't even know that. I think at some level I was hoping for a pat on the back or some recognition. That they would think it was great that I would graduate late so that I could do a job that I felt was a better fit. That was not going to happen. And I guess that is probably more common than I'd like to admit. I'm not in Virginia anymore. People aren't going to buy my gas for me just because I'm in uniform."

It wasn't until November, Veterans Day, that she met Brown's other vets, only it turns out they weren't vets, just a couple of guys who had somehow been able to serve without being shipped overseas. The school's ceremony, which Miranda heard of only at the last minute, was sparsely attended, the "strangest fake veterans' day ever," as she wrote in her journal. There were a handful of professors and a few other students, but mostly the small crowd was made up of community members. The color guard was most likely borrowed from nearby Providence College, which unlike Brown had an ROTC program. The ceremony was somber. A bagpiper played a dirge that reminded Miranda of the "phantom piper" in Iraq, always heard but never seen.

The students on campus largely ignored the ceremony en route to class, in laughing gaggles of twos and threes, to bright futures, where the strains of a bagpiper wouldn't evoke funereal memories. A few stopped to glimpse what was going on, but not many, just as day in, day out they passed through the gate commemorating the World War I vets, a war that could have been as distant as the one currently playing out on television screens. The two other former service members read aloud letters from Brown alumni who had served in World War I, which bothered Miranda for a couple of reasons. First, she was jealous that the school hadn't thought to ask her to participate. Miranda, unlike these two guys, had actually served in war. Second, why were they reading letters from World War I when there was a war going on right now?

After the ceremony, Miranda got to talking to a National Guard official who was on hand. He mentioned that he'd been trying to get ROTC reinstated on campus. Brown had abolished its program in the early 1970s in response to the Vietnam War, and there was little hope of its coming back because the military's prohibition on gays' serving openly through "Don't Ask, Don't Tell" violated the university's nondiscrimination policy. Students could participate in Providence College's ROTC program across town, but Brown wouldn't offer academic credit for it, and by 2007 there was but a single student who enrolled.

When Miranda said she was hoping to transfer to the Civil Affairs unit soon, the man's eyes lit up. You should hold your enlistment ceremony here in the middle of campus, he suggested. What better advertisement for the ROTC than a display of one of Brown's own with her right hand raised in the middle of campus, swearing to "support and defend the Constitution of the United States"? Miranda actually found herself considering the idea, for a moment anyway. She'd be used, she knew, as a recruiting prop. But the idea of her standing tall in her dress uniform, combat patch on her shoulder, Iraq service pin on her chest, her door gunner experience, her commitment to country and her sacrifice on display pleased her. She'd be able to get across what she'd been trying so hard to say in class with a single, wordless deed, no Etch-a-Sketch jokes needed.

It was a cold December day, and Miranda shivered as she stepped outside. But the dreary New England weather was not about to sour her mood. She was finally on her way to pick up the paperwork for her transfer to the Army Reserve Civil Affairs unit, a move that as her recruiter promised would allow her to collect as much as a $40,000 bonus. She was ready. Good to go. This was after all one of the reasons she'd decided to go to Brown and take on its otherwise prohibitively expensive tuition.

She marched into the recruiter's office, ready and willing. But as soon as he saw her, his face dropped.

"Things have changed," he said.

Instead of signing up as a new enlistment, he told her, she would first have to serve three years of inactive duty and then would be eligible for only a reenlistment bonus, which now stood at $15,000, but could in two years change.

Miranda was stunned into disbelief. It was not denial, though she had a well-developed sense of that particular emotion, but rejection. She flat-out refused to believe this could be happening. She needed that bonus money. The promise of it had sealed her decision to go to Brown, and she had too much riding on that cash to let it slip away without a fight.

"This can't be right," she said, trying not to sound alarmed. "There has to be someone we can call."

The recruiter shook his head. "I'm sorry."

"No, you don't understand, I'm well qualified for this position. I deserve it. I need it," she said, realizing that at some point she had stood up and was now looming over the recruiter. Miranda rarely lost her temper; the expression didn't really apply to her because when she got this furious she didn't lose anything, especially control, and she didn't get flustered. It was odd that someone so self-conscious would become more focused the angrier she got. Never was she quite as articulate as she was when she was furious.

She was talking fast. "You couldn't have brought this up six months ago? Before I made the decision to go to this really expensive school? Before I up-ended my life to move here?"

The recruiter sat there and took it, as if he had been expecting to get hammered and was riding it out until Miranda was finished. When she was done, he shrugged. There was nothing he could do but refer her to his boss, the head of the recruiting station. Miranda let him have it, too, even though he was an officer. "I can't believe this," she said. "You're really going to look at me and tell me this is the best you can do? That despite my degrees and everything I've put into my military career, you can't get around this? I can't believe it."

"I can't either," he said, sounding genuinely contrite. "We really screwed you."

It was his frank acknowledgment of the situation—his use of the word *screwed*—that made reality sink in and prompted Miranda to start thinking about what she would do next. Much as it killed her, there really wasn't much of a choice but to give up on the Army Reserve and stay in the National Guard, where she would at least be immediately eligible for the $15,000 reenlistment bonus.

But as if the last ten minutes hadn't just happened, the reserve recruiter was still pushing her to sign a contract with him—even though she'd get nothing in return.

"What are you, crazy?" Miranda said. "Do you really think I'm going to sign this now?"

She was done with this guy. He was more like a used-car salesman than an actual soldier.

"I need the number for the National Guard recruiter," she said dismissively.

He balked. The National Guard recruiter was his competition.

"Don't you want to sleep on it?" he said.

"Look," Miranda said, "I know you have the number. Give it to me now, or I'm going to find it on my own."

After taking a long time clearly pretending to fumble around in his desk, he finally handed it to her, and she stormed back out into the cold, her anger turning to despair, trying to figure out what just happened.

She'd been Jodied. Again. She had already expanded the definition of Jody from the person sleeping with your boyfriend or girlfriend to all the things that happened while you were away. Jody could take many forms. She knew this. But never did she imagine that she could be Jodied by the U.S. military itself.

Epilogue

Citizen-Soldiers: The Conscience of a Nation

On Drill weekend in May 2008, nearly a year and a half after getting home from Iraq, all Kate could think about was that she had just six more drills left before getting out of the army for good. After eight years in the service, she was done wearing the uniform, sick of all the army bureaucratic B.S. This drill was more of the same, with even more forms, this time an online questionnaire allegedly designed to assess her well-being. Kate groaned at what she considered another lame attempt by the army to look after the soldiers it sent to war.

What a load of crap, she thought.

Frustrated with the VA, she had completely given up on getting any help. Yes, the nightmares continued. Yes, her hand continued to shake and every once in a while she would wake up scared and disoriented. But by now she had just gotten used to those periodic spells, the way an epileptic accepted that life came with the occasional seizure. Life, for the most part, was good. David had proposed a few months earlier, and they were to be married that summer in Las Vegas. She had finally reenrolled in college and was taking it seriously this time, making mostly As and Bs. And even though it was weird to be in classes with nineteen-year-olds with whom she had nothing in common, she enjoyed her professors and feeling productive again.

She looked over the online form, which stated under the heading of "PRINCIPAL PURPOSE(S)": "To assess your state of health after deployment in support of military operations and to assist military healthcare providers in identifying and providing present and future medical care you may need."

The first few multiple-choice questions seemed generic. Then question 4 read, "During the past 4 weeks, how difficult have emotional problems (such as feeling depressed or anxious) made it for you to do your work, take care of things at home, or get along with other people?"

She scanned the possible responses:

Not difficult at all.

Somewhat difficult.

Very difficult.

Extremely difficult.

Well, her problems weren't "extremely difficult." She still functioned. She had finally reenrolled in college and kept her grades up. She was getting married in a few months. But who was she kidding? She was still having serious problems, so she marked, "Very difficult."

Question 12 read:

Have you ever had any experience that was so frightening, horrible, or upsetting that, IN THE PAST MONTH, you . . .

a. Have had nightmares about it or thought about it when you did not want to?

b. Tried hard not to think about it or went out of your way to avoid situations that remind you of it?

c. Were constantly on guard, watchful, or easily startled?

d. Felt numb or detached from others, activities, or your surroundings?

She marked "Yes" for all of them. On it went.

When Kate finished, she pressed submit and then called the 800 number as instructed, where a physician would go over the form with her. He pulled up her questionnaire, studied it for a minute while Kate waited on the line.

"It looks like you're suffering from some depression and PTSD," he said, "but you've only been to the doctor once. Why is that?"

"It's not for a lack of trying," she said. "I went to the VA and explained that I had been diagnosed with PTSD. But instead of getting a referral to see a mental-health counselor, I got a referral for smoking cessation."

She talked about how the chaplain at Fort Dix had promised to follow up with her but never had. She talked about all the time she waited on hold, trying to get through to the local VA hospital. Perhaps she had given up too easily. This wasn't entirely the VA's fault; she had bailed on the whole process. But admitting you needed help was hard enough. Asking for it was even more difficult—and in the macho culture of the army, having to ask for help repeatedly was harder still.

"First off," the physician on the line said, "let me apologize. You're not the only one to complain to me about this. But outside of the VA's hospital system, which provides just six free counseling sessions, there's another route I want you to try."

In a very calm voice, he told her about the VA's Vet Centers, which provide all sorts of services free of charge, for as long as it takes. He looked up the phone number for the one in Richmond and told her that if she ran into any more trouble to give him a call.

Promises—she'd heard them before and was, justifiably, skeptical. But something about this man's voice made her believe for the first time in a long time. And so two days later, she made the appointment. One week after that she was walking nervously into a nondescript building, which was dwarfed by the nearby Target department store. She opened the door to reveal a waiting room, with three men, all much older than she was, in jeans and polo shirts with sad, sagging eyes under tightly drawn baseball caps with the flags of that other war. Vietnam. Of course. She had not known what to expect exactly, but somehow the fact that she would end up in a room full of Vietnam vets took her completely by surprise. But here they were, huddled together on a warm spring afternoon, a Thursday, waiting for their group counseling session, where they would hash out the lost days of the jungle forty years past, struggling to reconcile memory with nightmare, truth with fantasy, just as she had been doing these past few months. It made perfect sense. The problems of the previous generation finally bubbling to the surface, and that's when it hit her: These old, grizzled men had been wrestling with their demons for years, for decades, and here they were in the same place she was, still trying to sort it all out.

It was at once frightening and comforting to know there would be no easy fix, that she could be struggling with Iraq for years to come. But above all the presence of these men made her realize in an instantaneous and permanent way that she was in the right place. She had finally found the sanctuary she'd so desperately been looking for. And these graying men, three decades her senior, were in a sense her contemporaries, only just a little further down the road.

She checked in and quietly took her seat, not wanting to disturb, and took out her book, a biography of the writer and feminist Mary Wollstonecraft called *Vindication*. One of the older vets caught her eye and nodded.

"How are you doing today?" he asked.

"Fine," Kate said, grateful that he had acknowledged her existence. Grateful that she was not invisible.

Her therapist came out after a few minutes. He was tall and balding with soft eyes and a deep, southern accent. He shook her hand, smiled, and said with a welcoming wave, "Come on back."

A few weeks later, the therapist called her. The Secretary of Veterans Affairs was going to be coming by the Vet Center in a few days, he told her, and given everything Kate had been through, she should show up and let him know how difficult getting help had been. He should hear what you have to say.

When she showed up, the director of the center urged the vets there not to turn the event into a bitch session, but simply tell the secretary how the center is helping. Kate scoffed. This man is fucking crazy if he thinks I am going to keep my mouth shut, she thought. With her waiting were two other Iraq War vets, six Vietnam, and one Korea. But Kate, who had to stop by the unit that morning, was the only one in uniform, and when Secretary James Peake arrived he went right to her. She didn't hold back. This was her chance to tell the man in charge how screwed up his agency was—or at least how terribly she had been treated.

"i let the man have it," she wrote in her journal afterward. "told him the truth about my disappointment in the medical care provided. told him of the hours i had spent on hold and the disinterested care I had been given. I told him that i knew what his budget was for this fiscal year (77 BILLION DOLLARS) and asked him what exactly he planned to do to help me and the other returning soldiers."

He sat there listening quietly, letting Kate vent. And when she was done, he took her into an empty office, pulled up the department's Web page, and showed her exactly what resources were available for her. He wrote down the names and numbers of people who could help. Then he gave her his personal e-mail address and told if she ever had any other problems to write him right away so he could take care of them personally.

Kate was impressed. Clearly the man cared about veterans, even if the bureaucracy he led had on occasion slipped. His reassurances made her feel safe, reassured. She knew the man in charge. He had promised to take care of her, and she believed him, which after all she had been through was no small gesture. She was going to be okay. She was sure of that now. But what, she wondered, about those vets who didn't get to sit down one-on-one with the secretary? What about those who didn't know about the Vet Center?

Who was looking after them?

. . .

Veterans Day 2007 was a picture-perfect autumn day. The November foliage was just past peak but still brilliant, holding on for an encore before fading away. The sun was out. The air was crisp. A friend had asked Ray to ride on the Veterans Day float the St. Mary's County Republican Party planned to enter in the county parade, and he was happy to oblige. So he took his uniform out of the closet and put it on for what could be, he knew, the last time.

On his birthday two months earlier, he had officially retired. Or, rather, he woke up and was retired. He was sixty. His time was up, that was all. No ceremony marked the occasion. Like Cinderella's spell breaking at midnight, there was simply an expiration date past which Ray was suddenly no longer a soldier. Not that he minded. Having survived forty-two years in the service, two wars, and countless bullets, including one that brought down his helicopter, he was ready for retirement.

The Main Street parade was quintessential small-town America, coming out to support its heroes. Throngs two and three deep jammed the sidewalks before the mom-and-pop storefronts. Babies in strollers, children in ball caps, their parents and grandparents lined the street, every last one of them waving a small American flag handed out by volunteers. Ray could feel himself choking up a bit as he waved like a celebrity to the cheering crowd. Everything about it was just as he had imagined.

But it was all just a little too perfect, as if the Rockwellian scene belonged to another, bygone era, circa V-J Day, 1945. Ray's war might have been over, but the country's was not. Other American troops were at this moment on their way in. Up the road in Rockville, Maryland, a little over an hour's drive away, word was spreading through the ranks of the Army Reserve's 352nd Military Police Company that it had been called and would soon ship out to Iraq. Maybe by this time next year its soldiers would be coming home. And maybe there'd be a sun-drenched parade just like this one to welcome them. Maybe by then the war would be over, and they'd be able to bask in the glow of victory, knowing they wouldn't be called on again. One could hope.

As much as he enjoyed cruising along on his float, Ray was skeptical that in a year the war would come to the kind of conclusive end that would make everyone happy. In which case what he meant in his CNN interview—"I see a lot of suffering"—was that the suffering was not his alone, but theirs as well. And even though he had used the present tense, the suffering Ray sees was not only in the here and now, but in the future, and it extended to this entire generation of soldiers, and it would for some time.

From his perch on his float, Ray waved to the adoring crowds. A wave that said both hello and good-bye.

A few weeks after the parade, Ray emerged from his basement office with an ad from the *Veterans of Foreign Wars* magazine about vacation tours for Vietnam vets.

"How would you like to go to Vietnam?" he asked Diane.

She was shocked. Twenty years of marriage and barely a peep about that place, and now he wants to go visit? This was out of the blue. He'd just gotten back from Iraq, and she thought he was dealing with what he went through in that war, not Vietnam. Maybe he was. It was a long road between the two, measured in miles and years and memory, and to get from one to the other, he first had to go back to the beginning.

·   ·   ·

About two weeks before the start of the school year, the school system's assistant superintendent left Craig a message offering him his
job back, but by then Craig had already made up his mind. He
wouldn't take it. It was too late. He needed a job desperately, but
he told himself he wasn't desperate enough to return to a place that he
felt had treated him so poorly and was now, in his view, offering him
a position at the last possible minute to cover themselves. The school
system, however, had a much different take. The fact was that Craig
was offered his job back. And as the superintendent would later say,
it was not unusual to fill positions just before school started. "We
honor his service and wanted to do right by him," he said.

Craig called back. Thanks but no thanks. As he would later say,
"If they were more receptive, it would have been a different story. If
they showed any interest in getting me back, I might have gone."

Instead, he continued the job hunt, reaching out even more
aggressively to friends and contacts, convinced that personal con-
nections were a far better way to go than sending out résumés in
response to Internet postings. By November, a friend who worked
for CACI International, the huge government contractor, promised to spread Craig's résumé around the company. And while they
were out having drinks, she even introduced Craig to her boss
when they happened to run into him. Craig was as hopeful as he'd
been in months. His friend's boss seemed genuinely interested in
him and thought his Guard experience was a huge asset.

"We should be able to get you in here no problem," he had
said.

"No problem." Craig had heard variations of that line before
and had fallen victim to it every time, like Charlie Brown lining up
to kick the football, assured that Lucy wouldn't pull it away at the
last minute. But this time Craig felt confident. He had a friend on
the inside, advocating for him. He had made face-to-face contact
with the boss. He had heard the phrase "no problem," as if it were
already a done deal.

But by January, when Craig had still heard nothing back, he was no longer in a position not to work. He'd been back nearly an entire year, and it was well past time to get rolling. So he took the only job where he could salvage some self-dignity and also be assured that his military service would be a plus. In fact, it was a requirement. The job at the Virginia National Guard's Joint Operations Center at Fort Pickett was the nerve center for the state's citizen-soldier corps. Here Craig would serve as a glorified 911 dispatcher, ready to alert Guardsmen in the event of natural disasters and coordinate with local emergency authorities, if need be. He'd keep tabs on the state's Guardsmen serving all over the globe and would, in a moment of crisis, be at the center of it all in what was surely important, gratifying work. The problem was that those periods of emergency were few and far between, and instead of feeling vital he was just plain bored most of the time. He read the reports that came in and monitored the weather, but mostly he watched television and then surfed the Internet. Worst of all, Fort Pickett was two hours away from his Charlottesville home. And because of his work schedule—four days on, four days off—it made more sense just to stay there while he was working, even if that meant he had to share a bathroom, eat in a chow hall, and live a life that closely resembled the one he'd led in Iraq. But what bothered him most of all was that by taking the job he was acknowledging, if tacitly, that he had been rejected by the civilian world. He had tried to get a "normal" job, by which he meant anything where he didn't have to wear his army uniform, and failed.

He hadn't given up all hope, though. After a few months at Fort Pickett, the tedium of the job made him pursue CACI even more vigorously. He e-mailed his résumé directly to CACI's recruiter, and that spring had even followed up with a phone call. His persistence finally paid off. He landed an interview. A few weeks later, on a Wednesday in early June, the man called back.

"Hey, we got your résumé," the recruiter said. "We just got a new contract we think you'd be good for, and we want to get you in here as soon as possible, say Friday or Monday. How does that suit you?"

This was the moment Craig had been waiting for ever since he got home more than a year and a half ago. A real job offer. His first one, and it was exactly the kind of job he wanted, too, not some youth counseling position. But he felt his stomach turn in knots. He couldn't be there by Friday, or the following Monday. He had just been called up to active duty for a three-week tour patrolling the Arizona border. The timing could not have been worse, which is what he tried to explain. Any other time he'd be available on a moment's notice. "Was there any way you could wait until I got back?" he asked.

"Unfortunately, no," the recruiter said. They had a new contract and needed to get up and running right away. He was gracious, though clearly disappointed, and told Craig to give him a call when he got back. "Maybe something will open up in the future," he said.

Craig promised he would call when he returned. But he couldn't help but feel that this was his chance, and he was missing it. He hung up in disbelief, trying to sort through what had just happened. All along he had refrained from blaming the Guard for his employment problems. His trouble with Fluvanna High was because of his principal, not the army, he told himself. And even if he suspected that other employers refused to hire Guardsmen because they could be shipped out at a moment's notice, there was no explicit proof of that, and he held on to the belief, perhaps naively, that his service made him a better job candidate. But this missed opportunity was undeniably linked to his service. The cold truth was that if he weren't in the Guard, he would be starting his dream job as soon as Friday. There was no way around it. Maybe there would be another opportunity, as the recruiter had said. Craig was by nature an optimist, and he wanted to believe what the man had said. But employers had to be able to rely on their employees, and Craig had just demonstrated in stark terms that he might not always be available.

"Bad timing," he had said to the recruiter. But it wasn't just that. Craig had always believed that you made your own luck with dedication and hard work and by keeping your nose clean. Things would work out, he kept telling himself. But they weren't working out. Not by a long shot. After a year and a half of setbacks, this was the tipping point that made him rethink his commitment. He loved the Guard, the camaraderie of the 2-224th, and flying and being in charge of an entire company of soldiers. He wanted to serve, and he'd known what he was getting into when he'd signed up. He was a volunteer, after all. No one had forced him to join.

But now he wondered if the sacrifice was worth it. If he resigned his commission and focused solely on landing a job in the civilian world, he wouldn't have to answer the "Will you be deployed?" question. He wouldn't have to worry about being called up and having to give just a few days' notice. He'd be able to settle into a career and begin that part of his life that had been so severely stunted.

How much longer did he have before he could get out? The thought had never really occurred to him. He was content with the military and with how he was progressing. But now he was convinced that it was interfering not just with his civilian career but with his life as well. He had to think on it a minute before coming to the disappointing answer: four years. A long way away. Maybe things would change between now and then. Perhaps it would all work out, and he'd figure out how to be both a citizen and a soldier. Being an optimist, he liked to keep his options for the future open. Who knew what he'd do in four years? He didn't want to believe he'd resign his commission, and hoped by the time he could it wouldn't even occur to him to do so. But after everything he'd just been through, he knew what he would do if his time were up today.

A few weeks after Craig's return from Arizona, the recruiter did call again. He had another job opening. Could he start Wednesday?

"You better believe it," Craig said.

He woke up early for work, excited by the prospect of gainful, satisfying employment. Normally the traffic on his commute would have driven him crazy, but not today. Today he was happy to be up, showered, beating his housemate out the door. He was thrilled to inch along the highway with everyone else on their way to work, to be part of the mainstream.

He was grateful his new employer seemed pleased to have him and apparently willing to work around the fact that he served in the National Guard.

Still, he did not mention the rumors that had been floating around the 2-224th the past couple months. Next summer's two weeks of annual training were supposedly going to be in the snow-capped mountains of Canada, where the pilots could get used to flying at high altitude. Some guessed that meant one thing for the battalion: Afghanistan as early as 2010.

.   .   .

Mark's father died Friday, the day his new unit left without him. Mark took care of the arrangements and comforted his mother. He stood at the freshly dug hole in the ground, roots exposed, as his father's ashes were buried. His mother wept quietly next to him, her hand delicate and quivering in his, while he unsuccessfully tried to hold back the tears beginning to form in his own eyes. Iraq was the last thing on his mind, which was how he knew it was where he was supposed not to be. But that didn't mean he knew where he did belong.

His father's death had been a distraction, but now at home he had to face his future, which did not include Iraq. It had been a week since he bowed out, but it was still hard to believe he wasn't going. Back in Richmond, he was exhausted, and so too, he noticed, was his house. He had bought it before he went to Iraq for $45,000, thinking he could renovate it from top to bottom, live in it a while, then flip it for six figures, viewing the act as much as an exercise in profitable real estate acumen as the noble resurrection of a once solid, if not grand, specimen. Before Iraq, before his fiancée left him, he saw so much potential in the place. It had good bones, as they say. A wide front porch for sipping whiskey and watching the neighbors go by. A large den with the perfect spot for a twelve-foot Christmas tree. A formal dining room for family dinners. And enough room for the children he had hoped to one day have with his ex. He had made some steady progress putting in new sub-flooring in the bedroom, heated tiles in the bathroom, and the new windows in the dining room. One night he even put on his bulletproof vest under his jacket and told the drug dealers on the corner that he didn't care where they did their business, but they were no longer going to do it in front of his house.

But now nearly two years later, the house was in even worse shape than it had been the day he bought it, with cracked pink siding, a faltering, no doubt rotted roof, and a charred upstairs bedroom and hallway, victims of a fire presumably started after the careless junkies who previously owned the house passed out stoned. Weeds had annexed every strategic inch of the periphery and appeared to be mounting an offensive. The porch sagged, the windows leaked, and underfoot the steps' creaks sounded like tired wheezes. It seemed the whole house would raise its hands, give up, and collapse under the slightest gust.

Now that he was no longer going back to Iraq, he could finally focus his attention on the house again. Day after day he told himself he'd get to it. Put in the new drywall, replace the kitchen floor, patch the roof. Then he'd start scouting for new properties to buy with the money he'd saved, and flip those. He'd make his million. But he was stuck, unable to get going. Since he had come home from Iraq, every single second brought him closer to his return. He had girded himself for combat, kept his calluses tough, his cara-pace hard, his switch on. He guarded the inner ferocity required in combat, waiting for the day he would need it, and now, just like that, he didn't. Where was all that pent-up energy and angst supposed to go? Would it just disappear? Throughout his military career, from VMI, to Army Ranger School, to flying in the pitch black over Baghdad, he had learned how to stay cool under fire, to keep the switch on. But no one told you how to turn it off.

He was like a cancer patient who'd been given six months to live, then was unable to accept that fact that the cancer was gone and a whole life lay ahead. It wasn't that Mark wasn't relieved about his change of fortune; it was that he was just completely unprepared for it.

The house in all its disrepair—the exposed plumbing, the charred walls, the cobwebs that seemed sturdier than the rickety banister—was, he knew, a metaphor for his life. It was also a way back; he had once seen so much potential in this place, and in himself. But the more time passed in which he did nothing, the more difficult it was to begin, and the house now just seemed like a lost cause.

Then on a sunny, spring Saturday his new girlfriend came over with several trays' worth of flowers. "Come on," she said. "Let's build a flower bed." Gardening was not his forte and with all the structural work that needed to be done on the house, planting flowers seemed frivolous. But she was insistent, saying you had to start somewhere, and they spent the better part of the day pulling up the ivy that coursed through the yard like snakes. It was tough, backbreaking work. The ivy was stubborn and entrenched. Sweat soon began to soak through his shirt. This was a far more difficult job than Mark had imagined. But it felt good, cathartic even, to work outside in the warm, spring sun alongside his new girlfriend, whose smile, even with a smudge of dirt on her cheek, made her all the more beautiful.

The flowers, yellow and red pansies and stolid, long-leafed caladiums, were, in the context of the house's vast problems, small changes, mere flecks of color in an otherwise dark canvas. But they held immense promise, even Mark could see that. Maybe he would still have those family dinners and twelve-foot Christmas trees. Maybe the future he had imagined wasn't lost after all, only different. It was too early to tell, and there was a lot of work left to be done, but at least it seemed possible. And it was what in the weeks and months ahead kept him going.

In the meantime, it felt good to live in the moment and feel the sun at his back. To watch the woman working next to him. To get his hands dirty in the cool, moist earth and part the soil, making way for these flowers that would soon take root and grow.

. . .

In the end, Miranda's reenlistment ceremony wasn't a ceremony at all. While running errands on a Thursday, she stopped by the National Guard recruiting station, raised her right hand, and affixed her signature to a document that would commit her for another six years, and in all likelihood one more deployment, if not two. Given the stakes, it was an anti-climactic finale to what had been a gut-wrenching ordeal, and a small part of her felt the tug toward holding a public reenlistment ceremony on campus as the National Guard official had suggested on Veterans Day.

There would have been the satisfying irony of such a public display on a campus that in another era would have been engulfed in the flames of anti-war protest. If nothing else, it would have served as a reminder that there was a war going on, and that the university's students, or at least one of them, were involved. That was her responsibility, wasn't it? To be a soldier was much more than shooting guns and driving tanks and flying helicopters. It was also to be an ambassador to the civilian world, a living, breathing paragon of the warrior ethos, a bridge between the civilian and the military. That had been long been the citizen-soldier's burden. But it had become especially true in an era in which such a small percentage of the population served. The role had often made Miranda feel as if she were a traveling circus act—Come, ladies and gents! See a real live soldier! Uniform and everything! A blond door gunner girl!—even though what she really wanted to be was just part of the continuum. She just wanted to do her part.

It sounded like such a cliché, the sort used in the obituaries of those killed in Iraq by their grieving families. "All he ever wanted to do was serve." She knew after she said something like that—"I just feel like it's something I was supposed to do"—she'd get the curious, "Is she serious?" stares and feel as antiquated as a gladiator, and as misunderstood. But how else to explain it? And why should joining the army be so hard to understand? What compelled her and, presumably, those of her contemporaries who had made the same choice was what had compelled previous generations of soldiers who had followed the script laid out by the founders. When the country goes to war, the whole country sacrifices—not just the 1 percent who through inclination or need volunteer to serve. It was that simple. The credo was even etched into the granite of the World War II Memorial: "This was a people's war, and everyone was in it." War was ugly and horrible and tragic, and that was precisely why its heavy burden needed to be carried by the entire population, not a select few. Robert E. Lee had said at Fredericksburg, "It is well that war is so terrible, lest we grow too fond of it." What happened instead is that America had grown ignorant of war, which was just as dangerous, if not more so.

The framers, having thrown off a king who could wage war without the hindrance of popular sentiment, knew this, and they had designed the system so that the burdens of war were spread throughout the population. Citizen-soldiers, then, weren't a mere check against executive power, but rather the conscience of a nation. The cause had better be worthy of their sacrifice. Those are our sons and daughters. Wasn't that understood to be part of the American DNA? Wasn't it lauded, even at Brown, where the Soldiers Arch commemorated the fallen of World War I, the engraved plaque had urged generations hence "to respond as loyally to their country's call," and reminded that there was honor in dying for your country?

In its greatest moments, the country had come together, sacrificing, from the Revolution on through World War II. And when for the first time the reserves were sidelined in Vietnam, General Creighton Abrams had, with Jeffersonian zeal, vowed that the country would never go to war again without its citizen-soldiers and therefore, theoretically, without public support. It was a democratic sentiment through and through, a noble effort to ensure that the nation's centuries-old civil-military pact was never abandoned again.

Only Abrams was too late. After the ignominy of Vietnam, and the long scars left by an unjust draft that exempted the privileged, the country, and its leaders, had started to swing away from service. In the years to follow, a generation of parents decided they would shield their children from the terror that had lurked in those

Southeast Asian jungles and before then in the Ardennes Forest, and before then in the fields at Gettysburg and before then at Valley Forge and before then in countless battle after countless battle. War was plainly awful; that was evident if not from firsthand experience then by the absent expressions of the homeless vets in camouflage asking for spare change on the corner. No wonder rational people wanted no part of it and would hang up on the recruiters who constantly called. Volunteers, and volunteers alone, would fight our wars for us. So we spawned the first of who knows how many American generations who felt it their entitlement to be exempt from combat. We justified this two-tiered system by pledging that even if we didn't see combat, we would support the volunteer soldiers. Plaster our cars with yellow ribbons, no matter if we opposed the war they had sacrificed so much for. This was progress. Or so it seemed throughout the 1980s and 1990s when flare-ups here and there—Panama, Grenada, Kuwait—were all handled tidily by the all-volunteer force. And if there was trouble, death, or injury, well, that was horrible, of course. But they had volunteered for it. They knew what they were getting into. And we could always change the channel, avert our gaze.

The country had successfully saved its children from combat. But in doing so it had allowed the ties between citizens and soldiers, between society and war, to collapse. As a result we forfeited the moral authority necessary for one of the most important tenets of American democracy: the ability to check a government from committing troops. War should belong to all of us. Not just the few and the proud, not just the 1 percent. That was what the founders had intended, what Abrams tried to resurrect, and what generation after generation assumed until the draft ended in 1973.

The public spectacle of Miranda in full dress uniform, her right hand raised under an American flag in the center of Brown's Common, wouldn't have changed that. It wouldn't have inspired awe or respect or even brought home the message Miranda would have hoped for: I am of you; we are of you. The truth was that soldiers were not of society any more than Miranda was of Brown.

The chasm was too deep, the disconnect too distant. The bridge between the civilian and military had collapsed.

Taking her oath on campus would not be seen as patriotic, as Miranda had momentarily hoped, but as curious, even misguided, because surely reenlisting in this day and age guaranteed a trip to the front lines. Perhaps to some she was, as a soldier, even a vulgarity. But no matter how she was perceived, the public display of patriotism would have demonstrated that Miranda was indeed, as the recruiting ads promised, an Army of One, though not in the way the military had intended. And that's why she ultimately decided against it: Because except to her, it would have meant nothing.

This was her decision, and hers alone. Service, and therefore war, had become a choice, and it didn't matter if no one around her understood, or was making the same decision. She didn't need anyone else's approval, or empathy. She just needed that fifteen grand paid for in full by the American taxpayer, thank you very much, even if it could be interpreted as the many paying the few to go fight in their stead. Miranda knew who she was, what she believed, and what she was getting into. If she was risking getting shot at on the taxpayers' dime, so be it. They owed her at least that much.

And so on a Thursday afternoon, in between errands, almost exactly one year after getting home from her first deployment, knowing full well there would be other deployments, she raised her hand and signed her name, without hesitation.

Six weeks later, the long-awaited $15,000 landed in her bank account. Only it wasn't $15,000, but $10,185 instead. The government had taken its share—one-third—before she even had the chance to spend it. She didn't have a problem paying taxes, but on her reenlistment bonus it somehow didn't seem fair.

Hadn't she already paid enough?

Index